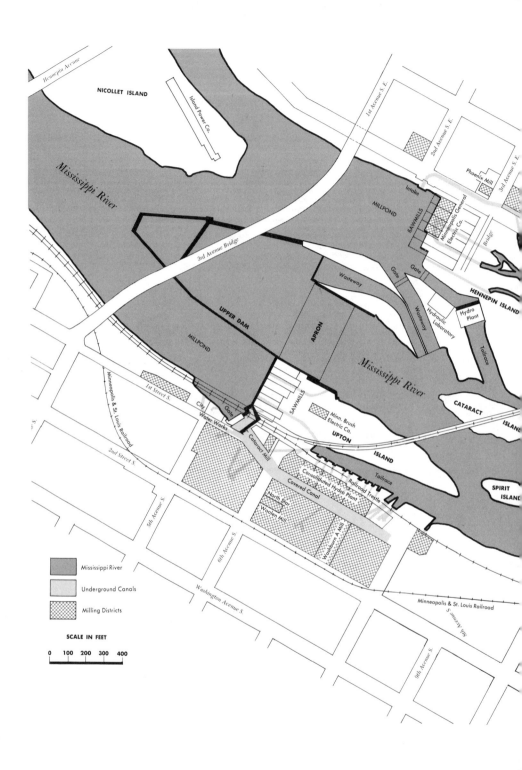

NICOLLET ISLAND

Mississippi River

Island Power Co.

Hennepin Avenue

1st Avenue S. E.

3rd Avenue S. E.

3rd Avenue S. E.

Phoenix Mill

Intake

MILLPOND

SAWMILLS

Minneapolis General Electric Co.

Bridge

3rd Avenue Bridge

Wasteway

Gate

Gate

HENNEPIN ISLAND

UPPER DAM

APRON

Wasteway

Hydraulic Laboratory

Hydro Plant

MILLPOND

Mississippi River

Tailrace

Minneapolis & St. Louis Railroad

1st Street S.

City

Gate

Water Works

SAWMILLS

Minn. Brush Electric Co.

CATARACT

ISLAND

2nd Street S.

Cataract Mill

UPTON

ISLAND

SPIRIT ISLAND

5th Avenue S.

Tailrace

Consolidated Hydro Plant

Railroad Trestle

Covered Canal

North Star

Woolen Mill

Washburn A Mill

6th Avenue S.

Washington Avenue S.

Minneapolis & St. Louis Railroad

7th Avenue S.

8th Avenue S.

9th Avenue S.

▓	Mississippi River
░	Underground Canals
▨	Milling Districts

SCALE IN FEET

0   100   200   300   400

WATER-POWER INSTALLATIONS AT THE FALLS OF ST. ANTHONY, 1850s-1950s

showing the main features built to develop the power and preserve the falls

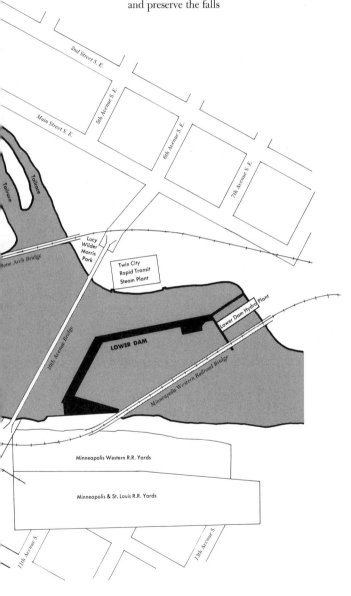

The Falls of St. Anthony

The Falls
of
St. Anthony

The Waterfall
That Built Minneapolis

LUCILE M. KANE

MINNESOTA HISTORICAL SOCIETY PRESS • ST. PAUL • 1987

MINNESOTA HISTORICAL SOCIETY PRESS, St. Paul 55101

Originally published as *The Waterfall That Built a City: The Falls of St. Anthony in Minneapolis*

Copyright © 1966, 1987 by the Minnesota Historical Society

International Standard Book Number 0-87351-205-7
Manufactured in the United States of America
10 9 8 7 6 5 4 3 2 1

Library of Congress Cataloging-in-Publication Data

Kane, Lucile M.
  The falls of St. Anthony.

  Updated ed. of: The waterfall that built a city. 1966.
  Bibliography: p.
  Includes index.
  1. Minneapolis (Minn.) — History. 2. Saint Anthony
Falls (Minn.) I. Kane, Lucile M. Waterfall that
built a city. II. Title.
F614.M557K36 1987   977.6'579   86-31194
ISBN 0-87351-205-7

Dedicated to my parents

EMERY J. KANE
RUTH M. KANE

Contents

Illustrations

Preface to the Reprint Edition

The Falls of St. Anthony: The Waterfall That Built Minneapolis is an updated edition of *The Waterfall That Built a City: The Falls of St. Anthony in Minneapolis*, originally published in 1966 by the Minnesota Historical Society. Many changes have come to the falls area since the book first appeared. At that time the area seemed like a quiet oasis within a bustling city. Tourists who visited the falls saw remnants of an industrial district that once had been the vibrant core of a young city. Although three hydroelectric plants and one flour mill were still operating, the decayed district had long ago lost its importance in the city's economy. A short distance away, urban renewal was transforming downtown Minneapolis. At the falls, the only significant sign of change was the new lock that extended navigation to terminals upriver.

Soon after the book appeared, Reiko Weston built a riverfront restaurant on the west bank in the old milling district. The Fuji-Ya, opened in 1968, heralded the beginning of new life at the falls. Slowly at first, then with a quickening tempo, reclamation got under way. Growing enthusiasm for making the riverfront once more a vital part of the city stimulated developers, who adapted old structures and erected new ones for use as restaurants, shops, offices, and housing. The city acquired land for riverfront parks. And, somewhat tardily, preservationists moved to protect the remaining historical fabric.

This reprint edition includes a new epilogue that briefly describes, within a historical context, the rehabilitation of the falls area occurring from the 1960s to mid-1986 — a somewhat perilous effort considering the great changes still taking place there and the complexity of the issues involved. Also added are new illustrations and a map locating the redeveloped sites.

For assistance generously given, I am indebted to Scott Anfinson, Elisabeth Doermann, Leona Kane Eder, Dennis Gimmestad, Deborah Miller, Kathy O'Brien, Ann Regan, and Albert D. Wittman, and to the librarians of the Minnesota Historical Society and the Minneapolis History Collection at the Minneapolis Public Library and Information Center.

October 1986   LUCILE M. KANE

Preface

THE STORY OF THE FALLS OF ST. ANTHONY, the only major waterfall in the Mississippi River, spans almost three centuries from the period of discovery and exploration in the 1600s to the present. During that time the waterfall built a great city. Its story mirrors a developing economy and technology and reflects changing attitudes toward natural resources. Since the mid-nineteenth century the Falls of St. Anthony have been one of the nation's ranking water powers. Along the cataract's banks rose towering mills that made Minneapolis for a time the foremost flour producer in the nation. Its waters powered sawmills, foundries, furniture factories, woolen mills, and a host of other enterprises important in the economic life of the city. It has been my purpose to chronicle the waterfall's changing role in the founding and growth of Minneapolis, its transformation from a scene of natural beauty to a developed water-power site, its use to turn the wheels of industry, and its evolution from a source of direct water power to a hydroelectric site.

The story has been shaped by the research materials available. Chief among them are the business records of the water-power and electrical firms that developed the falls. Most of these are in the possession of the Northern States Power Company of Minneapolis, which not only allowed me complete access to them but also generously provided research funds and technical assistance. In large measure the key records of the St. Anthony Falls Water Power Company and the Minneapolis Mill Company determined the type of book which could be written. They are meager for the years before 1880 and weak in financial and personnel information, but they offer a store of data on water-power management, engineering, and hydroelectricity. Supplementing them in other depositories were several groups of personal papers, notably those of Franklin Steele — the businessman who pioneered the development of the falls — as well as voluminous legal files, city records, and the reports of the United States Army Engineers. To the many people who aided me in my work in these abundant sources, my sincere thanks.

I am indebted, too, to the previously published studies of Mildred L. Hartsough, Herbert W. Meyer, Charles B. Kuhlmann, and Agnes Larson, who laid down broad concepts that stood the test of re-examination, offered guidelines for analyzing the Minneapolis water power, and traced the development of flour and saw milling — the two major industries fostered by the Falls of St. Anthony. Richly supplementing these works were local histories written by men who participated in the city's development, newspapers, reports of commercial bodies, and two trade journals — the *Northwestern Miller* and the *Mississippi Valley Lumberman*.

Special thanks are due Russell W. Fridley, director of the Minnesota Historical Society and friend of scholars, and my colleagues on the society's staff who cheerfully aided me in innumerable ways and extended many courtesies. A particular expression of gratitude is due to June D. Holmquist, the society's talented book editor, Anne A. Hage, Helen M. White, and James Taylor Dunn. All pictures in this book not otherwise credited were furnished by the society's picture department. The maps are the work of Alan Ominsky.

Others whom I wish to thank for their assistance are William R. Greer, Leona Kane Eder, and Mrs. Louise Braasch, who made available the papers of her father, William de la Barre. For reading all or part of the manuscript and making helpful suggestions I am grateful to Rodney C. Loehr, Herbert W. Meyer, Walter N. Trenerry, Mrs. Ralph W. Hidy, and Roger Williams.

In addition, I am indebted for their patient help to the personnel of the offices of the Ramsey County Register of Deeds, the Ramsey County Clerk of District Court, the Hennepin County Register of Deeds, the Hennepin County Clerk of District Court, and the City Clerk of Minneapolis.

LUCILE M. KANE

St. Paul, Minnesota
February 8, 1966

The Falls
of
St. Anthony

1.

A Landmark in the Wilderness

WINDING ITS WAY SOUTHWARD THROUGH MINNESOTA, the Mississippi River leaps over a sixteen-foot precipice known as the Falls of St. Anthony. This waterfall, which was responsible for the birth of Minneapolis, is the most abrupt drop in the Mississippi's entire 2,200-mile course from its source in Minnesota's Lake Itasca to the Gulf of Mexico.

The cataract was discovered in 1680 by Father Louis Hennepin, a Franciscan priest. At the time he first beheld its roaring waters the upper Mississippi Valley was largely unknown. From settlements in the St. Lawrence River Valley in present-day Canada, the French were probing southwestward for the fabled river they believed would lead to the Orient. Father Jacques Marquette and Louis Jolliet reached the upper Mississippi in 1673. Daniel Greysolon, Sieur du Luth, visited what is now Minnesota in 1679. A year later the intrepid La Salle sent Michel Accault, with Father Hennepin and Antoine Auguelle as companions, on the sortie up the Mississippi that led to the discovery of the Falls of St. Anthony.[1]

Setting off from La Salle's Fort Crèvecoeur on the Illinois River in February, 1680, the men traveled northward until they were captured early in April by a Sioux war party. The Indians carried the three men to their villages on Mille Lacs Lake in what is now east-central Minnesota. There, stripped of his vestments, the forty-year-old Hennepin endured the uneasy hospitality of the Sioux for over two months. In July he secured permission from his captors to travel with Auguelle to the mouth of the Wisconsin River, where La Salle had promised to drop supplies. Leaving Accault behind as a hostage, the two men canoed down the Mississippi to see for the first time the only major falls in that mighty river.

Although Hennepin had earlier viewed the much higher falls of the Niagara River, he was nevertheless impressed by the cataract in the Mississippi. He ascribed to it the exaggerated height of fifty or sixty feet, and remarked in some awe that the falling water "of itself is terrible, and hath something in it very astonishing." Honesty apparently compelled him to add that the Mississippi falls "doth not come near that of Niagara." Taking unto himself the prerogatives of discovery, Hennepin named the cataract for his protector, Saint Anthony of Padua.[2]

More sensitive perhaps than Hennepin, the Sioux and Chippewa Indians who inhabited the area nearby had given the cataract names evoking sight and sound. Looking upon the masses of limestone broken from the ledge that formed the falls, the Chippewa called them Kakabikah, meaning "the severed rock." The Sioux, mindful of the rushing torrents, called them Minirara (curling water) and Owahmenah (falling water). Long after Hennepin's discovery an artist viewed the "sublime spectacle of the whole volume of the Mississippi rushing and foaming" over the precipice and regretted the loss of the Indian names. "Shall we ever forgive Father Hennepin," he wrote, "for hiding" the names "beneath the brown mantle of St. Anthony of Padua?"[3]

To the Indians the falls were sacred, and many legends surrounded them. For example, Hennepin saw an Indian in an oak tree weeping bitterly as he fastened to a branch a beaver robe decorated with porcupine quills—a sacrifice to Oanktehi, god of waters and evil, who lived beneath the falls. "I could hear him say," wrote Hennepin, "as he was addressing himself to the Cascade, with Tears in his Eyes; Thou art a Spirit grant that Those of my Nation may pass here without any Disaster; That we may meet with a great many wild Bulls; and that we may be so happy as to vanquish our Enemy, and take a great many Slaves, whom, when we have made them suffer according to their Merits, we will bring hither, and slay in thy Presence."[4]

Another spirit—that of Ampato Sapa, or Dark Day—haunted a rocky, wooded island at the foot of the falls. According to legend, she was the wife of a Sioux hunter and the mother of a small son. When her husband's fame grew with his success in the hunt, he decided to show his prosperity by taking a second wife, according to the custom of his tribe. Ampato Sapa was heartbroken, but she went about her work quietly, caring for her son and awaiting her moment of release.[5]

In the spring when the Sioux were passing the falls, Ampato Sapa paddled a canoe to an island located in mid-river above the cataract. There she dressed in her bridal raiment—an embroidered robe, a crown of eagle feathers, and strings of beads. She placed the child in the canoe where he could be seen by her husband. Then, singing her death song, she guided the craft past the frantic father, over the precipice, and into the boiling waters below. The memory of Ampato Sapa was kept alive by tellers of tales, who reported that her lament was heard in the winds and that she was seen rising from the foam near Spirit Island, which was named for her.

> Yet that death-song, they say, is heard
>   Above the gloomy waters' roar,
> When trees are by the night-wind stirred,
>   And darkness broods o'er wave and shore!
> In haste, and with averted eye,
>   Benighted travelers pass near;
> And when that song of death is heard,
>   Stout-hearted warriors quake with fear.

Soon after discovering the falls Hennepin was rescued by Du Luth. He returned to France where he wrote an account of his travels. His book, which appeared in 1683 and in many editions thereafter, made the cataract a widely known landmark in the wilderness. Drawn by Hennepin's account and by increasing curiosity about western America, a few explorers visited the spot in the eighteenth century. They perpetuated the impression of the falls' great size. Jean Pénicaut, a member of a French exploring party in 1700, wrote that "the entire Mississippi" fell "suddenly from the height of sixty feet, making a noise like that of thunder rolling in the air." Jonathan Carver, a Connecticut adventurer exploring under the British flag in 1766, ascribed to them a height of thirty feet.[6]

Twelve years later Carver published the earliest known sketch of the falls in a book which became a bestseller and increased the cataract's fame as a landmark in a little-known region. Carver gave his readers considerably more information about the waterfall than its discoverer had offered. "We could distinctly hear the noise of the water full fifteen miles before we reached the falls," he wrote, "and I was greatly pleased and surprised, when I approached this astonishing work of nature. . . . This amazing body of waters, which are above 250 yards over, form a most pleasing cataract; they fall perpendicularly about thirty feet, and the rapids below . . . render the descent considerably greater, so that when viewed at a distance, they appear much higher than they really are. . . . These falls vary much from all the others I have seen, as you may approach close to them without finding the least obstruction from any intervening hill."

After describing the six nearby islands which added to the beauty of the scene, Carver concluded that "a more pleasing and picturesque view cannot, I believe, be found throughout the universe."

During the century following their discovery, the Falls of St. Anthony were shifted by treaty makers from one empire to another. They belonged to the domains possessed successively by France, Spain, England, and the United States. France, which had laid claim to the interior of North America in 1671, ceded to Spain in 1762 the area west of the river, and in 1763 relinquished to England all its lands east of the Mississippi with the exception of New Orleans. England held sway until 1783 when it recognized the sovereignty of the American colonies over the region stretching from the Atlantic seaboard to the Mississippi. And in 1803 the falls came wholly within the area of the United States after the new nation acquired Louisiana Territory from France (which three years earlier had reacquired it from Spain).[7]

The Louisiana Purchase ushered in a new period of exploration. Caught up in a westward movement that carried the crest of settlement through the Appalachian Mountains and on toward the Mississippi, the new nation eagerly gathered information about the vast domain in the distant west. In 1803 President Thomas Jefferson dispatched William Clark and Meriwether Lewis on their long trek across the continent to the Pacific Ocean. Two years later, impelled by the same quest for knowledge, the government ordered Zebulon Montgomery Pike, a young army lieutenant, into the northern reaches of the Louisiana Purchase. By sending Pike to what is now Minnesota, the United States government made its first gesture toward opening the land for white occupation. Pike's mission, in addition to gathering data about the country, was to secure from the Indians permission to erect "military posts and trading houses, at the mouth of the river St. Pierre [Minnesota], the Falls of St. Anthony, and every other critical point which may fall under your observation."[8]

Pike acted boldly on his instructions. As soon as he arrived at the junction of the Mississippi and Minnesota rivers in 1805, he called together the Sioux who occupied the area. Meeting on the island which now bears his name, under a bower formed from the sails of the bateaux which had carried him on his long journey up the river, he asked the chiefs for land cessions at the mouths of the Minnesota and St. Croix rivers. "As we are a people who are accustomed to have all our acts written down," he told them, ". . . I have drawn up a form of an agreement which we will both sign in the presence of the traders now present." [9]

The Sioux responded readily to the "young warriors," as Pike called the Americans, who asked them for a possession the Indians had in abundance. Ignorant of the momentous consequences of their act, Chiefs Le Petit Corbeau and Way Ago Enagee placed their marks upon an agreement ceding to the United States the two areas Pike requested — the first Minnesota land to be acquired by the white man. The tract at the St. Croix's mouth was nine miles square. The cession at the Minnesota's mouth embraced an area stretching "from below the confluence of the Mississippi and St. Peters up the Mississippi to include the falls of St. Anthony, extending nine miles on each side of the river." Over this land the chiefs granted the government "full sovereignty and power" forever. In return, the Sioux were promised an unspecified payment.[10]

Instructed to record precise information about the country he explored, Pike described the falls far more accurately than had earlier visitors. He recorded the height of the cataract as sixteen and a half feet. "As I ascended the Mississippi," he wrote, "the Falls of St. Anthony did not strike me with that majestic appearance which I had been taught to expect from the descriptions of former travelers. . . . The width of the river above the shoot is 627 yards; below, 209. . . . In high water the appearance is much more sublime, as the great quantity of water then forms a spray, which in clear weather reflects from some positions the colors of the rainbow, and when the sky is overcast covers the falls in gloom and chaotic majesty."

For some unknown reason, the government was slow to implement the quick stroke of Pike's diplomacy. Not until March 29, 1808, did President Jefferson transmit the treaty to the Senate for ratification; the Senate then provided that the Sioux be paid two thousand dollars in money or goods for the estimated 155,520 acres in the two cessions.[11] After this act the land purchase in the distant west was apparently forgotten. The president did not put the treaty into force by proclaiming it, and the government neither paid the Sioux nor took steps to occupy the ceded area.

But the period of negligence was brief. After the War of 1812, the lessening of British influence in the Northwest and the impetus of westward expansion encouraged the migration across the continent, and the Minnesota country lay in its pathway. Fort Crawford on the upper Mississippi River at what is now Prairie du Chien, Wisconsin, was established in 1816 as the nation's northwesternmost military post. Beyond it in northern Minnesota British fur traders still flew the Union Jack over American land, warring Indian tribes made the area their battleground, and not an acre outside the Pike tracts had been ceded to open the way for white occupancy.[12]

Determined to lay a firm hand upon the region, the government in 1817 dispatched Major Stephen H. Long to the upper Mississippi to re-examine the ceded tracts as possible locations for a military post. Long confirmed Pike's land selections on the Minnesota and St. Croix rivers and added to his predecessor's description of the Falls of St. Anthony. His engineer's mission did not dull his pen, for he wrote of the verdant shrubs and trees upon the nearby islands and shores. The "majestic cataract" in its wilderness setting, he said, was "romantic in the highest degree," and the "most interesting and magnificent" scene he had ever witnessed.[13]

Soon after Long's inspection, the war department chose the cession encompassing the falls as the site for a new military post, and in 1819 Lieutenant Colonel Henry Leavenworth was ordered to build it. The government then tardily remembered that it had not paid the Sioux the compensation promised them in the Pike treaty. Major Thomas Forsyth, Indian agent at what is now Rock Island, Illinois, was dispatched upriver to remedy matters. When he gave the chiefs presents, Le Petit Corbeau freely acknowledged that the Sioux had sold the land. As the troops moved in, however, the Indians began a sniping campaign against the incursion. Leavenworth tried to quiet their objections in 1820 by making a second treaty for a grant overlapping the Pike cession, but the Senate did not ratify it. Finally, in 1838, the government settled the matter by paying the Sioux four thousand dollars to allay doubts about the transaction, and the falls, it seemed, were enclosed in the military reservation.[14]

Forsyth, who made the trip upriver with Leavenworth's troops, had been at the site selected for the new military post only a few days when he set off with the commandant, several other officers, and Mrs. George Gooding to see the Falls of St. Anthony. Mrs. Gooding, the wife of a captain in Leavenworth's regiment, was doubtless the first white woman to view the cataract.

The Indian agent supplied a fresh impression of the falls and the adjacent country: "In going out of a thick woods into a small prairie," he wrote, "we had a full view of the Falls from one side to the other, a distance of about four or five hundred yards. The sight to me was beautiful; the white sheet of water falling perpendicularly . . . over the different precipices; in other parts, rolls of water, at different distances, falling like so many silver cords, while about the island large bodies of water were rushing through great blocks of rocks, tumbling every way, as if determined to make war against anything that dared to approach them. All this was astonishing to me who never saw the like before. After viewing the Falls from the prairie for some time, we approached nearer, and by the time we got up to the Falls, the noise of the falling water appeared to me to be awful. I sat down on the bank and feasted my eyes . . . in viewing the falling waters, and the rushing of large torrents through and among the broken and large blocks of rocks, thrown in every direction by some great convulsion of nature."

In 1820, before Leavenworth got the construction of the new military post well under way, he was relieved by Colonel Josiah Snelling, who took immediate steps to erect a permanent fort. On a commanding site overlooking Pike Island and the junction of the Minnesota and Mississippi rivers seven miles below the falls, he built a stone fortress first named Fort St. Anthony and then Fort Snelling. With the erection of this post, white men for the first time took up permanent residence in the Minnesota country within sound of the thundering cataract.[15]

The establishment of Fort Snelling provided an island of civilization in the wilderness and acted as a magnet for an increasing number of travelers who soon made the Falls of St. Anthony one of the best-known tourist attractions on the North American continent. From 1823, when the "Virginia" inaugurated steamboat travel to the post, until mills and dams began to obscure their beauty thirty-four years later, the falls were a prime objective of hundreds of artists, writers, politicians, and curious tourists who ascended the Mississippi to see for themselves the cataract Hennepin and Carver had made famous in their books. Dr. Nathan S. Jarvis, surgeon at the fort, noted in August, 1835, that the number of visitors to the falls was "constantly increasing & I should not be surpris'd that in a few years this place will become as great [a] resort as Niagara. The number of visitors already this season is between 1 & 200." [16]

In thousands of words disseminated in books, newspapers, and letters, these travelers from many lands described the charm of the cataract and of the islands — three above the falls that were later called Boom, Nicollet, and Hennepin, and three below the precipice, later named Upton, Spirit, and Cataract. Giacomo C. Beltrami, an Italian nobleman who visited the falls in 1823, wrote of "the magic play of light and shade" upon the river rushing over the cataract and the "white foam and glittering spray" thrown up by waters crashing at its foot. Twelve years later an English traveler, Charles Joseph Latrobe, echoing Forsyth, noted the "long line of the Fall, which is in all its parts more or less interrupted by the fragments of the limestone which fall down as the force of the water undermines them by the removal of the soft sand underneath," of the islands near the cataract, and of the "vast size of the body of water thus seen leaping from a higher to a lower region." He thought "the scene truly majestic." Another English traveler, Francis Wilkinson, despairing of words, commented in 1855 that the cataract "must be seen before any idea is gained of its awful grandeur." But a lady who viewed it five years earlier was not so tongue-tied. Fredrika Bremer, a well-known Swedish writer of the day, described the falls as the Mississippi's "last youthful adventure" on its way to the Gulf of Mexico.[17]

Henry R. Schoolcraft, the widely traveled student of Indian life who later discovered the source of the Mississippi in Lake Itasca, passed the Falls of St. Anthony in 1820. His feelings about the cataract were mixed. "The scene," he wrote, "presents nothing of that majesty and awe which is experienced in the gulf below the cataract of Niagara. We do not hear that deep and appalling tone in the roar of water, nor do we feel that tremulous motion of the rocks under our feet which impresses the visitor at Niagara. . . . The falls of St. Anthony, however, present attractions of a different nature, and have a simplicity of character which is very pleasing. We see nothing in the view which may not be considered either rude or picturesque, and perhaps there are few scenes in the natural topography of our country, where these features are blended with more harmony and effect."[18]

An acute observer, Schoolcraft added that the falls were "in fact the precise point of transition, where the beautiful prairies of the upper Mississippi, are merged in the rugged lime stone bluffs which skirt the banks of the river from that point downward." Raising his gaze, he also perceived a change "in the vegetable productions, and the eye embraces at one view, the copses of oak upon the prairies, and the cedars and pines which characterize the calcareous bluffs. Nothing can exceed the beauty of the prairies which skirt both banks of the river above the falls. They do not, however, consist of an unbroken plain, but are diversified with gentle ascents and small ravines covered with the most luxuriant growth of grass and heath-flowers, interspersed with groves of oak, which throw an air of the most picturesque beauty over the scene."

Another well-known visitor was less impressed. George Catlin, an artist famous for his paintings of Indian life, published a sketch of the falls in 1841. He remarked that they presented a "picturesque and spirited scene," but were, after all, only "a pigmy in size to Niagara." A few years later a newspaper correspondent, sharply disappointed in the cataract, belittled it mercilessly: "The falls are remarkable for nothing except the encomiums produced by sluggish fancies at seeing the 'awful and sublime' spectacle of water pouring over a slightly inclined plane, broken here and there by jutting rocks, which, when the water is high, flirt the spray *almost* a foot, obliquely. Love-sick girls and victims of unrequited love may admire the fizzle, for either malady is supposed to be soothed by falling waters."[19]

The primitive beauty of the falls impelled Carver, Pike, Schoolcraft, Catlin, and others to sketch and paint it. Seth Eastman, commandant at Fort Snelling in the 1840s, did so, and Henry Lewis, an artist who visited the falls in 1848, included a view of them in his much-traveled panorama of the Mississippi Valley. As photography reached the frontier in the 1850s, B. F. Upton and others distributed stereopticon views of the famous landmark.[20]

Most of the travelers who made their way to Fort Snelling and then went overland or up the river to the falls were interested in them merely as a scenic spot. Only the military men who built the fort saw a functional use for the falling waters. As early as 1819 Leavenworth suggested to the war department "the propriety and advantage of erecting a saw mill and a grist mill" at the falls. His energetic successor as commandant, after considering briefly the high but narrow Minnehaha Falls located on a creek nearer the fort, proceeded to implement Leavenworth's plan. Under Snelling's direction, the soldiers built the mills and two barracks on the falls' west bank in 1821–23. Later commandants enlarged the installations; by 1833 Dr. Jarvis, the post surgeon, reported that "a large farm house & stables" for "near 200 head" of cattle had also been erected at the falls.[21]

In 1824 Colonel Snelling penned the following description of the first mills to utilize the water power of the cataract: "The Grist Mill is a fine building of stone, twenty five feet high from the bottom of the Cog-pit to the eaves; it is furnished with an excellent pair of burr stones and the flour manufactured the last year was equal to any in the world. The saw mill is a wooden frame building, in the ordinary form, the machinery is of the best kind, we have sawed in twenty four hours, three-thousand five hundred feet of pine plank; both of these mills are supplied with water from the falls, it is taken out at the table rock and conducted to the Mills by a race placed on the right bank of the river." [22]

Although the army's mills evoked some comment from visitors, none viewed the falls as a potential source of water power which would stimulate the growth of a city. Indeed, James E. Colhoun, who saw the mills in 1823, wondered why they had not been built closer to Fort Snelling. In 1837 another visitor, Peter Garrioch, called the water-driven mill an "ingenious invention," but he did not look beyond it to the cataract's unexploited power. [23]

Snelling's mills were nevertheless prophetic of the future. Ascending the Mississippi to the Rum River, soldiers from Fort Snelling logged in the same pinery which would yield a bountiful cut for subsequent mills at the falls. On the military reservation they planted grain to supply the gristmill—pioneer fields preluding the mantle of wheat which would later cover Minnesota, the Dakotas, and eastern Montana and supply giant flour mills at the Falls of St. Anthony. [24]

Fort Snelling influenced the cataract's future in other ways, for it also served as a nucleus of settlement. When the troops began raising the walls of the post in 1820, no permanent settlers inhabited the wilderness that later became the Twin Cities of Minneapolis and St. Paul. Along the streams, rivers, and lakes of the Minnesota country a few fur trade outposts punctuated the empty land. With the establishment of Fort Snelling, white civilization took root in the area. Making their homes at the post were soldiers and their wives and children as well as civilian employees. Other men opened farms and grogshops nearby.

Soon after the fort's establishment, a few settlers gathered at Mendota, located across the Minnesota River within the shadow of the post. The village's founder was Jean Baptiste Faribault, a French Canadian who entered the Minnesota River fur trade early in the nineteenth century. In the 1820s he was joined at Mendota by his son-in-law, Alexis Bailly. Appointed by the American Fur Company to foster the Minnesota trade, Bailly established at Mendota the area's first business center. In 1834 Henry Hastings Sibley replaced Bailly as the firm's representative at Mendota. Under his vigorous administration, the settlement grew from a collection of rude log huts to a more imposing trading hamlet. From the stout stone house which he completed in 1836 Sibley ruled over a fur empire extending west to the Missouri River and north to British America. In his manorial establishment he was host to Indians, voyageurs, officers from Fort Snelling, and famed travelers, statesmen, and fellow traders who learned from him about the resources of the surrounding country, including the Falls of St. Anthony.[25]

Within these two centers of white settlement in the mid-1830s were venturers who regarded the falls as something more than a beautiful cataract and a convenient power source for the garrison's mills. They saw them as a valuable and unexploited natural resource which could be claimed by those with the foresight to seize it. Major Joseph Plympton, commandant of Fort Snelling, and Franklin Steele, the post storekeeper, would chart the strategy for acquiring the eastern shore. From the fertile brains of Sibley, Samuel C. Stambaugh, Steele's predecessor at the fort, and Robert Smith, a friend of men at the post, would come plans to gain possession of the government mill and thus open for development the west side of the falls.

With men poised to snatch the prize, the Falls of St. Anthony, a valuable resource locked up in the Fort Snelling military reservation, entered the first phase of a turbulent history which led to their development as one of the nation's great water powers and the foundation of Minnesota's largest city.

2.

The Rise of St. Anthony

THE FIRST STEPS in wresting the falls' eastern shore from the government were taken in the 1830s by Fort Snelling's commander, Joseph Plympton. He knew that if the area could be detached from the military reservation and if the Indian title could then be extinguished, settlers exercising a pre-emption privilege could stake claims even before the land was surveyed. By showing evidence of settlement (usually by building a shanty), pre-emptors could later purchase the land at the minimum price whenever the government offered it for sale. Those fortunate enough to secure claims to the shore abutting the falls would control half of the water power, for land ownership would carry with it the "riparian right" to use the water flowing by the eastern shore.[1]

With so alluring an inducement before him, Plympton in 1837 took a close look at the Fort Snelling military reservation's vague boundaries. The cataract seemed well within them, for the Pike cession made by the Indians in 1805 extended nine miles along both sides of the Mississippi from a point below its junction with the Minnesota northward to a point above the falls. The commandants of Fort Snelling had never drawn exact lines, however, and they had exercised little control over the area. As a result, it soon swarmed with squatters. Farmers as well as fur traders and whiskysellers conducted their activities on the reservation near the fort.[2]

As squatters moving onto the reservation threatened to engulf the post, Plympton saw a way to do his duty as commandant and at the same time open the east bank of the falls to pre-emption claims. Soon after he arrived to take up his duties at the fort in 1837 he ordered an officer to study the extent of the squatters' encroachment. The survey, which was completed in October, 1837, revealed that 157 persons not connected with the military establishment were living on the reservation and that nearly two hundred horses and cattle were ranging over it.[3]

When Plympton transmitted this information to the war department, he was ordered to define the reservation and assert military control over it. In 1838 he forwarded to the department a map delimiting a reserve of approximately 34,000 acres. He also moved against the squatters, ordering all but the inhabitants of Mendota to leave the reservation. A few tenacious settlers ignored the command, but in 1840 — after a second map was made — a detachment of soldiers from the garrison forcibly evicted them. The refugees fled beyond the reservation limits and established a new settlement on the east bank of the Mississippi downstream from the fort. They called it Pig's Eye, the nickname of Pierre Parrant, a squint-eyed whiskyseller who resumed his business at the new location. A year later Father Lucien Galtier built nearby the rude chapel of St. Paul. He selected a spot favorable for steamboat landings, and newcomers gravitated to it. In eight years Pig's Eye was to become St. Paul, the capital of Minnesota Territory and the center of its burgeoning commerce.[4]

Plympton had in mind a more important objective than evicting squatters. When he drew the boundary line at the falls, he excluded from the reservation the eastern shore that had been considered part of the Pike cession, while including the western bank where the government mills were located. By his action the eastern shorelands again reverted to the Indians. In 1837, however, shortly before the commandant transmitted his map to the war department, the government negotiated with the Sioux and Chippewa two treaties extinguishing their title to the land lying between the St. Croix and Mississippi rivers, including the area lopped off the reservation. Only ratification by the Senate was needed to open the falls' eastern shore to pre-emption claims.[5]

The canny commandant, who with a pen stroke had made a most fortuitous jog in the reservation line, planned to stake his own claim at the falls, and during the summer of 1838, he awaited news from Washington that the treaties had been ratified. But someone else was waiting too. Franklin Steele, a twenty-five-year-old Pennsylvanian who had gone to Fort Snelling in 1837, also knew that the first man who staked his claim on the eastern shore would control half the falls' power. A tall, dark, attractive, young man of erect bearing, Steele had already tasted the fruits of western enterprise, for in 1837 he and his associates had secured control of the falls of the St. Croix (located some fifty miles up that river to the north) and had organized the St. Croix Falls Lumber Company. In 1838, after he became a storekeeper at the Fort Snelling post, Steele responded to the roar of the St. Anthony cataract and decided that this, too, was within his reach.[6]

On July 15, 1838, the steamboat "Palmyra" brought news that the treaties had been ratified, and Minnesota's first land rush was on. Steele, forewarned of impending ratification and fearing that Plympton also had the news, sped to the falls. One version of the story asserts that by the light of the moon, he and his crew built a cabin "cob-house fashion," paced off the claim, and blazed trees to mark its boundaries. At sunrise, their work done, they had settled down to a breakfast of savory pork when Captain Martin Scott tardily arrived from the fort with a party of soldiers to stake Plympton's claim. Entrenched beside the waterfall, the victorious claimant, according to an account published years later in the St. Paul Daily Pioneer, hospitably invited the latecomer to breakfast. Scott, who was in no mood for sociability, reportedly accused Steele of occupying a claim the captain had made "some months ago," and announced his intention to take possession of it. "Very well," Steele is said to have replied, "you can put me off by force . . . but I shall not leave willingly." Outmaneuvered by a superior strategist, the captain retreated and paced out for himself and his commandant less desirable plots near Steele's land.[7]

Other Fort Snelling officers and frontiersmen also built rude shacks on claims near the falls. They included voyageurs, traders, scouts, whiskysellers, farmers, and businessmen, half-breeds, French Canadians, Scots, Irishmen, and Americans. Among them were Pierre Bottineau, a well-known scout, Joseph Rondo or Rondeau, a Red River refugee evicted from the reservation by Plympton, Samuel J. Findley, one of Steele's clerks, Roswell P. Russell, who later built the first store in St. Anthony, and Baptiste Turpin, a voyageur.[8]

Although Steele hired a man to occupy his claim while he lived and worked at the fort, he could not rest easy in his possession. His only legal sanction was his pre-emptor's right, and his only protection was strategy and the shrewdness of a canny frontiersman. His property was a favorite target of claim jumpers, enemies of pre-emptors on every frontier. In one instance an invader took over the cabin while the hired occupant was gone, and upon his return threatened to shoot if he entered. Rather than engage in a gun fight over the property, Steele paid the jumper two hundred dollars in cash as well as a hundred dollars' worth of store goods.[9]

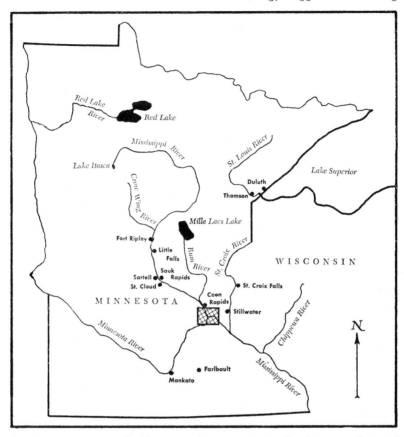

Red Lake River
Red Lake
Mississippi River
Lake Itasca
St. Louis River
Lake Superior
Duluth
Thomson
Crow Wing River
Mille Lacs Lake
Fort Ripley
Little Falls
Rum River
St. Croix River
WISCONSIN
Sauk Rapids
Sartell
St. Cloud
St. Croix Falls
Coon Rapids
MINNESOTA
Stillwater
Chippewa River
N
Minnesota River
Faribault
Mississippi River
Mankato

THE RIVER COMPLEX *significant in the water-power development discussed in this book is shown above. A detail of the shaded, boxed area of the Twin Cities appears on page 17.*

Steele had good reason to congratulate himself upon winning the falls' eastern shore. Within his claim the Mississippi River dropped fifty feet, creating falls greater than those which nourished Lowell and other leading industrial cities in Massachusetts. Nature and circumstance were ready to give more, but the water power could not be used profitably without raw materials, markets, transportation, and capital. Three of these four elements were at hand. A few miles above the falls, stretching northward into present-day Canada, was a forest exceeding in area the entire state of Maine, with trees reaching two hundred feet toward blue northern skies. These magnificent stands of pines and hardwoods covered 70 per cent of the land which was to become the state of Minnesota. Draining the pinery as it flowed from Lake Itasca to the falls was the Mississippi River, a natural transportation artery to carry logs from woods to mills. Below the falls the river coursed southward through a potential market of prairie lands opening to the plow. The pine, a prophet declared, would "supply the whole valley of the Mississippi" for two hundred years, and the falls' water power was extensive enough to "manufacture all of this lumber." [10]

North of the falls Steele had no competitors to cut off the flow of logs down the Mississippi to the cataract. Although men were already active on the St. Croix River, where Minnesota's first great lumber centers were created in the early 1840s, they had not yet tapped the rich stands bordering the Mississippi in what is now central Minnesota. Upriver from St. Anthony not a saw turned, and the only blots upon the forest were the decaying logging camps where Fort Snelling soldiers had cut logs for the government mill.[11]

With such bright prospects before him, the energetic Steele was not a man to let water run wasted over the falls. In 1847 he was ready to begin operations, but he lacked one vital element — capital. Since he was rich in property, he began a quest for partners who would provide the funds to build a dam and sawmills in exchange for a share in his claim.

The first capitalists Steele drew into his net were Caleb Cushing and Robert Rantoul, Jr., prominent Massachusetts lawyers and politicians. These distinguished gentlemen had plunged into western investments in 1845 when they organized the St. Croix and Lake Superior Mineral Company. In the same year Benjamin H. Cheever, a Boston broker, interested them in water power at St. Croix Falls, the site where Steele began his western business career. In July, 1846, as Cushing prepared for a trip to St. Croix Falls, Cheever gave him another tip. Steele, he said, "desires to have a conversation with you in relation to your visit West. . . . He is full of information in relation to this new country." Cushing rose to the bait, and in October he visited the Falls of St. Anthony.[12]

The easterner must have been impressed, for on July 10, 1847, Cheever, acting as Cushing's agent, met with Steele to "finish up" arrangements for a partnership to develop the falls' power. At an all-day conference in Steele's home, Cheever argued that his host's pre-emption claim was not adequate security for the capital necessary to improve the water power, since title had not yet passed from the government and the quantity of pine above the falls was at that

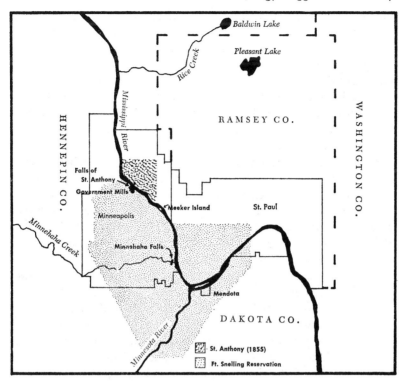

time unknown. The two men nevertheless reached a provisional agreement. Cheever waived temporarily the claim's dubious legal status and agreed to buy an interest in the property for Cushing and Rantoul. Before the investors decided upon the sum they would pay, however, Cheever insisted that Steele send a lumberman into the pineries to explore the timber resources, examine the Mississippi and its tributaries for navigability, and make a report.[13]

For this critical task, Steele selected Daniel Stanchfield, a lumberman who had recently arrived in Minnesota from Maine. Setting out in September, Stanchfield traveled north to the Mille Lacs region, approximately ninety miles above the falls. "I made it a practice," he reported, "to climb a tall tree every six miles . . . and to look from its top across the woods which reached far away in every direction." Although he admitted that his informal cruising methods gave him only a glimpse of the vast forest, he concluded that the pine was "almost inexhaustible." Stanchfield's findings were relayed to the waiting eastern partners, and they reputedly agreed to pay $12,000 for a nine-tenths interest in the property. In March, 1848, Stanchfield traveled downriver to Galena, Illinois, to collect the funds.[14]

While he was still negotiating with his eastern partners, Steele began to develop the property. After the provisional agreement was made in July, 1847, his crews built at the falls a mess hall, carpentry and blacksmith shops, stables, and a bunkhouse, and then prepared to construct the dam and sawmill. Work on the dam began in October, while a logging crew was still in the pinery near the Rum River cutting the timber needed to complete it. The logs were assembled in a boom at the mouth of the Rum. On November 1 the boom broke, releasing them prematurely for a pell-mell trip down the Mississippi and over the falls. Watching the logs drift past Fort Snelling, Steele sadly concluded that the accident would delay the work for a year. The resourceful dam workers, however, cut hardwood timber on Hennepin Island, hauled lumber from St. Croix Valley mills, and completed both the dam and sawmill in 1848.[15]

Located a short distance above the edge of the falls, the dam crossed the east channel, running from the shore to a point twenty feet above the head of Hennepin Island and then to the foot of Nicollet Island. The structure was approximately 700 feet long, 16 feet high, about 40 feet wide at the base, and 12 feet wide at the top. It was anchored to the river bed, and it had flumes placed at intervals to admit water. Upstream behind the dam was a millpond where logs were stored until they could be sawed. A low wooden sawmill equipped with two up-and-down saws was completed near the eastern end of the dam in September, 1848. In front of the mill stood a fifty-foot-wide platform for piling lumber.[16]

Meanwhile crews that were to work under Stanchfield's direction left St. Anthony for the woods on December 1, 1847, to harvest logs for the mill's first cut. Since the pinelands were still occupied by the Chippewa, Stanchfield bargained with Chief Hole-in-the-Day for cutting rights. After the chief agreed to sell the trees at fifty cents each, the loggers began their work near the mouth of the Crow Wing River. Three months later in March, 1848, the crews broke camp after cutting 1,500,000 feet of logs. These were placed in the river, and men were left behind to bring the drive down the Mississippi.[17]

The mill at the dam began cutting on September 1. Operating day and night for six days a week, it turned out approximately half a million feet of lumber by the close of its first season. "I have sold all the lumber as fast as it is sawed," Steele reported jubilantly in December. "I ran both saws up to the first of this month, and one since."[18]

While he was launching the first mill on the falls' eastern shore, Steele was also preparing for the day when he could buy the property from the government. To consolidate his holdings, he acquired Boom Island in 1848 as well as additional land adjoining his claims.[19] Since the sellers did not yet own the property they conveyed to Steele, these purchases were transacted in a legal shadowland. No one, however, seemed to dispute the aggressive frontiersman as he meshed enough claims to ensure his water rights and give him space for a townsite near the cataract.

Concerned about his investment, Cushing aided Steele in getting title to the property by using his political influence to hasten the government surveys. After they were completed, President James K. Polk on May 8, 1848, proclaimed the first sale of land in the area that became Minnesota. Ignoring more flourishing communities at St. Paul and Stillwater, the government established a land office at St. Croix Falls, Wisconsin. From this remote spot, officials sent out announcements listing the townships that would be offered for sale on specified days. Included were the lands Steele had pre-empted as well as the rest of the territory the Indians had ceded in 1837. From July 14 to 26 and from August 28 to September 11, 1848, a crier sang out land descriptions and knocked down the properties to bidders who offered the minimum price of $1.25 an acre. The area in which Steele and others were interested was auctioned on September 8. Steele bought for the minimum price 332 acres at the falls, including shorelands and Nicollet Island. Others who acquired substantial holdings near him were: Pierre Bottineau, a frontier scout, Calvin A. Tuttle, a farmer who had gone to Minnesota in 1838, and William A. Cheever, Benjamin's brother, who had settled below Steele's claim in 1847. In the bidding no one tried to wrest from Steele the prize he had won in the turbulent decade preceding the sale.[20]

Mindful of the townsite he had envisioned when he bought claims from other pre-emptors, Steele subdivided the land, and in 1849 he registered the plat. Upon the map the surveyor wrote "Saint Anthony Falls." Declaring that the name was "too big a mouthful for a man to spit out at once," Steele shortened it to "St. Anthony." Soon hundreds of settlers flocked to the townsite, and a newspaper—the *St. Anthony Express*—was founded in 1851 to give voice to the community's hopes.[21]

But even as Steele gained legal title to the St. Anthony property, he lost his partners. In 1848 Cushing, "abandoning speculation in water privileges," girded on "sword and buckler" and sped off to battle on the "plains of Mexico." Rantoul was left to face alone the consequences of an overextended partnership which could not meet its financial obligations. Early in 1848 Steele sent William Cheever to Boston to secure from Rantoul the payment of drafts totaling $13,000. After waiting vainly for almost a month, Cheever wrote his brother on March 7 that he believed Rantoul could not "get the money." He added, "I can see no other way than for Mr Steele to take back the property." [22]

Steele saw the matter in the same light, and in the fall he traveled to Boston to face the hard task of finding new investors. His partners quickly agreed to sell their interest back to him on terms which are unclear but which required Steele to raise $2,000 in cash. When he tried to borrow the money by mortgaging the property, he found that he could do so only at 1½ per cent interest a month—a rate he would not pay. Paul R. George, Cushing's friend and business associate, then offered a solution by advancing the money and taking Steele's power of attorney to sell a half interest in the property for $20,000. [23]

St. Anthony's citizens long regretted Cushing's withdrawal from the water power. On October 27, 1855, when he was serving as United States attorney general, the *Express* lamented: "How different might have been the results both for St. Anthony and Gen. [Franklin] Pierce's Cabinet, had Caleb continued steadfast here in his purpose of improving this gigantic water power! St. Anthony might by this time have outstripped Lowell," the Massachusetts city it regarded as a model, "and the Attorney General been a quiet, respectable citizen, attending to his lumber mills and cotton factories, under the soothing influence of the roar of the Cataract, instead of inhaling the poisonous political atmosphere of Washington."

Steele was more realistic than his townsmen about Cushing's departure, and never in all the years he labored to bring the water power into productivity was he known to express regrets. His eyes on the future, he extricated himself from the Cushing-Rantoul tangle and worked to further his enterprise. He took an important step forward in October, 1848, when he arranged with Ard Godfrey, a Maine millwright who had helped build the mill and dam, to supervise the St. Anthony business at a salary of $1,500 a year. He also offered Godfrey an option to buy a one-twentieth interest in the property, an option Godfrey exercised a year later. [24]

Paul George, seeking buyers in Boston, did not fail Steele in his need for capital. Through his efforts Arnold W. Taylor of Dorchester, Massachusetts, purchased a half interest in the property for $20,000 on March 31, 1849. At that time it included 250 acres which Steele still owned in the St. Anthony townsite, Hennepin Island, Boom Island, and frontage on Nicollet Island, as well as the water rights and the dam and mill. The sale price demonstrated the property's increased value, for Taylor's half interest cost him almost double the amount Cushing and Rantoul had agreed to pay for a nine-tenths interest two years earlier.[25]

At first Steele's new partner remained aloof from the St. Anthony scene. He appointed George as his business agent, and he left to Steele the responsibility for local management. Within a year, however, Taylor began to take a more active role. On frequent visits to the little town he injected into the situation a personality "running over with eccentricity," as the *Express* put it, and both Steele and the citizens of St. Anthony soon had reason to regret the agreement that brought him into the venture. Accustomed to Steele's liberal policies in selling lots and giving generous support to civic enterprises, another newspaper attached to the stingy Taylor all the opprobrium westerners were wont to heap upon absentee landholders, considering him a "thorn in the way of the advancement of the town."[26]

As early as October, 1850, a St. Anthony resident reported that Taylor was at "heads and points" with Steele and was talking of a "division of the property." Acting independently in 1850 Taylor offered to sell or lease St. Anthony's "unequaled hydraulic power." He also engaged a builder to construct a row of seven sawmills at the dam, at least one of which was built in 1851. In December, 1851, Taylor brought suit against Steele, claiming $10,000 in damages because the 1849 agreement had purportedly conveyed a bona fide interest in Hennepin Island, when actually Steele had only a pre-emption claim to it. This suit came about because two other pre-emptors had registered conflicting claims to the island after it was surveyed in April, 1851, thus threatening Taylor's interest through Steele. In a second action begun in the same month, Taylor sued Steele and Godfrey, who were doing business together as the St. Anthony Mill Company, for $10,352.59 — a sum Taylor alleged the two men owed him for using the sawmills and for his share in jointly held real estate Steele and Godfrey had rented or sold.[27]

Harassed by a partner who was strangling the enterprise, Steele bought out Taylor's interest on January 17, 1852, agreeing to pay his vexatious associate $25,000. The contract defined precisely the method of remittance. Steele was to pay Taylor $1,000 on January 17 and the remaining $24,000 within sixty days. He was to deposit the $24,000 in either the Merchants or the Suffolk bank in Boston, then deliver a certificate of deposit to Taylor at St. Anthony. Taylor was to retain his interest until Steele transmitted the certificate, and the two lawsuits were to continue until the sum was paid.[28]

On March 17, 1852, the scheduled day of payment, an agent acting for Steele in Boston tendered $24,000 first to the Merchants Bank, then to the Suffolk. When both banks refused the money, allegedly on the grounds that they did not issue certificates of deposit, the agent on the same day executed the transaction at the Bank of Commerce. Steele, who was in Washington, D.C., at the time, offered the certificate to Taylor when he returned home early in May. Claiming that the delay in delivery and Steele's failure to secure the certificate from a specified bank had nullified the agreement, Taylor refused to accept it. On May 20 Steele again tried to fulfill the agreement, this time offering Taylor $24,000 in lawful money and $240 for the exchange he would have to pay in transferring the funds to Boston. Again Taylor refused the payment.[29]

When his partner declined the second proffer, Steele acted quickly. On May 21 he took complete possession of the St. Anthony property, and four days later he brought suit against Taylor to force compliance with the January agreement. The court ruled on July 30, 1852, that Steele had fulfilled the spirit of the agreement and restrained Taylor from alienating title to the property until a final hearing could be held. Nearly a year later on May 4, 1853, the court issued its final decree, upholding Steele.

By that time—despite the court's order—events had put some of Taylor's interest into the hands of other men. Even before the January agreement was signed, as well as during the interval between that date and Steele's offers of payment, Taylor had acquired debts in St. Anthony, allegedly for improving the joint property. To pay them the county sheriff on November 5 and December 31, 1852, sold at auction Taylor's share in several St. Anthony blocks as well as in one saw. When the purchasers received their deeds, they in turn parceled out the property to others. Thus by the spring of 1853 fifty-two men held title to Taylor's interest. They knew that a court decision favorable to Steele would nullify their ownership.

Also alarmed about the impending decree was David A. Secombe, a St. Anthony lawyer, who on January 28, 1853, secured a judgment for debt against Taylor in the amount of $1,214.35. At a sheriff's sale held on March 17, 1853, Secombe bought Taylor's interest in a piece

of shoreland carrying water privileges and in four saws in the partners' mills. At the same sale, John W. North, who was also a St. Anthony attorney, purchased Taylor's interest in another saw, bringing
to fifty-four the number of men who owned portions of Taylor's
share in the partnership property.[30]

When the 1852 sheriff's sale occurred, Steele had lulled the purchasers into a feeling of security by assuring them that he would
make no settlement with Taylor depriving them of their "just dues"
as long as the sales did not involve property necessary to the water-
power development. The 1853 sheriff's sale did involve such property,
and rumors reached the purchasers that Steele and Taylor had pri-
vately agreed on a settlement which excluded the claims of purchasers
under both sales. As a result, in March, 1853, they petitioned the
court to admit them as codefendants in Steele *versus* Taylor for the
purpose of sharing in the $24,000 Steele would pay Taylor when
the final decree was issued. In its decree of May 4 favoring Steele the
district court dismissed their petitions, awarding the entire sum
to Taylor alone.[31]

Two days later the petitioners appealed to the Supreme Court of
Minnesota Territory asking that the order dismissing the petitions
be set aside. One of the purchasers reported that this move "damp-
ened" Steele's "ardor" considerably, and placed him "in great per-
plexity about the possession of his Mills." [32] He responded to the
new crisis by trying to buy the property from the litigants. In 1854,
when it became clear that he could not acquire at his price the fragments necessary for developing the water power, he sued the purchasers in district court to quiet the title.

Two suits concerning the same matter were now before the courts,
and both were disposed of in Steele's favor during the next three
years. In 1855 the district court sustained Steele in the suit he had
instituted. When the defendants appealed, the territorial Supreme
Court on February 2, 1856, upheld Steele. The defendants then carried the suit to the United States Supreme Court under a writ of
error, and that tribunal in 1857 again affirmed that Steele's title to
the property was good. In the meantime, in 1855, the territorial Supreme Court had sustained him in the purchasers' first suit, and
their cause was lost.[33]

In the early stages of his struggle to free the water power from
Taylor's grasp, Steele had the hearty public support of the people
of St. Anthony. Its citizens honored him with a banquet when he

bought his partner's interest in 1852. During the litigation with Taylor, the local papers portrayed Steele as a public-spirited man devoted to the town's interest, while they clothed his partner in villain's robes. The contentious Taylor was accused by the *Express* of January 24, 1852, of tying up the "immense water power" and rendering St. Anthony's "unrivalled natural advantages" useless. With his departure the town would grow at a rate "unknown even in the most prosperous western cities." On October 27, 1855, the *Express* opined that the like of the large, ruddy-complexioned Taylor was not to be found in "all the characters ever drawn by pen. . . . He stands by himself, solitary and alone, in all this surging world of humanity. . . . Childish simplicity, yet withal shrewdness, difficult to a fault, now communicative, now silent as the grave, delighting in the ring of metal, clutching close and tight to the 'evil root,' and then again when fancy pleased, full lavish — and more than all, a bachelor, of full forty, such an assemblage of incongruities and contradictions were never before united in a single character."

Although the press cheered on the town's champion, Steele's conflict with the local purchasers engendered private resentment. Some of it undoubtedly stemmed from a general sentiment against monopolies. Steele's association with the Mendota fur interests through his sister's marriage to Henry H. Sibley, as well as his position in St. Anthony, made him a natural target. Attorney North, one of the purchasers, forcefully expressed the private hostility toward Steele as early as 1850. He confided in letters to his family that the day had passed when St. Anthony's founder could assume he owned the town and pursue his interests without regard for others. With the motley group of French-Canadian and half-breed pre-emptors who had originally staked out the east side he might safely act the role of leader, commented North, but now St. Anthony had an articulate "American population" that would not accept Steele's patronage. According to North, the conflict over the Taylor interest sharpened this feeling. The purchasers, he wrote, felt that Steele had treated them like a "pack of fools," and they believed that he had manipulated district court judges to win his cause against them.[34]

Steele's serious financial troubles during the years he shared the property with Taylor were complicated by the multiplicity of his business interests. In addition to the Fort Snelling store, the water power, the mills, a ferry, and St. Anthony real estate, he owned a warehouse in St. Paul, and shares in two boom corporations, several railroads, and a bridge company.[35] He did not have enough capital to keep all his enterprises afloat and at the same time develop the water power at the falls beyond a pioneer stage.

The limits to which he was driven in meeting financial crises are illustrated by the measures he took in 1851 to pay a $12,000 note due in New York. Lacking funds to satisfy the debt, he sent his devoted friend John H. Stevens east to raise them. He was ready to pay 10 per cent annual interest on the loan and give as security "the best real estate in the Territory." Should Stevens fail, Steele asked Sibley to negotiate a mortgage on the falls property. Discouraged by his continual need for money, the weary man declared he would either "connect" himself with men of ample capital or close up his business.[36]

Laboring in New York, Stevens extricated his associate from the creditors' "clutches" by signing another note using the firm name of "Steele & Stevens," an organization that did not exist. Chagrined by the subterfuge he had to practice, Stevens expressed a hope that in the future Steele would "manage closer" or sell the property. "God knows," he confided to Sibley, "that I care more for him . . . than any other live man — not excepting my brothers — but through his noble and generous heart he too often, neglects his business."[37]

Steele, however, was not neglecting what to him was the most important requirement for developing the falls — capital. Safely past the immediate crisis the note had precipitated, he enlisted Sibley's help in finding a third set of partners. He was fortunate in his brother-in-law, for through the American Fur Company Sibley had acquired contacts with New Yorkers in that organization. Among them was John F. A. Sanford — the son-in-law of Pierre Chouteau, Jr. — who later figured as a defendant in the Dred Scott case. Sibley had known Sanford since the 1830s, and through the Mendota trader Sanford stepped forward in 1852 to buy an interest in the St. Anthony property.[38]

Sanford, in turn, brought two other New Yorkers into the business — his brother-in-law, Frederick C. Gebhard, an importer and banker, and Thomas E. Davis, a merchant. In an agreement signed on April 8, 1852, Steele conveyed to the three men for the sum of $50,000 a half interest in the St. Anthony townsite, the dam, four sawmills, the gristmill, the St. Anthony boom, Hennepin Island, Boom Island, Boom Landing, frontage on Nicollet Island, and water rights attached to all the real estate conveyed.

Although Steele at first enjoyed better relations with his new partners than he had with Taylor, at least one irritation sprang up early in the association. In 1853 both Sanford and Gebhard complained to Sibley that in twelve months Steele had sent them only one letter. "I feel easy myself," wrote Sanford, "but my friends do not. They went into it alone on my knowledge of Mr Steele. . . . Will you my Dear Sir," he urged Sibley, "see friend Steele & press on him the propriety of writing them or myself." Steele must have heeded the admonition, for the New Yorkers not only continued the partnership, but in 1853 bought out Ard Godfrey's interest in the property.[39]

In 1854 the easterners assumed closer supervision of the falls enterprise by appointing as their local agent Richard Chute, an energetic man who had become well acquainted with Minnesota while a member of the fur-trading firm of Ewing, Chute and Company of Indiana. The tall, spare, fair-complexioned Chute first saw the falls in 1844, when he was traveling in the area. He visited them again in 1848 and yearly thereafter. Upon his appointment as agent, he moved his family from Indiana to St. Anthony. For the rest of his life, this able and charming man was to be closely associated with the water power and the community's interests. In 1855 he became a partner in the St. Anthony enterprise as did John S. Prince, a representative of the Chouteau fur interests in St. Paul.[40]

Although Steele had to scramble to secure the capital needed to develop the water power, he emerged in 1855 with five strong partners and a prosperous manufacturing development. When a great flood washed three million feet of logs over the dam in 1850, he and his partners raised the structure several feet at a reported cost of $30,000. To increase the water supply in the eastern channel, he built in 1853 a temporary dam from Nicollet Island across the western channel to the opposite shore. And in 1855 he constructed a 3,500-foot sluice for carrying sawed lumber from the mills to a point below the falls for rafting downriver.[41]

In this period sawmilling was by far the most important industry at St. Anthony. Between 1849 and 1852 the number of mills increased from one to four, and daily production capacity went from 15,000 board feet to about 50,000. When a gang saw was added in 1854–55, total sawing capacity rose to about 100,000 board feet a day and 12,000,000 a year. The mills were run by various operators. For a time Steele and Godfrey, associated in the St. Anthony Mill Company, ran some of the saws themselves, while Taylor used others to saw for lumbermen on a contract basis. After Godfrey withdrew from the enterprise in 1853, Steele no longer tried to operate the mills. Initiating a practice that later became common, he leased them at various times to such lumbermen as Caleb D. Dorr, Sumner W. Farnham, Henry T. Welles, and Dorilus Morrison.[42]

The expansion of sawmilling facilities at the falls stimulated a large log harvest in the upper Mississippi pineries. Millions of feet came into the St. Anthony pond and thousands more crashed over the cataract on their way to downriver markets. In 1851, when over eight million feet floated to the falls, Steele and other lumbermen organized three boom companies to handle them. The St. Anthony Boom Company built works above the cataract to catch the logs, sort them by log mark, and turn them over to their owners much as cattle wranglers on the western plains later cut herds by brands. Below the cataract, the Mississippi Boom Company performed the same function, and in 1852 Sumner W. Farnham and his associates incorporated the Rum River Boom Company to organize the drives nearer the source of cutting. The moving ranks of logs then passed in a more orderly fashion from the pineries to St. Anthony.[43]

From there much of the lumber was rafted downriver, particularly to St. Louis, but the local community and nearby St. Paul also provided a substantial market. St. Anthony took pride in the "busy clack and din" of the sawmills. "The *Lion* of the place," wrote a young lawyer newly arrived from the East, ". . . is a sawmill operated by water power."[44]

But this was not always to be so. In 1851 Richard Rogers constructed at the end of the sawmill row a little grist and flour mill, which was a harbinger of the future. A year later Steele joined Rogers as a partner in the small custom mill which produced corn meal, feeds, and flour. Some notion of the capacity of this pioneer establishment can be gained from the fact that thirty-two bushels of grain brought to it by a farmer in 1853 were called "the largest grist ever ground at the falls." Although the mill produced only a tiny amount of flour, the press congratulated the community upon liberating itself from the tyranny of importing this commodity. "Persons who expect to get eight and ten dollars per barrel for flour before the opening of navigation might as well 'hang up their fiddles,' " advised the *Weekly Minnesotian* (St. Paul) on December 25, 1852. Minnesota spring wheat, claimed the *Express* of May 6, 1853, "is nearly if not quite equal" to the winter variety raised farther south, and the local mill's flour "is fully equal to the average imported."[45]

Merchant flour milling — as distinct from grist or custom milling — was born at the falls in 1854 when John Eastman, John Rollins, and Rufus P. Upton built the "Minnesota" or "Island" mill and prepared to buy grain, grind it, and sell the product. Leasing water power and a site on Hennepin Island from Steele for two hundred dollars a year, the three men erected a flour mill measuring forty by sixty feet at its base and rising three stories above the basement. It had four run of stones and machinery procured in Milwaukee, Pittsburgh, and Buffalo. The owners engaged an itinerant millwright who built it, said the *Express,* "in the same happy-go-lucky way a carpenter would make the frame of a house." The reckoning came when two floors collapsed soon after the machinery was put into operation. "A good laugh was enjoyed at the expense of the owners," recalled the *Northwestern Miller,* "but they repaired the break without serious trouble." In 1854 the *Daily Minnesotian* (St. Paul) urged householders to " 'hurry up' the Johnny cakes," for the new mill had established the astonishing record of grinding 160 bushels of corn in four hours. The following year the *Express* triumphantly reported that the mill had turned out a hundred barrels of flour in a day. With its opening, farmers were encouraged to market their wheat in St. Anthony at "remunerating prices," but local production was so small that the owners had to import supplies from Iowa and Wisconsin.[46]

In their loyalty to home manufacturing, residents of the community tried hard to be proud of the flour made by the Island mill. The *Express* of February 17, 1855, declared, "It is as fine and soft as any flour we ever saw, and excepting a slightly dark color, is superior to our best imported brands. . . . The time is not distant," the paper predicted, "when Minnesota, with the superiority of her soil and seasons for wheat culture, and her unparalleled water power for manufacturing flour, will export largely of this article. Farmers need but to attend more carefully to cleaning well their wheat fields and keeping them free from noxious weeds, or cleanse their wheat . . . before sending it to the mill, and our mills will turn out wheat, superior in quality and appearance to any now manufactured in the West."

As the mills at the falls prospered, so did the community of St. Anthony. In 1848, when Steele bought the land, an estimated three hundred persons lived in the town. By 1850 the population had more than doubled, and five years later St. Anthony had approximately three thousand people. To serve the growing community, stores, schools, churches, and a hotel were built, and hundreds of laborers and professional men moved in. Evolving from a collection of makeshift claim shanties, Steele's village rapidly took on the appearance of a thriving town.[47]

Sprawled over a lightly wooded prairie sloping gently to the river,

St. Anthony at first glance looked like a New England village. Gleaming white houses, surrounded by gardens and cattle grazing on the open land, gave easterners the feeling that they had traveled into the distant West only to find a bit of home transplanted to the falls. But a second look reminded them that St. Anthony was not a peaceful New England town resting quietly in maturity. Houses built of green lumber cured on their foundations to the annoyance of housewives who mopped up the oozing moisture. "Nasty, piratical looking pigs" roamed at will, and streets were filled with stumps. Stagecoaches, carts, and wagons rumbling in from St. Paul—the head of Mississippi River navigation where steamboats carrying people bound for St. Anthony tied up—spilled out passengers with mountains of baggage and freight. Indians wandered through the town, strangers to the noise and bustle around them. Piles of logs and lumber from the sawmills dotted the landscape, and the whine of the saws could be heard above the roar of the falls. In 1855 Steele's town was incorporated as a city. Fittingly its new seal bore a view of the falls, framed by a saw, a sheaf of wheat, and a barrel of flour. The wheels were turning, lumber and flour were flowing from St. Anthony's mills, and the first city to be born at the falls was launched on its brief period of glory.[48]

3.

The Birth of Minneapolis

WHILE THE EAST SIDE WAS EMERGING as a city under the aegis of Franklin Steele, men who shared the aggressive frontiersman's vision fixed their sights upon the land across the river. Unlike the shore property Steele had seized in his dramatic maneuver, the western bank was well within the boundaries of the Fort Snelling military reservation. But it was a tempting prize, for the person who shared the falls with Steele could develop the other half of its water power — a resource that might well yield a fortune. With so rich a prize sealed into the reserve, ambitious men began in the 1830s to storm the wall barring their entrance.

The targets of the first assault were the saw and grist mills the government had built in 1821–23 to supply the Fort Snelling garrison. In 1836 Samuel C. Stambaugh, who like Steele was a sutler at the post, launched the first of a series of devious campaigns to pry the mills from the government when he boldly proposed to Quartermaster General Thomas S. Jesup that he be permitted to buy them. Jesup, who seems to have been indebted to Stambaugh for past political favors in Pennsylvania, countered with an offer to grant the sutler a ten-year lease on the condition that he turn over to the Fort Snelling garrison one-third of the lumber sawed. Dissatisfied with this offer, Stambaugh went to Washington, where he was confident of the support of Secretary of War Lewis Cass. Both Cass and Jesup were absent from the city, however, and even an appeal to President Andrew Jackson failed to produce the desired results. All Stambaugh's pleas eventually wound up on the desk of Acting Quartermaster General Trueman Cross, who doubted the "propriety" of granting mills and land located in "Indian country" to a private individual. Cross also suggested seeking the opinion of Lieutenant Colonel William Davenport, who preceded Plympton as commandant at Fort Snelling. In 1837 Davenport wrote a stinging criticism of

Stambaugh and his project. He termed the sutler's maneuver a "treachery to the public," and stated emphatically that the post command did not recommend either the lease or sale of the mills. Stambaugh continued unsuccessfully to exert pressure on the war department, increasing his offer in 1841 to ten thousand feet of free lumber a year. By that time, however, he had competition.[1]

In 1838 Robert Harris of Harrisburg, Pennsylvania, asked his Congressman to find out if the secretary of war would grant him "any portion of the water privilege at the falls of St. Anthony." He was unsuccessful, and in 1838–39 three other applicants joined forces in an attempt to wrest the mills from the government. They were Henry Sibley, Kenneth Mackenzie, a St. Louis fur trader, and Adam D. Stuart, an officer formerly stationed at Fort Snelling. Requesting that the "whole affair" be kept *"sub rosa,"* Sibley confided to Senator Lucius Lyon of Michigan that the three men had determined to "make an effort . . . to obtain from the Government, a release of the mill privilege . . . upon engaging to furnish any lumber necessary for the garrison at a low rate. As it would be our object, should we succeed in our purpose[,] to erect permanent mills and other necessary buildings forthwith," he continued, "it would be the means of opening the Upper Mississippi to our enterprising lumber men, who are at present excluded from that pine region in consequence of the falls' remaining in possession of the Government."[2]

Although they enlisted the aid of Congressmen, government officials, and other influential friends, Sibley and his associates failed to secure the lease. The decision was penned early in 1839 by the army's acting quartermaster general, who observed — as had Major Cross three years earlier — that the "insuperable" objection to granting the lease "is presented by the fact that the mills are situated in the Indian country: and that, although the United States may have had the right to construct and maintain them, as necessary appendages to a military post, it is believed that the 'Government cannot consistently with our obligations to the Indians sell or lease them out to individuals.'"[3]

Where Sibley, a Minnesota resident knowledgeable in the ways of frontier land acquisition, had failed to secure the mills, an outsider succeeded. Tall, brisk Robert Smith, an Alton, Illinois, businessman and representative in Congress, visited the falls in 1848. He had supported Sibley while the latter labored in Congress to have Minnesota made a territory, and he said that he played a "humble part" in fixing its boundaries. In 1849 he purchased lots in St. Paul, and his interest in Minnesota became so well known that he was suggested for appointment as territorial governor.[4]

Early in 1849 Smith asked the war department to grant him a five-year lease on the mills at the falls and on a house that had been built near them. "I shall move into the Territory of Minnesota after the adjournment of Congress," he wrote, "and I wish to procure this house for my family to live in, and to fix up the old grist mill to grind corn and other grain, there being no grist mill now [*operating*] in that region of the country." The commandant at Fort Snelling warned his superiors in Washington that Smith intended to gain a foothold on the reservation rather than to establish a home, but the war department leased the property to him in spite of the officer's protest.[5]

Although Smith did not move to Minnesota, he apparently allowed the department to believe that he was living on the property. Late in 1849 he wrote the secretary of war, using the following argument to secure additional land: "I am repairing the mills and the house at considerable expense, and, in order to carry them on at all profitably, I must have ground to raise something to live upon. . . . Provisions are dear and scarce, while there are tens of thousands of acres of excellent land, with no one within six or seven miles (on the same side of the river) cultivating an acre. . . . I cannot but believe," he concluded, "that it will be decidedly for the interests of the government to permit me to make a farm adjoining the mill." The secretary, falling into Smith's trap, granted him the favor.[6]

While Smith was securing the government mills, Franklin Steele also found a way to gain a toehold on the west side of the falls. He suggested to his friend John H. Stevens, the genial Canadian whom he employed as a bookkeeper in 1849, that Stevens bargain with the war department to obtain 160 acres above Smith's mill in exchange for maintaining a ferry at the falls. Steele reasoned that a ferry would be useful for troops and teams passing between Fort Snelling and newly established Fort Ripley on the upper Mississippi near present-day Brainerd. Steele's surmise that the government would entertain such a proposal was correct, for the secretary of war granted Stevens' request soon after it was received. To consolidate his gain, Stevens built during the winter of 1849–50 the first permanent home on the site of the future city of Minneapolis. Dwelling with his bride in the white frame house by the falls, Stevens was reminded that this was indeed frontier country. "We have often gone to bed at night . . . ," he wrote, "waked up in the morning and seen that while we were asleep, the wigwams of either the Sioux, Chippewa or Winnebago, had gone up." [7]

The next move to secure the west half of the falls came from Smith. In 1850 he sold an interest in the mill lease to Alexander Mitchell, Minnesota Territory's first marshal, and Henry M. Rice, a St. Paul fur trader and businessman who succeeded Sibley as territorial delegate to Congress. Two years later Smith audaciously asked the government to sell him the mills outright. The war department consented in 1853, and for $750 he became the owner of the buildings. "The means taken to obtain a foothold on the reserve," wrote an early historian of Minneapolis, "calls to mind the fable of the camel, that begged leave of a tailor just to warm his nose at his open window, but when his modest request was granted, pushed his demands until the tailor was driven out and the camel left in undisputed possession." [8]

By the time the sale of the mills was completed, Smith had new partners. Alexander Mitchell had withdrawn from the arrangement; Smith offered a share to Sibley, but the "Squire of Mendota" refused the invitation to the feast. In 1853 Rice, too, made his exit, selling his interest to Benjamin F. Fridley, George Huy, and Benjamin F. Brown. The land adjoining Smith's mills was quickly taken up. In 1852 Anson Northup, who was already the owner of a hotel and other property in St. Anthony, crossed the river to claim forty-eight acres next to Smith's property. Unlike Smith, Northup lived on the tract, built a house there in 1853, and cultivated eight acres. At approximately the same time, Charles B. Russell claimed twenty-six acres next to Northup; in 1854 he moved upon it and began farming. [9]

Although the land on the west side of the falls was still in the military reservation, pressure for its release was mounting. Under the land practices accepted on the frontier, settlers and speculators believed that if they could enter the forbidden area, establish a residence, and cultivate land, they might be considered first settlers. Anticipating the eventual day when the government would be forced to offer the reserve for sale, doctors, lawyers, merchants, laborers, real-estate dealers, soldiers, and a host of others badgered the war department and the Fort Snelling command with requests for permits to settle. In the absence of a cohesive policy, the officials yielded haphazardly—as they had in the instances of Smith and Stevens—to considerations of friendship, influence, and self-interest. [10]

John North of St. Anthony explained how such matters were handled. "I have got a claim on the Military reserve .. . . ," he wrote his father-in-law in 1851, "in company with one of the Officers at the

Fort. He has a written permit from the Commanding Officer, and I have an article of agreement by which I am to share it equally with him. Mr Finch my brother in law is going to move on to it in the Spring, in consideration of which I let him have one half of my share. We have enough included in the claim for three good farms, and the Lieut shares equally in the expense of all improvements except the building of a small shanty which will cost possibly five dollars, and which I build in consideration of his getting the permit from the Commanding Officer. . . . We hope in that way," he continued, "that a very trifling expense will secure to us the preemption right to a valuable piece of Land. Such chances can rarely be got, and in no case except in company with some Officer."[11]

When pressed to give the reasons for granting permits to some while refusing them to others, the Fort Snelling command replied that each case was judged according to its merits.[12] But military reasoning was not consistent enough for egalitarian frontiersmen. A facetious dialogue published in the *Express* of December 13, 1851, has "the boys" berating "Uncle Samuel" for the conditions that existed—the boys observing that the officers and the "biggest boys" in the territory had taken up so much land that soon nothing would be left for the "hard-fisted democrecy" but swamps and sand hills. The solution the boys suggested was for the government to open the reserve, sweep out everyone there, and then offer the land to all comers at $1.25 an acre. "We will then show you," continued the boys, "as pretty a fight as you can see at Donnybrook Fair."

In the early 1850s hundreds of settlers moved onto the reservation they regarded as a "useless and uncultivated blotch upon the finest portion of our Territory—a sort of military carbuncle." Invoking the code that protected the sacred rights of squatters, they took up claims covering almost every inch of the area. By 1854 reservation lands rolling back from the west side of the river were sprinkled with dwellings of almost every description. Although some were makeshift shanties built only to hold claims, many were neat frame buildings constructed of pine sawed by the mills at the falls.[13]

Since their residence on the reserve was illegal, the settlers were beyond the protection of law. And they had dire need of it. "A sort of frenzy seemed to possess people," wrote an observer, a frenzy which "dulled all sense of honor, and led them to trample on the most sacred rights." Men slept uneasily in their cabins, firearms by their sides. In outbursts of violence, they jumped one another's claims and moved across the reserve in gangs to give them courage.[14]

Such frontier anarchy spawned frontier regulation. The settlers themselves marked out their claims by informally extending the survey lines the government had laid out on the east bank. Some bargained away parts of their claims to community leaders in exchange for promises of support when the time came to legalize their settlement. But the most important weapon of self-protection was an association formed by the settlers to enforce a code of frontier justice. Organized in 1852 in John Stevens' home, it was at first called the Minnesota Protection Association; by 1853 it had become the Hennepin County Claim Association. In nearby areas other settlers on the reserve formed the Calhoun, Military Claim, and Mendota Claim associations. These groups co-operated in bringing order and in urging squatters to submit to discipline. The Minnesota Protection Association drafted regulations, recorded claims, and arbitrated disputes. It also administered punishment to violators, in one case by lashing a claim jumper and evicting him from the territory.[15]

The resolute invaders posed a real problem for the Fort Snelling command. Although officers had staked claims on slender legal pretexts and granted permits to the privileged, they were obligated to keep the area clear as long as it was a military reservation. Steering around pitfalls in logic, they chose to free their hands by distinguishing between men who took claims by permit and those who were squatters. They ordered illegal occupants from the reserve and implemented the command in 1852 by razing the cabins of those who defied them. These actions did not prevent squatters from swarming back into the reserve, but they added bitterness and uncertainty to an already chaotic situation.[16]

Mind and heart with the settlers, Minnesotans urged legislative action to reduce the reservation and guarantee the squatters' rights. The territorial assembly, gathered in its first session in 1849, opened the campaign when it passed a resolution requesting that Sibley, as Minnesota's delegate in Congress, urge the war department to reduce the reserve and secure pre-emption rights for the squatters.[17] The legislature's action mirrored the temper of the place and time, for frontiersmen considered the government only a temporary custodian of land which should be turned over to them as soon as they needed it.

Although Sibley was uncomfortable in the knowledge that a law including a pre-emption clause would protect the claims of favored persons like Smith as well as the squatters, he considered himself "virtually instructed" to secure its passage. After one effort failed, Congress in 1852 passed a bill severing 26,023 acres from the 34,000-

acre reserve, leaving approximately 8,000 acres for military use. The act did not contain a pre-emption clause, but it stipulated that the area was to be surveyed immediately and offered for sale at public auction.[18]

Passage of the law brought new anxieties to the settlers on the reserve. Since the act did not contain a pre-emption clause, they had no assurance of being the successful bidders at a public sale. Rumors flourished that Smith and others planned to grab the choice lands near the falls where a town would surely develop. Reacting sharply to the reports, the *Express* took up the cry for squatters' rights, the "common law" of the West. In the coming sale, it warned on June 24, 1854, any man who bid against a squatter "would be the most unfortunate of human beings. To the goadings of a guilty conscience . . . would be added the scorn and curse of an outraged community, upon whose lips his name would forever become a byword and reproach." [19]

The community at the falls had no chance to test the honor or courage of men who might bid against the settlers, for the sale scheduled for September 18, 1854, was delayed when the plats did not arrive at the land office in time.[20] After the sale was postponed, agitation began for an amendment granting the settlers pre-emption rights. In 1854 the territorial legislature sent a memorial to Congress requesting that protection be given to these pioneers who had made the "wilderness to blossom like the rose." Throughout the anxious months that followed, Minnesotans traveled to Washington to add the force of their personal influence to the effort.[21]

The reserve's fate was finally settled in 1855 when an amendment granting the pre-emption right became part of the law. Although some Congressmen felt that the amendment would favor persons who had claimed the most valuable parts of the reserve, the influence of western representatives dedicated to the general principle of settlers' rights carried the day. When a Congressman, uttering the cry of the West, declared that the policy of protecting first settlers had carried the American flag "to where it is now floating upon the other side of the continent," the fight was over and the bill passed.[22]

Even before its passage, men at the falls were busy snatching claims like "luscious fruit, dropped from the hands of a grandfather," as the *Express* of February 24, 1855, put it. Sleighs and horses in St. Anthony were pressed into use to carry lumber for shanties across the river. When the bill passed, the *Express* of April 28 declared that

Congress had removed from the west side the "mighty incubus, which like a mountain of lead, has crushed her to the earth."

With their rights ensured by the new law, members of the Hennepin County and Calhoun claim associations met to dissolve their organizations and plan a day of "general rejoicing." Declaring that they had the "utmost confidence in the officers at our Land Office," the settlers yielded the weapons with which they had fought for squatters' rights. In 1855 and 1856, 187 persons quietly trooped into the land office to buy 20,661 acres of the reserve at the minimum price of $1.25 an acre.[23]

By 1855 the mills on the west side and the nearby lands had been consolidated into a partnership holding of twelve men. Smith retained a 25 per cent interest. Ten owners held an interest amounting to 62½ per cent. Among them were Fridley, Huy, and Brown, who had bought out Rice's share of the mills; Roswell P. Russell and Marquis L. Olds, land office officials; and Leonard Day, a local lumberman. The final 12½ per cent interest was owned by Dorilus Morrison, who was already operating a sawmill in St. Anthony. The transactions which led to this consolidation were carried on in the same legal shadowland where Steele had operated, for Northup and C. B. Russell—the original claimants—could not buy their claims until 1855. Nevertheless Smith and others readily purchased interests in them, and several of the transactions were duly recorded by the Hennepin County Register of Deeds.[24]

Morrison was easily the most important partner Smith acquired during the shuffle. A decisive and dignified businessman, he had come from Maine in 1854 searching for pinelands. He joined the enterprise through his cousin, Cadwallader C. Washburn, who since the 1840s had conducted a land agency and other businesses at Mineral Point, Wisconsin. Washburn's interest in Minnesota stemmed both from an acquaintance with Smith—to whom his firm had loaned money and sold land warrants—and from his substantial holdings in the territory's pinelands. As Washburn's agent, Morrison managed his lands above the falls, sawing logs at a mill on Steele's east-side row.[25]

The owners of the west-side water power did little to develop it or their mills in the years between 1849 and 1855. They remodeled the dilapidated government sawmill in 1850–51 and again in 1854, and leased it to various operators. Calvin Tuttle, George Huy, and Leonard Day ran it for a time, as did Charles King, a local lumberman. It remained in operation until 1857.[26]

The gristmill was even more neglected. The owners rented it to various millers and made no major improvements in the building or its equipment. Reuben Bean ran it in 1849, and Calvin Tuttle took over in 1850. He operated it until 1855 as a custom mill, grinding customers' grist for "lawful rates of toll." The *Express* of May 31, 1851, said that the little establishment accepted buckwheat, corn, rye, oats, peas, and "whatever else requires grinding, including Salt." As a special service to customers, Tuttle offered to pick up grists in St. Anthony and deliver them after grinding.[27]

Although the water-power owners at first did little to foster it, a settlement developed on the west bank of the falls. By 1854 the advancing flood tide of squatters had raised the population to an estimated 300, and two years later it had increased to an estimated 1,555. Schools, churches, and social and cultural organizations came into being; grocery, clothing, hardware, and furniture stores offered merchandise to the settlers. In 1854 the community acquired the voice so essential to frontier towns, when a newspaper, the *North-Western Democrat,* moved across the river from St. Anthony.[28]

The settlers who had so aggressively forged a town from the reserve vacillated when it came time to give the community a name. Among those suggested was Lowell, in honor of the industrial city on the eastern seaboard. Local citizens could find no higher praise than comparing the Falls of St. Anthony with the cataract at Lowell, and no ambition, it seemed, could be more exalted than to build in the West a city on this eastern model. But other citizens wished to name the town Winona, Albion, West St. Anthony, or All Saints.[29]

Many residents, as well as the neighboring *Express,* spoke up for a different choice. "It is bad enough," the paper declared on December 24, 1853, ". . . to have had the rivers, woods and villages of this Territory so thoroughly be-sainted by the Canadian voyageurs who first discovered this land of promise. For them however a plausible apology may be offered. But that at this day the saintly calendar should be [used] . . . to christen a thriving young city is past belief especially in the prodigality of beautiful and expressive Indian appellations still unappropriated." The name selected was indigenous to the locality. It was suggested in 1852 by Charles Hoag, one of the settlers. He coined the word "Minnehapolis" by combining Minnehaha, the Sioux word for "laughing waters" and the name of a small nearby falls, with "polis," the Greek word for city.[30] Although the town used such names as All Saints and Albion after Hoag made his suggestion, Minneapolis, the "h" removed, gradually won approval.

The community was as laggard in establishing a municipal government as it was in choosing a name. The settlers rapidly subdivided their holdings into blocks and lots even before they held formal title, but the semblance of a town was stronger than the reality. The first local governmental unit with jurisdiction over the area was Hennepin County, created in 1852. Two years later the territorial legislature strengthened this tie by naming Minneapolis as the county seat. In 1855 twenty-one persons filed a plat for the "Town of Minneapolis"; the legislature authorized the establishment of a municipal government in 1856, but not until 1858 was the first election held.[31]

At first the west-side village looked to flourishing St. Anthony for leadership, and little rivalry existed between the settlements. St. Anthony men crossed the river to take up land, build stores, and open offices. The two towns, joined by the cataract that had created them both, shared a sense of common destiny. St. Anthony men fought beside the Minneapolis claimants in freeing the reservation, and the older town's residents assumed a generous attitude toward the settlement. "A city is to grow up on the opposite bank . . . ," the *Express* declared on November 29, 1851, "the interests of which are to be identical with our own." On October 27, 1855, the *Express* stated that it expected St. Anthony and Minneapolis soon to be "united under one corporation, and constituting one great city which will know no superior North-west of Chicago."

The two communities had more in common than a waterfall. Their inhabitants, drawn heavily from New England and the Middle Atlantic states, developed a similar civic consciousness in which pride and a kind of inverted humility were mingled. Social and cultural institutions grew as luxuriantly as they had in the fertile ground "back East," and the local inhabitants watched with pleasure the evolution of a "polished and refined society" at the falls. They were inordinately proud that the new towns were "peopled from the colleges, court-rooms, pulpits, counting rooms and workshops of the East." Affirming this identification, the *Minnesota Republican* claimed: "We are Yankees by birth and profession, by inclination, education, habits and *twang*."[32]

While the inhabitants boasted of living in the "New England of the West," they were conscious that the claim was not really valid. Toward easterners who viewed the towns as rough and the inhabitants as "below par in point of morality and intelligence," they were defensive, and they countered with bitter criticisms of the older society from which they had sprung. More positively, they pointed out that for all the similarities with the East, this was the West — a region bursting with new vitality, ambition, and resources which would become a formative influence in the nation as the pendulum of economic and political power swung to the Mississippi Valley.[33]

The unity between Minneapolis and St. Anthony was strengthened in 1854 when a group of citizens constructed a beautiful suspension bridge spanning the Mississippi from the western shore to Nicollet Island. It met a bridge built earlier between the eastern shore and the island to form the first span ever to cross the Mississippi River at any point. A gala celebration on January 23, 1855, signaled the opening of the bridge linking the two towns and the "Eastern and Western valleys of the Mississippi." Minnesota Governor Willis A. Gorman, addressing a crowd assembled to celebrate the occasion, saw the completion of the bridge as a significant event in the emergence of the West. "This is a wonderful enterprize," he said, "when we consider that we are standing at the Falls of St. Anthony, 2200 miles from the mouth of this great river, and when but yesterday . . . we were crossing its turbid waters in a log canoe, and pushing as with the palm of our hands the red man of the forest and prairie, farther and farther back from the habitations of civilized men." Then looking to the future, he exhorted the people not to let pass the opportunity "of making known to the Congress of the United States, the accomplishment of this great work. Point them to the fact that it is upon the [*proposed*] line of the Northern Branch of the Pacific Railway. Who knows but this mighty structure may yet bear . . . the commerce of the Pacific, as it mingles with that of the Atlantic!"[34]

Identifying themselves as a single manufacturing center with the falls as their hope for a bright future, the two communities — in the ambitious booster fashion of the times — drew together to make common cause against their rival downriver. St. Paul, with an estimated population of well over four thousand in 1855, was a formidable adversary, drawing great strength from its position at the head of navigation. Its busy levees teemed with steamboat traffic, and its thriving commercial center enjoyed prestige as the territorial capital. The falls communities, on the other hand, seemed destined to be manufacturing towns. "The interests of the two places are in direct opposition," the *Express* declared in 1854. "One must . . . be a hamlet; and as to which . . . will be the hamlet we apprehend none doubt."[35]

Expressing confidence in the falls, Paul R. George declared in

1850 that "man made Saint Paul, but God made Saint Anthony." After quoting this assertion, the *Minnesota Pioneer* of December 26, 1850, retorted: "This is in part true. God made the thundering cataract there, and Franklin Steele put a yoke upon its neck . . . but the same God also made eighteen miles of very crooked river below the Falls, and very swift, and scattered flocks of boulders, and ridges of ledge in the channel. The same God also left a very pretty spot for a steamboat depot, where Saint Paul is."

The newspaper had a point. Below the falls was a rock-filled channel that frightened even courageous captains accustomed to the treacherous Mississippi. Determined to remove this obstacle to progress, community leaders launched a crusade to bring cargo and passengers directly to the falls without "running the gauntlet" at St. Paul. They encouraged captains to make the hazardous trip by offering bonuses, building warehouses and landings below the falls, making exclusive cargo agreements with captains and steamboat lines, organizing a company to build boats dedicated to the service of the towns at the falls, raising money to remove the worst obstructions from the river, and petitioning Congress through the Minnesota legislature for federal funds. With every successful steamboat run, the newspapers toasted the communities' fair future in commerce as well as in manufactures and looked forward to St. Paul's impending demise. The *Express* of July 5, 1851, maintained that when the falls were acknowledged as the "true head" of navigation on the Mississippi the "CITY (?) of St. Paul will retrograde to a modest little village, — grass will grow in the now crowded, and busy Exchange; the owls will build their nests in the City Hall, grand even in ruins." But the battle was a futile one. While a few steamboats responded to the bribes, St. Paul remained the practical head of navigation. Passengers headed for St. Anthony and Minneapolis continued to disembark at St. Paul, while freight was forwarded from the capital in wagons.[36]

In 1855 the fate of the three communities seemed to depend on the Mississippi River. It was a question whether the towns at the cataract, deprived of the navigation essential to commerce in this prerailroad age, would develop manufactures rapidly enough to avoid becoming a milling suburb of the ambitious port city of St. Paul. It was a question, too, whether St. Anthony, with its lead in water-power utilization, would retain its dominance over Minneapolis. The answers lay with the men controlling the falls, for the way in which they used the water power would determine the outcome.

4.

East Side—West Side

As HORSE-DRAWN SLEIGHS DASHED OVER the new Suspension Bridge in the winter of 1856, the twin towns were at peace. The harsh sounds of conflict attending the fight over the reservation were stilled, and Minneapolis and St. Anthony were as calm as the river slipping beneath its frozen sheath to break free for its plunge over the falls. The shoreland owners busied themselves with plans for developments that would infuse new life into the communities. Steele's associates— weathering the first stormy years of their western venture—were ready to join him in forming a permanent organization to develop the eastern half of the cataract. Smith and the eleven other men who controlled the west side were also ready to take a long look at the future.

Acting independently but simultaneously, the two groups secured from the territorial legislature on February 26 and 27, 1856, per-petual charters incorporating companies capitalized at $160,000 each. They borrowed names from the towns at the falls. Smith's group called its organization the Minneapolis Mill Company, and Steele and his partners named their firm the St. Anthony Falls Water Power Company.[1]

Under the common law recognized in Minnesota, the incorporators through their shoreland ownership already possessed the privilege of using water flowing past their lands. The charters, acknowledging this riparian right, granted the new organizations authority to main-tain dams already placed in the river and to build additional instal-lations for the purpose of improving the water power. They divided the river between the two companies, empowering Minneapolis Mill to construct installations to the mid-point in the western channel, which was the main stream, and leaving to the St. Anthony firm the other half of the main stream as well as the eastern channel. The firms were allowed to use the water, but they did not own the river. The obligations conferred by the charters were as specific as the privileges granted. Since the Mississippi was a navigable stream, the charters required the firms to provide a passage for logs through their dams and restrained them from interfering with the rights others might have in the Mississippi.

The fact that they shared a river created the companies' first major problem. Because each organization planned to use water on its own shore, they had to find a way to divide the flow. This necessity inspired a co-operative plan for constructing a dam across the river above the falls that would drain part of the water into a millpond on the west side and part into the St. Anthony pond. In 1856–57 the St. Anthony firm reshaped Steele's dam by removing the section between Hennepin and Nicollet islands and extending a wing into the western channel. In 1856–58 Minneapolis Mill built — as a counterpart to the old Steele dam — a structure projecting into the western channel against which sawmills were to rest. It also constructed a wing which angled upriver to join the portion built by the St. Anthony firm. When the co-operative project was completed, a single large dam shaped like an inverted V angled out from both shores and met upriver in the middle of the western channel.[2]

The dam "is a monster affair," boasted the *Daily Minnesotian* of December 22, 1858, "and for strength and durability equals any thing of the kind that has yet been constructed in the United States." Built on a scale to meet the challenge of the Mississippi, the structure was fashioned of rock-filled timber cribs covered with planks on the upriver side, and it was anchored to the river bed with oak bolts. Its base, sixty feet wide at the ends near the shores, narrowed gradually to sixteen feet at mid-channel. Twenty feet high near the banks on the west side and some fourteen on the east, it declined to four feet at the apex. The main structure was 2,206 feet long; with connecting dikes, gates, and other shore installations, it measured 3,574 feet. The *Falls Evening News* of November 28, 1857, observed that the new dam would "stand for ages" and would make available for manufacturing "the most magnificent water power in the country."

The co-operatively built structure drastically changed the appearance of the cataract and represented the first major assault upon its natural beauty. It drained the river above the falls and left them exposed in low water as a barren mass of limestone rock. Only during periods of high water, when the swollen Mississippi rushed over the dam, did the Falls of St. Anthony again exhibit the splendor which had so delighted tourists and travelers.

After building the dam, each company withdrew to its own shore, pursuing an independent course. Although they shared equally in the cataract, had the same access to raw materials, and enjoyed identical corporate powers, other factors influencing their development created two dissimilar organizations. Under aggressive and harmonious leadership, Minneapolis Mill seized its opportunity to develop the west-side water power, while the St. Anthony company—obstructed by the same discord among its owners that had clouded Steele's earlier ventures—foundered on the shoals of mismanagement.

The St. Anthony company began its corporate existence promisingly enough. Gathering in New York City in April and May, 1856, the incorporators forged an organization hopefully designed for operational efficiency. John Sanford, Frederick Gebhard, and Thomas Davis, who together owned half the stock, recognized that direct responsibility for conducting the firm's business must rest on the westerners. Thus the incorporators elected Franklin Steele president and Richard Chute secretary-agent. They appointed Steele, Chute, and Prince of St. Paul as an executive committee empowered to act on the company's behalf.[3]

Accustomed to changes in the water-power organization, St. Anthony received phlegmatically the news that the owners had formed a company. The *Express* of February 9, 1856, observed cautiously that development of the water power would "redound to the benefit of the whole City." The owners, on the other hand, enthusiastically declared in a statement published in the *Express* of August 9, 1856, that the city, vitalized by water power, would become the "Key to the North-West."

Though their words seemed to presage a bright future, not many months passed before a nationwide panic, breaking in 1857, blighted the young city, paralyzing its financial institutions, blocking the flow of eastern capital to its enterprises, and stemming the tide of immigration. In the wake of depression came the Civil War.

During these bitter years, the company had difficulty in renting its sawmills and selling town lots. Its revenue was not sufficient to meet operating expenses, to say nothing of extending the water-power development. The Minnesotans were in no position to furnish the additional capital needed. Steele was so deeply involved in other enterprises that the company was only one strand in the web that entangled him; Prince had no funds to give the organization; and Chute, a man of small means, could contribute only his managerial skills.

Hope rested, therefore, in the New Yorkers' willingness to extend credit, supply capital, and use their influence with other moneyed men to extricate the company from its financial morass. Unfortunately for this hope, Sanford died on the eve of the 1857 panic.[4] He alone knew the Minnesota men, and it was he who had brought Davis and Gebhard into the business. With his death good will between the Minnesotans and the New Yorkers evaporated. The easterners accused the westerners of bad management and even dishonesty, while the Minnesota men suspected the New Yorkers of protecting their investment without regard for the corporate welfare.

Soliciting the distant partners' aid and understanding, the persuasive Richard Chute in 1861 laid before them a summation of the company's unhappy experiences in trying to pay taxes, promissory notes, and interest out of dwindling income. The "financial tornado that swept over the country throwed Minnesota on its beam ends," he wrote, "and took from us our available resources. After lying still 3 months . . . & sadly misjudging the extent & duration of the disaster," he continued, "we undertook *Man fashion* to 'Bridge the Crisis' but our timbers were too short."[5]

Efforts to resolve its financial problems plunged the company deeper and deeper into trouble. In 1859, for example, Henry Sibley (who held a mortgage on the property as security for money owed by the company on lands it had purchased from him) sold the paper to William H. Gebhard, Frederick's brother. Two years later Gebhard brought suit to secure payment, and the Hennepin County District Court entered a judgment in his favor for $48,524. In 1861, too, Davis and Frederick Gebhard sued to recover $20,000 they had loaned the company in 1857. Fortunately for the firm, the frontier mills of justice ground slowly, and in 1869 it was still awaiting orders that would put its property on the auction block to satisfy the judgments.[6]

Not content with borrowing from the easterners funds to sustain the company, the westerners also solicited money to develop other interests. Sometime in the 1850s Chute and Prince obtained $6,150 from the New Yorkers, and when the latter brought suit to recover in 1868, Chute complained that they did so in order to get control of his company stock. Steele dragged the firm into an even more involved financial situation in 1859 when he personally borrowed

$63,500 from Frederick Butterfield, a New York merchant known to the eastern partners, and pledged his stock in the St. Anthony company as security.[7]

Although Steele was president, a member of the executive committee, and the largest shareholder, he exerted no effective leadership in guiding the company. Fighting a defensive battle, he warded off disaster by signing new notes to pay past due obligations, pledging his property, and pleading for time. On all sides creditors pressed him for payment. "If you intend to come home soon," a St. Anthony employee wrote in 1860 while Steele was in the East trying to raise money, "I would advise you to bring a considerable amt of money with you, although parties are easy when you are away, as soon as they see you, you will have a hornet's nest about your ears." [8]

The Minnesotans, traveling back and forth between St. Anthony and New York, persistently knocked on their associates' doors soliciting money to carry the company through its crises. Suspicious, each group felt that the other was bent on getting control of the property. In January, 1859, Gebhard "utterly refused to advance or help with his Credit" when Chute appealed to him. "I then proposed," Chute wrote, "that we should sell the property West of Main St. with Water Power Mills &c. but to this he would not listen as he said that was the most valuable part of all." [9]

Two months later Chute, still in the East, was somewhat encouraged when Davis told him that if his interest could be sold for $100,000 in cash he would lend the money to the company. Spurred by the promise, Chute scurried after purchasers. "I shall pull this string hard," he wrote Steele, "& in meantime punch Gebhard up. I have talked very plain & will continue to do so & shall leave no stone unturned to accomplish what we need." [10]

Throughout 1859 and 1860 Chute crowded the New Yorkers for money, while he tried to find a buyer for the Davis interest. In his desperation, Chute urged Steele to join him in New York. "I know you would not stay away unless detained by important business," he commented in 1859, "but the *fire* is hottest at this end of the line." Davis frequently promised to help, but at every turn Gebhard blocked specific measures to extricate the company from its difficulties. "D will play the amiable," Chute wrote in April, 1860, "G. the Shylock." [11]

In the midst of recriminations and mutual suspicions, the associates had very little area of common understanding. Since the board of directors rarely met, the stockholders were dependent for communication upon letters and visits. Chute and Steele took the initiative in maintaining contact, for as local managers they were obligated to report on operations. The lead they took personalized the struggle, making them feel that they alone cared to save the property. Occasionally, however, even the beleaguered Chute showed some comprehension of how the absentee owners felt. "I do not expect that eastern parties can appreciate these things," he wrote of the difficulties the local managers were having, "it would be strange if they did." The solution, he thought, was for the New Yorkers to visit the falls and "see for themselves if all has been done on the square."[12]

The Gebhards went to St. Anthony in 1860 and 1861. William's trip in 1860 did not improve relations, but more amity and a course of action came out of Frederick's visit in 1861. Before he made the trip, he wrote Steele that he was eager to enlist his "valuable counsel and support" in considering plans "to relieve the property of its embarassments [sic] and ultimately save something for the proprietors." And he made perfectly clear the course of action he had in mind — sell the company. Showing more confidence in Steele than he ever had before, he wrote on his return to New York that he was satisfied the westerner could present facts to buyers in a way that would prove "the property is cheap and desirable."[13]

Gebhard's suggestion to sell was not the first time the stockholders had entertained the idea. In fact, they always returned to it as the only solution upon which all could agree. Devoid of local offers, Steele in 1860 had planned, as Chute put it, to go "over the Water" to England in an attempt to find buyers. When the president's plan became known, St. Anthony, eager for good news from the embattled water-power organization, reacted favorably. "People here say when I tell them that you are going," Chute wrote, " 'Well Steele has got good pluck at any rate' or 'I glory in his spunk,' & the report does us good." Although Steele canceled his plans, the proposal for a sale in England cropped up again in 1864.[14]

In 1866, after several other efforts had failed, the stockholders — their numbers reduced by Frederick Gebhard's death in 1865 — evolved a scheme for what Chute called a "home trade" that might "change defeat into victory." This plan, which matured in 1867, differed from those advanced earlier. Instead of selling the company outright, the men proposed to offer shares in it at $62.50 each. After buying the stock, the new owners would divide the property into millsites and then allot the sites. The organization, it was hoped, would be composed of men interested in developing water power for their own mills.[15]

The *Minneapolis Daily Chronicle,* enthusiastic about the opportunity for centralizing company ownership in St. Anthony, urged citizens on May 24, 1867, to buy the shares before they fell into the hands of "Eastern capitalists." The *Minneapolis Tribune* of June 27, 1867, predicted that the plan would cut the "gordian knot" and open a "brilliant future" for the east-side power. But the community's enthusiasm for the proposal was premature. Like the schemes gone before, it was entertained for a few months and then dropped.

The company, however, was in no position to continue plowing heavy seas of debt and conflict. In 1866 the firm's debts amounted to almost $200,000, and selling remained the only practical solution. Two years later the New Yorkers at last sold their shares to twelve local men for $160,000. Several of the buyers had strong interests in water-power development — David Secombe, who in the early 1850s had fought Steele for the property, and three lumbermen who had operated the company's mills, Sumner Farnham, John Martin, and John S. Pillsbury. On the evening of September 9, 1868, when news of the sale was announced in St. Anthony, the noise of cannon, steam whistles, and church bells sounded in a "jollification" celebrating the change in ownership of the company which controlled the city's destiny.[16]

The new stockholders immediately made trouble for Steele, Chute, and Prince. They obtained an injunction ejecting Chute from the firm's office and instituted a suit against all three men to recover $100,000 the company allegedly owed the New Yorkers. The complaint filed by the new stockholders was a litany of abuse. It charged that Chute conspired with Steele and Prince to hold his position as agent, that he withheld income from the New Yorkers while they poured $100,000 into the enterprise, that he fraudulently received $12,000 for services, that he used company funds to purchase judgments against it and then turned them over to his brother, Samuel H. Chute, without compensation, that he brought the company to the "very verge of bankruptcy" through mismanagement and prejudice against the New Yorkers, and that he was planning to sell company real estate and grant 999-year water leases. As if this were not enough, the complaint also charged that the Minnesotans were "insolvent and irresponsible men" who had already pledged their own stock as collateral for debts greater than its value.[17]

With the city in an uproar over the lawsuit, President Steele on

September 29, 1868, called to order the first stockholders' meeting held in five years. Chute must have somehow satisfied his critics, for he emerged from the meeting as the company's new president. John Pillsbury was elected secretary, and Henry G. Sidle, a stockholder and a banker, became treasurer. The new bylaws vested management in the board of directors instead of the executive committee, provided that the entire net income be used to pay debts, and declared that the company would hereafter push water-power development energetically. The board of directors consisted of President Chute, Pillsbury, Martin, Farnham, Samuel Chute, and Butterfield, who still held Steele's shares as security for the personal loan made in 1859. E. S. Brown, a local lumberman who had supervised construction of the dam in 1856–57, became company agent. The new president's position was strengthened a day after the reorganization when Butterfield appointed the two Chutes as his representatives. Two weeks later the stockholders withdrew the suit naming Richard Chute as the chief architect of the company's misfortune.[18]

In the heat of the struggle no one paused to memorialize the men who had fought so long for and over the water power. Steele, the moving force in the company's development since he made his first bid for partners in 1846, quietly relinquished his posts. The city press, usually so avid for memories, did not even remark upon the coincidence that he gave up the presidency in the thirtieth year of his victory in the 1838 land rush. Sanford, the man who brought together the ill-fated combination of easterners and westerners, was dead, as was Gebhard, who had been a thorn in the Minnesotan's side. Davis, the "amiable," gladly laid down the burden and departed for the sunny climes of Italy, while Prince, divesting himself of his St. Anthony interest, became wholeheartedly a citizen of St. Paul. Of these men no one wrote, for they belonged to a past full of frustrated hopes.

While the St. Anthony firm was enduring thirteen years of chaos, the Minneapolis Mill Company became a flourishing business organization. Differences that affected the development of the two companies were rooted in the natures of their owners. The St. Anthony proprietors split into two hostile factions, but the men who owned Minneapolis Mill worked together almost as one.

There were many reasons for this harmony. After the firm's incorporation, the men holding small interests gradually relinquished their shares, leaving of the original stockholders only Robert Smith and Dorilus Morrison. Cadwallader C. Washburn, Wisconsin lumberman and Morrison's cousin, bought shares in 1856, and the next year his brother, William D. Washburn, joined the group. By 1865, and probably earlier, Smith, Morrison, and the two Washburns held all the stock; Smith had seven-sixteenths of it and each of the others had three-sixteenths. Thus the ownership of Minneapolis Mill evolved smoothly toward consolidation in the hands of four able and aggressive businessmen.[19]

Although Smith and C. C. Washburn were absentee owners, the four men had a great deal in common. All shared similar viewpoints as westerners by adoption. Smith, who was born in New Hampshire, migrated in 1832 to Alton, Illinois, where he made his home for the rest of his life. He never moved to Minnesota, but he retained from his first visit in 1848 a concern for the commonwealth's future. C. C. Washburn left Maine in 1839, living in Iowa, Illinois, and Mineral Point, Wisconsin. After 1861 he made his permanent home at La Crosse, Wisconsin. It was he who encouraged his younger brother, William, to move from Maine to Minneapolis in 1857. Moreover, Morrison and the Washburn brothers had grown up together in Livermore, Maine, and they had a mutual interest in Minnesota pinelands.[20]

The two Washburns, while dissimilar in personality, made a strong team. Both were striking looking, elegant men who possessed great vitality and good educations. The comments of those who knew them indicate that C. C. was perhaps the more amiable of the two; William was given to positive opinions and "dogmatic and sometimes even arrogant ways." One Minneapolitan who knew him well wrote that William "insisted always upon doing things in his own way, regardless of restraint or advice of others, and was not always easy to work with."[21]

All four men were deeply interested in public affairs. Morrison, who served as mayor of Minneapolis in 1867 and as state senator, was active in politics all his life. The two Washburns belonged to a family of public officeholders. As a political rival remarked in the heat of a Congressional campaign, they seemed to assume they were born with "M. C." (member of Congress) stamped on the seat of their pants.[22] W. D. served in Congress as well as in the Minnesota legislature; C. C. represented Wisconsin in Congress and was that state's governor. Smith, too, was elected to Congress from Illinois and to the state legislature several times.

Three of the men had a bond even more important to the Minneapolis company's prosperity. Although C. C. Washburn did not move to Minnesota, he shared with his brother and Morrison great confidence in the city's potential as a manufacturing center. The three men believed that their future lay in building mills at the falls as well as in selling water power. Thus they fused their identities as manufacturers and water-power men, and it was this dual interest that moved them to harness the falls as rapidly as their resources permitted. Steele on the east side had entertained a similar idea when he constructed the first mills, and Taylor's plan for adding saws was part of the same philosophy. With the addition of partners who were not manufacturers, the plan crumbled, separating for years on the east side the functions of distributing and using water.

In the 1860s the two Washburns and Morrison gained complete control of Minneapolis Mill. C. C. Washburn, mildly discontented with Smith's position as president and majority stockholder, offered either to buy the Illinois man's shares or to sell his own. Disposed neither to "fish nor cut bait," the aging Smith in 1865 transferred his interest to his brother William, then relinquished the presidency to Washburn. Smith died in 1867, and two years later C. C. achieved his objective by purchasing William Smith's stock. At no time, however, did these transactions seriously disturb the firm's tranquility.[23]

The proprietors maintained their equilibrium despite keen financial anxieties. Like the St. Anthony owners, they faced the problems of launching a new business during periods of depression and war. Like their neighbors, too, they made heavy investments to harness the water power before returns could be reaped. C. C. Washburn worried a great deal about the prospects. "The total cessation of business knocks me badly," he wrote in 1858. Robert Smith, too, felt the pinch during the depression years. Faced with raising $22,000 to pay for water-power improvements in 1858, he wrote to Elihu B. Washburne, a brother of his partners: "I never want to live to see such another time as we have had."[24]

The owners' reaction to the financial crisis of the 1850s was totally unlike that of the east-side group. The Minneapolis men assumed that their investment in the water power was a long-term one, and they knew that they must tide the company over lean years to ensure the harvest. They provided for an initial capital outlay in their organization plan, reserving three-tenths of the company's shares to finance improvements when they exchanged their land holdings for stock in 1856. Nor did they contend against the fact that as individuals they must lend the company money and as stockholders accept assessments against their shares.[25]

Between 1856 and 1867, when investments in improvements were particularly heavy, the stock assessments amounted to $103,800. The size and number of levies created hardships among small stockholders and may have been the reason they gave up their interests to Smith, Morrison, and the Washburns. A bylaw and a charter amendment provided that the company might levy interest of 2 per cent a month against unpaid assessments, and that shareholders who did not honor the levies would forfeit their stock. In 1858, when several small holders had already given up their stock for nonpayment, a group of them protested against further assessments. The revolt was unsuccessful, however, and other company owners purchased the forfeited stock.[26]

Franklin Steele's ownership of land above Minneapolis Mill's property precipitated a minor financial crisis. In 1857 Steele forced the company to buy the land by threatening to build a dam which would expose Minneapolis Mill to lawsuits for infringements on his riparian rights. In order to forestall construction the company bought the land for $25,000, offering as security a mortgage on its own property payable in five years. During the panic years, the firm could not meet the interest payments, and the debt at maturity amounted to $37,500. Steele, however, compromised with the debtors, accepting $22,000 in personal notes signed by the owners in lieu of the total sum.[27]

The Minneapolis Mill Company's fortunes in the 1860s contrasted sharply with those of the St. Anthony firm, which was threatened with auction sales for personal and corporate debts. By the mid-1860s Minneapolis Mill's investment in revenue-producing installations was yielding a return. In 1867, when its gross income from rentals was $10,683.32, the company distributed its first known cash dividend of $19,872.85 — a sum probably made possible by sales of millsites and accumulations from earlier years. Moreover the stockholders, who were interested in manufacturing facilities for themselves as well as in cash returns, found another method of compensation, for in 1865 and 1867 they took a substantial amount of rent-free water power.[28]

The two companies' different approaches to business problems were also reflected in the facilities they built to develop the falls. After joining Minneapolis Mill in constructing the big dam in 1856–57, the St. Anthony company for ten years built no major installations to extend its half of the water power. As manufacturing establishments scattered along the east bank and over Hennepin Island, the St. Anthony firm transmitted power to them through a makeshift system of shafts and ropes, running from water wheels on the dam, which showed more ingenuity than engineering skill. The dam across the eastern channel remained, as it had in the partnership period, the location where water wheels were centered.[29]

At last in 1866 the St. Anthony group announced plans to expand the east-side water power by constructing a canal which would conduct water from the millpond, carry it through the shorelands, and discharge it into the river below the falls. The mammoth canal, one newspaper reporter prophesied, would drain the falls so dry that "the ghost of St. Anthony will take up his residence among his big, dry stones, and lament everlastingly his departed watery glory." But the canal did not progress very far. After workmen had dug several hundred feet into the shore, they encountered a great cave. Probably deterred by the costs of additional exploration and new engineering plans, the company then postponed construction.[30]

The west-side proprietors pursued no such haphazard course in expanding their portion of the falls' power. Instead they modeled their development on the well-established Atlantic seaboard water powers at Lowell, Lawrence, and Holyoke, Massachusetts. It will be recalled that in its admiration for one of these cities, Minneapolis had contemplated adopting the name of Lowell, and it was to New England that Minneapolis Mill now looked for guidance. In 1857 the company engaged Charles H. Bigelow, an engineer from Lawrence, to design the water-distribution facilities it planned to construct.[31]

Central to the design of the new installations was the company's objective of carrying water through a large manufacturing center. On the east side expansion of the industrial district was largely limited by the distance power could be transmitted from water wheels on the dam. Although Minneapolis Mill also included in its plan a dam which could be used by sawmills to draw power directly from the river, it was a minor part of the whole design. The most important feature in the west-side system was a canal angling inland from the millpond and then paralleling the shore. Reaching numerous sites and offering facilities for carrying water to other nearby locations, the canal opened a large area for mill building.

Work on it began in 1857. Men blasted their way through the surface of hard limestone and dug out the soft sandstone beneath to excavate a passage 14 feet deep, 50 feet wide, and 215 feet long. The "great canal," as it was dubbed, was lengthened in later years. More than any other part of the installations harnessing the falls, this waterway nourished young Minneapolis. Along its shores would rise the huge flour mills that were to bring the city world renown. "There is, probably," an engineer wrote, "no example in existence of so large an amount of power derived from so short a canal." [32]

Minneapolis Mill's plan also required such related installations as headraces to conduct water from the canal to the mills, pits in which wheels were set deep in the mills' subbasements, and tailraces carrying water from the wheels through underground tunnels or open canals to the river below the falls. The various firms which leased water from Minneapolis Mill installed their own wheels and built under the company's supervision a maze of surface and underground head and tail races. When they completed the system, the manufacturing district was honeycombed with 2.9 miles of tunnels and open canals. The character of all these installations was important to the water-power development. Extraction of the greatest amount of power from a given quantity of water depended upon using the water at the highest possible head or fall, which in turn depended upon the depth of the canals, races, and wheel pits. The extraction of maximum power depended, too, upon the mechanical efficiency of the wheels in using the volume and fall.[33]

The contrast between the two water-power organizations' leasing practices was as marked as the differences in their installations. The St. Anthony company, pressed to the wall for revenue, sold water in any way it could. It made both perpetual grants and leases with time limits, and it alternately charged for the water a lump sum and fixed annual rentals. It sold water alone, leased water and millsite together, and rented as a parcel water, site, and mill. Influencing the company's arrangements were financial crises which required quick sales, the legal difficulties which beset it, and the lack of a well-organized distribution system which would have enabled it to compute values.

An example of an agreement that included a dam privilege as well as water and mill rights was the lease the company granted to Orrin Rogers and Charles F. Stimson in 1856. The lease, which was to run for ten years at an annual rental of six hundred dollars, empowered the two manufacturers to construct on Hennepin Island a sawmill as well as a sash, door, and blind factory, to put a dam in the river, and to draw from the Mississippi an unspecified amount of water.[34]

The way the company handled its sawmills also illustrates the chaotic arrangements. In 1856 it rented the mills with attached water power for a five-year period at an annual rental of $15,000. When the operator abandoned them a year later, the company brought suit for back rentals and breach of contract, then leased each saw for whatever it could get. In 1861 it rented three gang saws for $2,500 each, a single saw for $350, and another for $250. Whenever it could not find renters, the water-power firm operated the mills, probably buying logs from contractors.[35]

More methodical than its neighbor, Minneapolis Mill again turned eastward for its leasing system and a plan for the manufacturing district. Copying almost word for word the lease form used by the Hadley Falls Company at Holyoke, Minneapolis Mill profited from eastern experience. The regulations it adopted in 1857 became part of every deed the organization granted. The compact between the company and those who bought land and water was perpetual, for a purchaser or lessee could not reconvey any property acquired from Minneapolis Mill without incorporating the regulations into the new instrument. Thus the company established tight control over the west-side manufacturing district.[36]

To ensure that the small area within range of the water-distribution system would be dedicated to manufacturing, it restricted land use to mills and the outbuildings necessary for their maintenance. Foreseeing fire hazards in so compact a manufacturing area, it specified that brick or stone building materials must be used near the canal and prohibited the construction of laboratories, powder mills, and chemical works.

The company assumed the obligation to construct and maintain the dam and canal, and, under penalty of paying rebates, to furnish the amount of water specified in the leases. It assigned to the lessees responsibility for building and maintaining headraces, tailraces, wheel pits, and other facilities necessary to conduct water from the canal, use it, and carry it away. It reserved the right to measure the amount of water being used and to inspect the lessees' installations for safety. If the purchasers drew more water than the amount granted, or if they refused to make needed repairs, the company had the authority to shut off the water or sue for damages.

The measuring unit the firm adopted for leasing water was a mill-power, which it defined as the amount of power that could be derived from thirty cubic feet of water per second used on a twenty-two-foot head. Theoretically this volume and head would create seventy-five horsepower. Given the energy loss in the entire installation, however, the Lompany estimated that a millpower would actually produce from fifty to sixty horsepower at the turbine shaft. This unit differed from the measurements used on the eastern seaboard, and it became known among hydraulic engineers as the "Minneapolis millpower." [37]

The company's leases granted perpetual rights to use a specified number of millpowers. Although the grants were really sales rather than leases, Minneapolis Mill required as compensation a fixed annual rental rather than a lump payment. The leases fixed the water use to stated locations, and a purchaser could not employ it elsewhere without securing the company's permission. Since the organization was liberal in allowing transfers as owners moved their mills or combined them into more efficient manufacturing units, the limitation did not produce a static situation. The company also sold millsites outright for lump sums, but it retained control over them by requiring the owners to obtain its consent before reselling and then binding new purchasers to the regulations.

Although it was far wiser than the St. Anthony firm in most of its planning, Minneapolis Mill made two blunders that later worked a hardship upon it. The first was its system of perpetual grants at fixed rentals. In the early years, when it was eager to encourage industry, the company set the millpower rates extremely low, increasing its charges per millpower only gradually from $133 to $500 annually.[38] Bound into the first error was a second. Early in its history the firm adopted a priority system that graded the right to use water according to the date of the lease. Since the earliest grants held the highest priorities, lease number one had first call on the available water in times of water shortage. Because the highest priority leases carried the lowest rental rates, the company in future years was forced to forego income from its most lucrative contracts. In a low-water year, for example, the firm had to honor a high priority lease which netted it only $133, foregoing the rental income on a low priority grant for which it would have received $500.

While Minneapolis Mill leased most of its water under the system copied from Holyoke, it made a few exceptions which were later to have far-reaching effects. Notable among them were the leases to lumbermen who rented sawmill sites at the dam. These leases fixed water use upon a specific location and defined the mutual obligations of lessee and lessor, but they bore a time limit which made them cancelable at expiration, combined rental of site and water, and allocated the water by volume rather than by millpower.[39]

In the span of thirteen years from 1856 to 1869 the divergent policies of the Minneapolis and St. Anthony water-power companies
created distinctly unequal manufacturing centers on the east and
west banks of the falls. In spite of its later start, Minneapolis quickly
outstripped St. Anthony, and by 1869 it was apparent that the differ-
ing fortunes of the two water-power companies had reversed the positions of the two communities. By dissipating its resources, the St.
Anthony firm dragged the east-side city down with it. The manufacturing center the company had spawned was not strong enough to
spur St. Anthony's growth, and from 1857 to 1870 its population
increased by only 324 persons. The resulting "city" of 5,013 people
fell far short of the western metropolis envisioned in the 1850s, and
the blame for the failure fell squarely on the company. By 1869 St.
Anthony's economic foundation was so shattered that few believed
it could ever be rebuilt.[40]

While the east-side company destroyed its city's metropolitan
dream, Minneapolis Mill became the life-giving force that raised its
community from a prairie village of 3,391 persons in 1857 to a city
of 13,066 by 1870. Typical of the firm's resolution and optimism was
an advertising campaign designed to crowd the west side with mills.
It got under way in 1857 with the publication of a circular letter
containing a prediction by the engineer, Charles Bigelow, that the
falls would make Minneapolis "one of the principal centers of manufacturing industry and business west and north of Chicago and St.
Louis." Bigelow said that lumber, flour, and machinery would pour
from plants at the cataract; wool from the immediate area would
be woven at the falls; and the "way is wide open" for the flow of
cotton from New Orleans "to the very door of the mill." Fulfillment
followed in the wake of prophecy. Manufacturing developed so rapidly that by 1869 the west-side district was turning out five times as
much flour and more than twice the amount of lumber produced on
the east side, and was laying the foundations for a textile industry.
Minneapolitans accorded the company a full measure of praise for
its contribution. To the firm, the *Minneapolis Daily Chronicle* observed on September 1, 1866, should go the "thanks and good will
of this community" for expanding the power and encouraging
industry.[41]

Despite the unequal development of the east- and west-side manufacturing districts, the communities regarded them as a single center.
After 1856 a Union Board of Trade, composed of businessmen from

both sides of the river, reported annually on the progress of all manufactures located at the falls. Recognizing the salient fact that both
sides shared the same water power, fostered the same industries, and
shared a common ambition to exceed the "manufacturing business . . . of Lowell or any other place," the board drew attention to
the many similarities which existed between the two areas. Lumber
ranked first in value among their products; flour took second place;
and metal items from shops and foundries were third. Other plants
turning out paper, wool, and wood products provided evidence of
the commonly held belief that the water power was extensive enough
to support many industries. In 1860 the total value of the communities' manufactured products was $357,900; by 1870, spurred by the
growth on the west side, it had increased to $6,810,970.[42]

During this period both Minneapolis and St. Anthony were dominated by the lumber industry. Both were sawdust cities, and their
calendar was governed by lumbering's cycles. As crews departed for
the pineries each fall, the streets were crowded with slow-moving ox
teams. Merchants hustled about their stores assembling supplies to
send north for the winter's work. After the loggers departed, quiet
settled over the cities. By November or December the saws stilled
their music, and until spring the community heard only the soft
rumble of the flour mills. When the water once more ran free in
the Mississippi, the cities again stirred to life. By late April or early
May, the advance guard of logs from the northern pineries floated
into the millponds. Soon the river was filled with logs as far as the
eye could see, and the streets again echoed to the shouts of loggers
returning from a winter of solitude in the woods. With a fresh log
supply on hand, the mills began a new sawing season.[43]

Lumber production grew steadily throughout the period; the annual output increased from about 12,000,000 board feet in 1856 to
90,734,595 in 1869. A large part of the production came from thirteen
mills on the east- and west-side rows. Six of the thirteen were on the
east side (five on the row and one built on Hennepin Island in 1856).
During this period the east-side saws were rented by more than two
dozen operators, among them Morrison, Joel B. Bassett, and John S.
Pillsbury. Between 1858 and 1869, Morrison, Bassett, William D.
Washburn, and others built on the west side a row of eight mills
resting against the dam. Modeled on the east-side row, the low
mills were so closely joined that they seemed to form one long structure. Like their counterpart across the river, they drew logs from

the millpond, sawed them, and deposited them on an adjoining platform.[44]

Although flour ranked second to lumber in value of product, the industry made such substantial progress that the relationship was soon to be reversed. As the wheat harvest from fields in southern and western Minnesota furnished increasingly abundant raw materials, flour production rose from 30,000 barrels in 1860 to 256,100 in 1869. Eight of the mills contributing to the output were located along the westside canal—the old government mill, after standing idle for two years, began grinding again in 1857, and seven new ones were built between 1859 and 1869. Only four were in St. Anthony. King of the stately west-side row was C. C. Washburn's imposing limestone structure built in 1866. Six stories high, it was touted as the largest mill west of Buffalo.[45]

The communities' third-ranking industry was represented at the falls by at least a dozen foundries and machine shops. Prominent among them were those of the Minnesota Central Railroad, which in 1867 was absorbed by the Milwaukee and St. Paul. These shops repaired rolling stock and constructed cars and locomotives. Other plants on both sides of the river made steam engines, saw- and flour-milling equipment, farm implements, and ornamental iron. Also attracted to the falls were a number of wood-using plants, many of which shared buildings and power with larger mills. Among them were planing mills for finishing rough lumber and factories producing blinds, sashes, doors, shingles, laths, pickets, flour barrels, tubs, pails, and churns.[46]

While saw and flour mills and metal shops dominated manufactures at the falls, neither the water-power companies nor the communities forgot that textiles had brought fame to eastern water powers. In its 1857 regulations, Minneapolis Mill—ignoring fire hazards—specifically allowed for shops "bleaching, dyeing and printing cloth," and in estimating the cataract's capacity local prophets frequently expressed the potential in terms of the number of looms and spindles it could propel. Encouraging the establishment of woolen mills, the *Minnesota State News* in 1861 urged the community to foster the industry, keep its money at home, and wear "homespun."[47]

A Minnesota sheep-raising boom in the 1860s initiated the woolen industry at the cataract. Established on the west side at mid-decade were two mills producing cassimere, flannel, scarves, and stocking yarn. Two carding mills—one on the west side and one on the east—also began to operate during this period.[48]

The manufacture of paper began at the falls in 1859 when a plant was built on Hennepin Island. The *Minnesota State News* announced on December 29, 1860, that the issue was printed on paper from the mill—the first to be manufactured in the state—and on July 20, 1861, it claimed that the plant was manufacturing most of the printing paper used in Minnesota. In 1866–67 a mill producing both newsprint and other paper was established on the west side. Both mills used rags shipped from as far away as La Crosse, Wisconsin. Although the citizens were proud of the new industry, they did complain about the stench.[49]

During these years, the similarities in the manufacturing districts, coupled with St. Anthony's decline, brought into focus the folly of maintaining two municipal organizations, and the communities moved rapidly toward consolidation. Since their identities as western towns and their common origins and institutions made the gulf between them a narrow one, a merger had been discussed as early as the 1850s. The first concrete step was taken in 1860 when the Union Board of Trade, the communities' joint commercial body, proposed a plan for uniting the two municipalities into a single city. Encouraged in 1866 by a joint citizens' committee appointed to work out the mechanics, the Minnesota legislature authorized Minneapolis to incorporate as a city and to include St. Anthony within its boundaries. The measure was subject to the approval of the voters in both communities. Although the voters rejected the plan and Minneapolis was incorporated as a separate city in 1867, union was to come in 1872.[50]

The two communities fostered by the falls had still another reason for joining forces. By the late 1860s it seemed that they must unite in order to compete with St. Paul. Despite the rise of Minneapolis, the capital city still remained in the lead, boasting a population of 20,030 in 1870.[51] Maintaining its commanding position as the head of navigation, it zestfully reached out for a network of railroads which would expand its commercial dominion. St. Paul business leaders were also taking an increased interest in developing manufactures based on steam and, as we shall see later, on water power purloined from the communities at the falls.

The growth of the manufacturing district at the falls gave substance to the faith of Minneapolis and St. Anthony that the cataract could support a major urban center on St. Paul's doorstep. With mills multiplying on a cataract with a potential rivaling "the largest improved Water Power in the World," it seemed possible that a prediction made in 1856 might come true: "Twenty years from this date, a city second only to Chicago in the west will occupy the ground upon which Minneapolis and St. Anthony now stand." If the prediction were to become a reality, however, the communities at the Falls of St. Anthony must successfully cope with a full-scale crisis — a crisis which had been in the making for many years.[52]

5.

The Falls Are Going Out!

CONFIDENT IN THEIR WATER POWER, the people of Minneapolis and St. Anthony in the early years gave little thought to the permanency of the falls that created it. Instead residents equated the fortunes of the two communities with the progress of the Minneapolis Mill and the St. Anthony companies in harnessing the water power for manufacturing. The "giant power," typically asserted the *Minneapolis Daily Chronicle* of September 27, 1866, was destined "to perform . . . the chief portion of the manufacturing labor required by the myriad populations of the vast Mississippi Valley." Allegations that the cataract might be less than eternal were usually discounted. The *Tribune* of April 28, 1869, for example, termed an "atrocious slander" a statement by a St. Paul newspaper that the falls might disappear, adding that the report "cannot fail to do us incalculable injury, and no pains should be spared to acquaint the public with the truth." [1]

Throughout the pioneering period the notion persisted that the geological formation in the falls area was especially well adapted for water-power development. Overlying the district was a thin layer of hard limestone, and beneath this sheath was a soft sandstone formation more than a hundred feet deep. The limestone formed a solid river bed to which the dams were fastened, while tunnels and canals were easily excavated through the friable sandstone along the shores. Had the geological structure been different the companies and their lessees would have had to invest considerably more money in building installations to utilize the water power. [2]

The formation, however, was treacherous. For centuries the falls had been eaten away as water, crashing over the ledge and spraying up at the base, eroded the sandstone layer which was beneath the limestone. Huge blocks of the harder rock sheath dropped into the river as its support was undercut. Once located near Fort Snelling,

62

the falls had been retreating slowly upriver for eight thousand years, leaving behind the deep gorge filled with boulders which deterred steamboat navigation above St. Paul. When the water-power companies built their dams in the mid-nineteenth century, only 1,200 feet of limestone sheath remained upriver. And this remnant was flimsy. Approximately twelve feet thick at the cataract's ledge, it dwindled to nothing a short distance above the apex of the dam. If the thin protective covering were to disappear, the cataract would quickly dissolve into swift-running rapids.

Seemingly unaware of the danger, most writers of the day were stimulated by nature's violence. In 1854, for example, a flood tearing through a log jam at the falls inspired a newspaper reporter to write: "The huge logs . . . are hurled lengthwise into the deep abyss, sometimes striking the concealed rocks with a force which causes the adjoining bank . . . to tremble beneath your feet. . . . These mighty monarchs of the forest . . . are caught up by the whirling eddies, and hurled ten feet heavenward, with the same ease that you would toss a shingle in the air." [3]

Intent on harnessing the cataract, the Minneapolis and St. Anthony water-power companies inadvertently contributed to the forces of destruction. The dam they built across the river diverted the water into millponds, causing the limestone sheath to be exposed to freezes and thaws during periods of low flow. By narrowing the channel, the dam also increased the devastation when floods battered the falls. Debris from the mills constricted the channel still more, and logs which escaped from booms or were carelessly driven over the falls pounded the crumbling ledge. [4]

The two companies reacted characteristically to the danger. Racked by dissension, the St. Anthony firm did nothing to halt the falls' retreat. Minneapolis Mill, on the other hand, delayed action only long enough to build the initial facilities needed for water distribution. In 1866 it moved to halt the erosion, engaging Franklin Cook, a civil engineer, to construct over the falls in the west channel a timbered water slide, called an "apron." This inclined plane was designed to ease the river's flow to a point below the caldron where its force would be harmless. [5]

As dozens of workmen hammered timbers into place, spectators realized that the mammoth apron would further tame the cataract. "Pay your respects . . . to old St. Anthony," the *St. Paul Daily Press* advised on September 21, 1866, for soon "the heavy plunge of the amber Mississippi will be heard no more." To save the falls, the engineers "will stifle the voice of nature with wooden aprons, and the water power company alone reign supreme."

The farewell was premature. Scarcely had the apron been completed when a devastating flood descended upon it in June, 1867. For weeks the river raged, inundating mills, battering dams, and releasing from booms thousands of logs which thundered over the falls. The apron was shattered beyond repair. Minneapolis Mill had spent $35,000 in building it, and—resourceful as the firm was—it could not repeat the investment. Turning to the St. Anthony company, it appealed for co-operation in protecting the cataract from further damage. When the ailing organization did not respond, Minneapolis Mill sought help from other quarters.[6]

The firm found that it was not alone in its concern, for the cataract was important in the economy of the state. Early in 1868 Governor William R. Marshall placed before General George K. Warren, a United States army engineer stationed at St. Paul, a report describing the dangers to the falls. Warren forwarded the information to the chief of army engineers in Washington, and added his warning to the governor's. "One more flood like that of 1867," he wrote, "might complete the destruction, since only about eleven hundred feet of the protecting rock remains, and its thickness diminishes up stream." The engineer recommended government intervention, declaring "there is cause for the most serious apprehension." Civic leaders in the falls communities, newly aroused to the danger, added their voices to the plea. The Union Board of Trade, the manufacturers using the water power, and the laggard St. Anthony company joined the effort to place responsibility for preserving the falls upon the federal government.[7]

In 1868 they urged Congress to approve an amendment to a navigation bill then under consideration which would provide for a 100,000-acre land grant dedicated to saving the cataract. Like Warren, local spokesmen warned that another great flood would probably destroy the falls, a calamity which they believed would be "ruinous" to Minneapolis and St. Anthony and which would affect "very seriously" the interests of the entire state. Responsibility for obtaining passage of the amendment rested upon Alexander Ramsey, Minnesota's influential senator, and Congressman Ignatius Donnelly. Ramsey easily carried the amendment through the upper chamber, but Donnelly encountered serious opposition in the House.[8]

He launched the debate on an exaggerated note when he declared that destruction of the falls would be a "calamity of almost national proportions, for that water-power is the greatest available . . . on the continent." Then came a disturbing question from James Mullins of Tennessee: "Who derives benefit from that water-power, the Government or individuals?" Donnelly answered stoutly that the individuals who owned the water power reaped benefits, but that the question was broader. Destruction of the falls would injure not only Minneapolis, St. Anthony, and the great agricultural area tributary to them, but also the Mississippi Valley which consumed products manufactured at the cataract. Congressman William Lawrence of Ohio then charged that if the grant were approved, public lands would be used to benefit private interests.[9]

Casting about for an argument to justify government support, Donnelly shifted ground. Recalling that steamboats had been navigating the Mississippi above the falls as far north as Sauk Rapids since the 1850s, he contended: "The bill is based not so much upon the preservation of this water-power, important as that is, as upon the preservation of the navigation above the falls for a distance of eighty miles. If you take away the magnesian limestone . . . which now constitutes a natural dam across the river, the sandstone rock will be swept away, the bed of the river will fall, and the entire navigation above that point will be destroyed." Unconvinced by the argument, the House defeated the amendment, but Donnelly had struck upon a stratagem which was later to be used successfully in securing federal aid.[10]

Citizens at the falls refused to accept defeat. The Minneapolis City Council gave the Union Board of Trade five hundred dollars to finance a study of the falls preparatory to renewing the request for federal aid; the St. Anthony company donated three hundred dollars to send a Union Board of Trade representative to Washington; and the board forthrightly declared that the government would save thousands of dollars by acting immediately.[11] Despite this spate of activity, the year 1868 closed without an encouraging word from Washington.

In the meantime, the problem was attacked on a second front by an effort to place the responsibility for preserving the falls on the municipal governments of Minneapolis and St. Anthony. The cities could not issue bonds to finance the project without authorization from the Minnesota legislature. At the request of local residents, the legislature in January, 1868, authorized Minneapolis to issue $31,500 in bonds and St. Anthony $8,500. The law provided that the question must be submitted to the voters in a special election, that Minneapolis would not be obligated to act if St. Anthony did not do its share, and that no bonds would be issued unless at least $35,000 were raised from other sources.[12]

The prospect of bonding the cities to save the falls brought up questions never before debated in the communities. Until this issue arose the people had assumed that the cities' existence and growth depended on the cataract, and that the communities' welfare was closely identified with the water-power companies. Residents frequently complained about the St. Anthony organization, not because it controlled a vital natural resource, but because it was not developing the water power fast enough. The bond question stimulated a new appraisal of the situation. Two business organizations monopolized the power. Was the public to be taxed to protect the financial interests of private corporations? Or was the water power so essential to the cities' welfare that the public interest transcended such considerations?

Before the vote on the bonds an editorial in the *Tribune* of February 7, 1868, called for a "full and free discussion" of these questions. On February 13 opponents termed the proposition "outrageously wrong in principle," and a "swindle." On the thirteenth and during the next two days, correspondents in the *Tribune* argued that the measure was an appropriation of private property through taxation to swell the companies' fortunes, a levy on the poor to benefit the rich, and a maneuver by the companies—who had no intention of letting the falls be destroyed—to get public funds for a project they should finance themselves. One angry letter writer asserted in the *Tribune* of February 15, 1868, that the proposal was unfair to the citizens in another respect: "That the city is dependent, in a great measure, on the water power at the Falls, none can deny," he wrote. "So also is the development of the vast agricultural regions lying north and west of us. And yet these are not laid under tribute." Another opponent stated in the *Tribune* of February 18: "My opinion is if we allow ourselves to be taxed for private purposes in the manner proposed . . . we shall then have as hard work to hold the people in Minneapolis as we now have to hold the Falls in the river."

Advocates of the proposal countered that those who opposed the bonds were myopic. Two of them set forth their views in letters published in the *Tribune* of February 16. One claimed that "every man in Minneapolis is dependent on the preservation of that water power for security against a fatal decline in the value of his property. . . . We are placed in a position where self-preservation demands that

FATHER LOUIS HENNEPIN *discovered and named the Falls of St. Anthony in 1680. This oil portrait, dated 1684, is the only known likeness of the Franciscan friar.*

THE EARLIEST KNOWN VIEW *of the Falls of St. Anthony is reproduced below from Jonathan Carver's volume of* Travels, *published in 1778. Exploring under the British flag, Carver saw the falls in 1766 and estimated their height at an exaggerated thirty feet. His book, which was widely read in Europe, helped make the falls a well-known landmark in the American wilderness.*

LIEUTENANT ZEBULON M. PIKE *was
sent to explore the upper reaches of
the Louisiana Purchase in 1805. He
chose the site upon which Fort Snelling was later built and visited the
Falls of St. Anthony. Courtesy National Archives.*

MAJOR STEPHEN H. LONG *went to
the upper Mississippi in 1817 to con-
firm Pike's choice of a site for a military post. Oil by Charles Willson
Peale, 1823; courtesy Eastern National Park and Monument Association,
Philadelphia.*

THE CONSTRUCTION OF FORT SNELLING, *on the site selected by Pike and Long at
the confluence of the Minnesota and Mississippi rivers, got under way in 1820.
This oil by James McC. Boal shows the post as it looked in 1852.*

A SAWMILL (at right) was begun on the west bank at the Falls of St. Anthony by soldiers from Fort Snelling in 1821. A gristmill (center) was completed two years later. This view of Minnesota's earliest mills, the first to utilize the falls' water power, was photographed by B. F. Upton in 1857.

AFTER THE ESTABLISHMENT of Fort Snelling many travelers and artists visited the Falls of St. Anthony. One of them was Henry Lewis, an American, who painted this oil of the scenic cataract as it looked in 1848.

EIGHT YEARS *after Lewis painted the Falls of St. Anthony, a large sawmill and a small gristmill (at extreme left) had been built by Franklin Steele and others on the eastern shore (foreground). This view, taken by Upton in 1856, looks west toward the infant city of Minneapolis.*

FRANKLIN STEELE, *who staked his claim to the falls' eastern shore in 1838, founded the village of St. Anthony and was the key figure in the formation of the St. Anthony Falls Water Power Company in 1856. Engraving from E. D. Neill,* History of Minnesota *(1882).*

JOHN H. STEVENS, *who built the first permanent home on the west side of the falls in what is now Minneapolis, was Steele's friend. They worked together during the troubled early years of the St. Anthony company.*

RICHARD CHUTE, *Steele's associate, bought a share of the east-side water power in 1855. After the St. Anthony Falls Water Power Company was organized, he served as its first agent and later as its president.*

SPRAWLING ST. ANTHONY *had a population of 4,689 in 1857 when this photograph was taken by Upton. The village resembled a small New England town with its many frame houses erected from lumber sawed in Steele's mills at the falls.*

DORILUS MORRISON, *a native of Maine, was active in the Minneapolis Mill Company, which developed the west half of the falls. Morrison also operated a sawmill on the east-side row.*

CADWALLADER C. WASHBURN *(left) and William D. Washburn (below), two brothers from Maine, joined the Minneapolis Mill Company in the 1850s and played large roles in the successful development of the water power and the city of Minneapolis. Engraving of C. C. Washburn from Isaac Atwater,* History of Minneapolis *(1893); of W. D. Washburn from A. I. Andreas,* Illustrated Atlas of Minnesota. *(1874).*

THE PRODUCTION *of lumber and pails was among the enterprises carried on in the manufacturing district which grew up on the Minneapolis side of the falls in the 1850s. The platform where lumber was piled can be seen in front of the mills. Photograph taken about 1860.*

MINNEAPOLIS *had a population of only 3,391 — less than that of St. Anthony — in 1857 when this photograph was taken by Upton. The towers of the first Suspension Bridge can be seen at right center in this view which looks northeast on Washington Avenue from Second Avenue South.*

THE LIMESTONE LEDGE of the Falls of St. Anthony was crumbling in 1863. Continuing the recession begun thousands of years before, huge boulders dropped from the crest of the cataract into the river below. By the 1860s the recession and the water-power installations threatened to destroy the falls. The St. Anthony skyline in the background was dominated in 1863 by its largest hotel, the Winslow House (left), which had been built in 1857.

THIS VIEW *shows the west-side sawmill row as it looked about 1865. In the foreground are the sluices which carried the sawed lumber from the mills to calmer waters below the falls. There the lumber was assembled into rafts.*

SECOND STREET IN MINNEAPOLIS *was unpaved, had board sidewalks, and was lined with unpainted frame buildings in 1867. This photograph looks southeast on Second Street from Nicollet Avenue. Visible at right center is the Cataract Hotel, which was an early Minneapolis landmark.*

IN 1869 HENNEPIN AVENUE *in downtown Minneapolis sported a variety of stores selling everything from tea and wallpaper to fishing tackle and boots. The Pence Opera House is the large structure at the right on the corner of Hennepin Avenue and Second Street. This photograph was taken from the roof of the Nicollet House, at the corner of Hennepin and Washington avenues, looking toward the Mississippi River.*

In *1867* William W. Eastman (*left*) and *J. L. Merriam received permission to excavate a tunnel under Nicollet and Hennepin islands. Two thousand feet of tunnel had been dug by October, 1869, when the Mississippi broke through the limestone sheath, and the cry "The falls are going out!" rang through the cities whose economies depended upon the cataract's water power.*

WORKMEN *are shown above building a wooden apron in
1870 to save the cataract. In that year the United States
Congress made its first appropriation to preserve the falls and
the almost nonexistent navigation on the upper river. From
1874 to 1884 numerous installations to protect the cataract
were built with federal funds. The apron, completed by
1880 under the direction of the United States Army Corps
of Engineers, is shown below.*

THE MILLING DISTRICTS *at the Falls of St. Anthony are shown as they looked about 1870. St. Anthony on the eastern shore is at the right and Minneapolis is at the left. The first Suspension Bridge appears in the background, and in the foreground from left to right are Upton, Spirit, and Cataract islands.*

THE WASHBURN A MILL, *completed in 1874, was intended by its builder—C. C. Washburn —to be the "finest flouring mill in the world." It exploded in 1878, killing eighteen men and leveling one-third of Minneapolis' milling capacity in a single night. Photograph by W. H. Jacoby.*

A NEW AND MUCH LARGER *Washburn A mill was built in 1879 on the site of the structure destroyed by the explosion as the powerful fraternity of Minneapolis millers moved swiftly to rebuild the city's milling district at the falls. A plaque listing the victims of the explosion still may be seen on the rebuilt mill.*

ONE OF THE MILLS *which helped make Minneapolis the flour-milling capital of the nation in the 1880s is still in use at Third Avenue Southeast and Main Street. It is the impressive Pillsbury A, completed on the east side by C. A. Pillsbury and Company in 1881 at a cost of almost half a million dollars. With various additions, it was later for a time the largest flour mill in the world. This photograph shows the A as it looked in 1886.*

JOEL B. BASSETT *incorporated the Minneapolis Eastern Railroad to build tracks to the expanding flour milling district on the west side, and precipitated a bitter fight with the Washburns and Minneapolis Mill.*

THE FRAME STRUCTURE *in the foreground at right housed the first hydroelectric central station to begin operating in the United States. It was constructed on Upton Island at the falls in 1882 by the Minnesota Brush Electric Company. Behind it in this photograph taken in 1886 is the Great Northern Railroad's Stone Arch Bridge, completed by James J. Hill in 1883.*

BRADLEY B. MEEKER, *a territorial judge, proposed in 1857 to build a lock and dam at Meeker Island (now gone) below the falls. His idea aroused a controversy between Minneapolis and St. Paul that continued throughout the 1870s.*

JAMES J. HILL *was president of the St. Anthony Falls Water Power Company throughout most of the 1880s. He was interested in water-power development, but is best known as a railroad builder. This photograph was taken in 1873.*

THE FALLS OF ST. ANTHONY *looked like this in 1884 after the installations had been completed by the United States engineers. Several of the sawmills on the west side may be seen at the left, and the Winslow House and the steeple of Our Lady of Lourdes Church may be seen in the background. The three-story building in front of the smokestack at top left housed the Island Power Company. Power was carried by ropes from the east-channel dam — an ingenious arrangement devised before hydroelectricity came to the falls.*

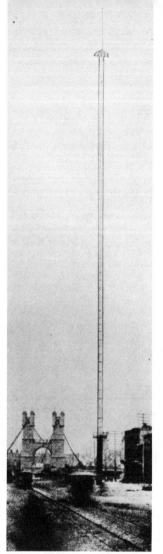

AT LEFT *is the 257-foot mast erected by the Minnesota Brush Electric Company on Bridge Square in 1883 to demonstrate the effectiveness of electric street lighting.*

ABOVE *is a close-up view of the eight arc lamps on the mast. In the background are the towers of the newly completed second Suspension Bridge.*

BELOW, *looking in the opposite direction, is another view of Bridge Square in 1886. The stone structure in the center is the Minneapolis City Hall, which stood at the junction of Nicollet and Hennepin avenues.*

BY *1890* THE INTERSECTION *of Nicollet and Washington avenues had begun to assume a substantial aspect, befitting its position as the junction of two principal streets in a city with a population of 164,738.*

A NEW GRANITE STRUCTURE *to serve the combined functions of the Minneapolis City Hall and the Hennepin County Courthouse was begun in the 1880s and opened to the public in 1906, when this photograph was taken.*

THIS IS THE MINNEAPOLIS MILLING DISTRICT *as it looked in 1905 when the city was still the largest producer of flour in the United States. By that time, however, the economy of Minneapolis was no longer totally dependent upon the milling and manufacturing district at the falls.*

THOMAS LOWRY, *the exuberant president of the Twin City Rapid Transit Company, became interested in Meeker Island in the 1890s. His plans to utilize its water power failed, and his firm became one of the principal purchasers of the hydroelectric power developed at the falls about the turn of the century.*

WILLIAM DE LA BARRE, *an Austrian engineer, was the key figure in the management of the water power from the 1880s until his death in 1936. The Lower Dam and the hydroelectric station completed by the water-power companies at the falls in 1897 were his inspiration. The undertaking was so bold it was dubbed "De la Barre's Folly." This photograph of De la Barre was taken in the late 1890s or early 1900s.*

THE DAM OF THE RESERVOIR *at Lake Winnibigoshish is one of six such installations built by the United States Army Corps of Engineers between 1880 and 1912. By helping to regulate the amount of water flowing over the Falls of St. Anthony, the reservoirs greatly aided the power development there.*

BELOW IS A MODERN VIEW OF LEECH LAKE, *one of the six lakes near the headwaters of the upper Mississippi which were utilized as reservoirs to improve navigation and flood control on the river.*

THE FALLS OF ST. ANTHONY *and the small remaining milling district can be seen in this aerial view taken in 1938 by Mark Hurd. Looking upriver, downtown Minneapolis is at top left. From the lower left, the bridges are the Tenth or Cedar Avenue, a railroad bridge, a footbridge (torn down in 1942), the Stone Arch, the Third Avenue, and the Hennepin Avenue. In the center of the photograph are the Lower Dam and the Northern States Power Company's hydro plant and steam station (the building with four tall smokestacks). The Upper Dam is at right; there near the east bank is Northern States Power's Hennepin Island plant.*

The High Dam, *or "Ford Dam," and lock below the Falls of St. Anthony were completed in 1917. A license to generate power there was granted to Henry Ford in 1923. The dam created a channel deep enough to extend navigation as far as the Washington Avenue Bridge in Minneapolis and made available 15,200 horsepower for conversion into electricity. Photograph by Alan Ominsky, 1965.*

The lock and dam *completed below the falls in 1956 drastically altered the area to bring navigation into the heart of Minneapolis and fulfill a dream that had been nourished since the city's pioneer days. At right are the hydroelectric and steam stations of the Northern States Power Company. Photograph taken in 1959; courtesy United States Army Engineers, St. Paul.*

THE UPPER HARBOR PROJECT, *begun in 1950 and completed in 1963 by the United States Army Corps of Engineers, extended navigation a little more than four and a half miles up the Mississippi in Minneapolis. The construction of the upper lock further altered the falls area. In the foreground of this view is the Stone Arch Bridge; beyond the upper lock is the Third Avenue Bridge. Photograph by Ominsky, 1965.*

THE SKYLINE OF MINNEAPOLIS *in 1965 had little to remind one of the pioneer villages that grew up beside the Falls of St. Anthony. No longer the center of the city's industry, the falls have also changed since their discovery nearly three centuries ago. This view looking across the Stone Arch Bridge shows the remains of the once all-important west-side milling district (left) and beyond that the downtown area of the metropolis fostered by the cataract. Photograph by Alan Ominsky, 1965.*

we should take some decided step at once, and secure for ourselves and our children the elements of our prosperity, viz: the Falls." A second correspondent, identifying himself as a laboring man, calculated that his share of the tax for paying interest on the bonds would amount to sixty-two cents a year. "This amount," he opined, "I would rather pay than have any fears about the Falls. I can make it up in good, sound sleep. . . . I can save more than sixty cents by not going to the next circus that comes to Minneapolis."

Despite such eloquent arguments, Minneapolis defeated the bond issue by a vote of 817 to 485 and St. Anthony rejected it 303 to 15. The reasons are difficult to divine in the light of the importance attributed to the falls in this era. Up to the day of the Minneapolis election, for example, the chauvinistic *Tribune* steadfastly maintained that approval of the bonds was essential to the cities' existence. When Minneapolis voters rejected the issue on February 18 and St. Anthony citizens followed suit two days later, however, the newspaper reported the votes without any editorial hand-wringing.[13] Many citizens presumably believed the companies should and would protect their properties by furnishing the necessary funds. It is also possible that the voters were not convinced of the danger to the water power.

Deeply concerned about the falls, the cities' representatives tried a new tack. At their urging in 1869 the state legislature approved another bond bill which made the companies and the cities partners in saving the cataract. The measure did not repeat the mistakes of the earlier law, for it required that the companies, or interested individuals, furnish $5,000 for each $20,000 in bonds issued by the cities, that the firms agree to provide any additional funds necessary for falls preservation, that the west-side organization deed to Minneapolis three millsites, and that the east-side firm convey to St. Anthony several lots for municipal use. The bill authorized Minneapolis to issue $60,000 in bonds and St. Anthony $20,000 if the voters of both cities gave their approval in a special election. It also provided that if either city refused approval, private subscriptions might be taken to raise the funds. Formalizing the partnership, the measure vested responsibility for administering the funds and supervising the work in a "Board of Construction," which included a representative from each company and city.[14]

Fortune now seemed to smile on the project. The mollified voters approved the bond issues in March and April, 1869; in June the St. Anthony company promised to donate the lots and Minneapolis Mill undertook to convey three millpowers as well as the required sites. Minneapolis Mill yielded, too, when the city council, protecting itself against the "averice [*sic*] of irresponsible persons who may in the future obtain control of the Falls," required the company to pledge its property as security against further demands for municipal bonds or neglect of the cataract.[15]

Confident that adequate provisions had at last been made to preserve the falls, the *Tribune* on March 17, 1869, characteristically extolled the future of the "Lowell of the West." In a front-page story entitled "JUBILATE!" it proclaimed: "Our destiny is now assured. Our fame is fixed as the future manufacturing metropolis of the Great Northwest. The Dual City will become not merely a Lowell, but the complement of many Lowells. The water power of Lowell is a baby compared to ours. When the great Northwest shall be as densely populated as Massachusetts, Lowell will be a baby compared to the metropolis at the Falls of St. Anthony!"

When it was ready to begin the project, the board of construction turned to the eastern seaboard for experienced engineers. In June it engaged Captain A. H. Kelsey of Boston to examine the falls and recommend preservation methods. Kelsey proposed the construction of an apron, such as Minneapolis Mill had built in 1866–67, at an estimated cost of $95,000. The board then hired J. T. Stevens of Lewiston, Maine, to supervise the work.[16]

Adoption of the plan created a great deal of interest in the communities at the falls. On June 27, 1869, the *Tribune* proudly reprinted a story which had appeared in the *Troy Times* of New York. "As the prudent wife, to save the wear on her dresses, provides herself with an 'apron,'" the distant journal observed, "the idea suggested the propriety of furnishing the Falls with a similar article, and when completed, Mississippi will . . . wear the biggest and most expensive apron of any lady in the land."

Construction began in mid-July, 1869, and progressed rapidly. The crew, which at times numbered a hundred men, built a temporary dam turning the river to the Minneapolis shore, tore away the remaining timbers of the old apron, and blasted tons of rock below the falls to obtain a level footing. By September workmen had installed part of the foundation for the apron, built one section of the rock-filled timber structure from the foot of the caldron to the brink, and fastened a plank covering over it.[17]

The local press, preparing once more for the final transformation of the cataract from a scene of rustic beauty to one of industrial power, reported frequently on the work. "Now is the time," advised the *Tribune* of August 12, 1869, "for all those who wish to take a final look at old St. Anthony Falls. . . . Its natural beauty, of which poets and writers throughout the world have said so much, will soon be gone forever, and nothing will be left but a continuation of rapids, made by the great apron. It is a stupendous work to accomplish; yet engineering skill . . . will overcome all obstacles, and so the mighty Falls of St. Anthony have been made to succumb to man, and are now as subject to his will as a child." [18]

The Mississippi, however, was not to be tamed so easily. Even as the press published farewells to the beautiful cataract, heavy rains in the northern drainage area swelled the river. When raging waters reached the falls in September, they tore loose the booms, and hundreds of logs crashed over the new apron.[19]

While workmen waited for the flood waters to recede, a new catastrophe struck the cataract with a fury that upset the plans for its preservation. The chain of events that caused the disaster led back to 1848, when Franklin Steele bought Nicollet Island from the government and acquired the usual water rights attached to riparian property. Over the years he transferred water rights to successive partners, but he retained ownership of Nicollet Island for himself. With the St. Anthony company's incorporation, the riparian privilege seemingly passed to it.[20]

Control of the Nicollet Island water rights was clearly defined in all the deeds conveying the St. Anthony water-power property. Steele's need for money, however, precipitated a difficulty he did not foresee. In 1851 he borrowed six thousand dollars from Hercules L. Dousman, a fur trader who lived at Prairie du Chien, and gave as security a mortgage on the island which did not specifically exclude the water rights. Ten years later, when Steele failed to repay the loan, Dousman foreclosed and took possession of the island. Although no one seemed concerned about the situation at the time, Steele's blunder gave both Dousman and the St. Anthony company a claim to the water rights.[21]

Dousman remained in quiet possession of the island until 1865, when he sold it to William W. Eastman, a Minneapolis lumberman and miller, and John L. Merriam, a St. Paul banker and stagecoach operator. In a surprise move, the new owners in 1865 brought suit against the St. Anthony company to force the removal of all installations it had placed in the river, on the grounds that Eastman and

Merriam owned the water rights attached to the island and that the water-power firm's dams infringed upon them.[22]

Puzzled Minnesotans wondered how the company could have been so careless about protecting the rights on which its existence was based. "The more the history of this strange and interesting question is investigated," stated the *St. Paul Daily Pioneer* of September 1, 1865, "the greater the wonder of the remissness of the Company, in a matter so vital to its very life. It has been sleeping upon a volcano all these long years in regard to this defect in its title."

Since the company was at this time in serious financial trouble, it chose to compromise with Eastman and Merriam rather than dispute the issue. The compromise was set forth in two agreements signed on May 20, 1867. They provided that Eastman and Merriam would grant the company flowage, dam, and boom privileges on Nicollet Island's shore, and that the company would grant Eastman the right to draw enough water from the river to create two hundred horsepower for use on their property. The seeds of calamity lay in an additional provision which gave Eastman and Merriam permission to excavate under Nicollet and Hennepin islands a tunnel which would serve as a tailrace for exhausting water.[23]

In 1868 Eastman and Merriam were joined in the tunnel project by two new partners—Amherst H. Wilder, a prominent St. Paul merchant, and William S. Judd, a Minneapolis lumberman and miller.[24] As the digging began, the *Tribune* cheered the "important enterprise" which would expand the industrial area served by the water power. "Perhaps few of our citizens," the paper commented on September 16, "while looking upon the numerous manufacturing establishments at the Falls . . . have for an instant dreamed of seeing the substantial walls of similar establishments rising upon Nicollet Island, and that locality, now so quiet, converted into a manufacturing centre second only to the Falls themselves. Such a result is to be accomplished, however, and at no distant day." Some three months later the paper was still praising the proprietors for their contribution to the cities' economic life. On January 9, 1869, it called the tunnel "a work of great magnitude and importance, the full extent of which will hardly be realized until it is completed, and those islands are covered with manufacturing establishments deriving their power from it."

The St. Anthony organization cast the first shadow of doubt on the tunnel project in May, 1869, when it warned the partners to stop work until they had taken "suitable precautions" against damaging the water-power company's property. Heeding the warning, Eastman and his associates installed a bulkhead around the upper end of Hennepin, then continued digging under that island toward Nicollet.[25]

In the first days of October, workmen were burrowing steadily through the sandstone beneath the thin limestone sheath. They had come a long way since they began work under the islands more than a year before. Behind them lay two thousand feet of completed tunnel; five hundred feet more would bring them to their destination. On the morning of October 4, they discovered water oozing into the tunnel through cracks near its upper end. Faster and faster seeped the water, until by noon it was coursing swiftly through the tunnel and pouring out its mouth beneath the falls. The workmen carefully probed for the source of the leak; accustomed to fighting the river, they were not particularly alarmed. The cities slept that night in peace.[26]

Then dawned black Tuesday, October 5, 1869, a date long remembered by Minneapolis residents. Early that morning the river broke through the limestone covering at the upper end of the tunnel. A huge maelstrom formed at the break, whirling, eddying, and plunging into the tunnel with tremendous force.

With lightning speed the cry spread through the cities, "The falls are going out!" One witness remembered that "Proprietors of stores hastened to the falls, taking their clerks with them; bakers deserted their ovens, lumbermen were ordered from the mills, barbers left their customers unshorn; mechanics dropped their tools; lawyers shut up their books or stopped pleading in the courts; physicians abandoned their offices. Thru the streets hurrying hundreds were seen on their way to the falls." Before their eyes the raging waters were ripping the tunnel to pieces. As the roof collapsed, the earth of Hennepin Island sank beneath the spectators' feet, and they hurriedly scrambled to safety. Expecting that the Hennepin Island mills would drop into the river, volunteers rallied to strip them of machinery. Momentarily the cities believed that the falls as well as the entire island would be swept away.[27]

Hundreds of people gathered on Nicollet Island near the point where the rushing waters plunged underground. What could they do, this curious and fearful crowd? George A. Brackett, the leader of the Minneapolis volunteer fire companies, stepped out of the milling throng, stripped off his coat, and said, "That water *must* be stopped." Accustomed to commanding crews of men, John Jarvis, yardmaster for the Milwaukee and St. Paul Railroad, moved up beside Brackett. "Boys," he said, "let's plug that hole." [28]

Throughout that long day, Brackett and Jarvis galvanized the man power of Minneapolis and St. Anthony into a working force. Every mill in Minneapolis sent teams, and hundreds of volunteers "sprang to their work like giants." They seized heavy timbers providentially piled on the island and quickly used them to build a large crib. Floating it over the chasm, they filled it with rocks and dirt until it sank into place over the break.

No sooner had the crib filled the breach than the river bed between it and the shore of Nicollet Island collapsed. The Mississippi then plunged with terrible power through the new break and into the tunnel. The crews built more cribs, whirled them into line over the hole, and dumped into them hundreds of wagonloads of rock, dirt, hay, brush, and trees. By the middle of the afternoon, workmen were strolling over the cribs, readjusting the timbers here and there, piling on more rock, and enjoying "the triumph of human skill and brain over the dumb force of nature."

Suddenly while the men were still on the cribs came a misfortune worthy of the malice of Oanktehi, the god of waters and evil who was reputed to dwell beneath the falls. A great suction drew the cribs downward "into the bowels of the earth." The whole mass heaved upward for a moment, allowing the men to escape, and then plunged from sight. Into the hole in the river bed, water rushed with a force that strained the descriptive abilities of those who viewed the scene. The torrent tossed huge logs "as though they were mere whitlings" and "as if in sport" stood them on end and then swallowed them, said the *St. Paul Daily Press* of October 6, 1869.

By the end of the day, the workmen knew that cribs alone would not stop the flow of water through the tunnel. To halt the destruction of the limestone sheath, they must not only plug the holes but build dams around the break to turn the river from the shattered area. All night long, by the light of lanterns and fires kindled on the shores, the men worked. And still the water, a "grand but fearful" sight, flowed through the tunnel with unabated force. [29]

As shocked citizens struggled to save the falls, the cities' newspapermen tried to make up their minds about the seriousness of the crisis. The *Tribune* of October 5 announced the break in a single sentence on the back page, devoting its front-page headlines to eastern floods. The next day it told readers: "Every moment of time, is how precious no man knows, so long as that mighty rush of water,

irresistible in its power of demolition, is free to undermine and sub-
vert the prosperity of these two cities."

The *St. Anthony Falls Democrat* was thrown into a state of confusion by the crisis. In the course of a single story published on October 15, it proclaimed that the cities could exist without the
water power, that excitement about danger to the falls "runs higher
than the waters," and conversely that the prospect of the falls' destruction would rally the nation to the defense of the cataract. The
journal concluded its split-focus report by saying that the "great
west, the seat of empire, the country needing this power as no other
country on earth needs it, cannot afford to have it destroyed."

While the local press vacillated, St. Paul newspapers offered readers
factual, sympathetic accounts of the disaster. Petty civic interests and
rancor gave way to a rush of regional feeling, and on October 7 the
Daily Press, which had often sneered at the pretensions of Minneapolis, offered the services of "hundreds of men" to help save the cataract. The "anxiety reaches over the whole State," the *St. Paul Daily
Dispatch* reported on October 6, "as all Minnesota has an interest
in that unrivalled water power." The *St. Paul Daily Pioneer* on the
same day declared that destruction of the falls would cause "incalculable injury." Striking the same note, the *St. Paul Daily Press* of
October 6 stated that the loss of the falls would be a "blow . . .
which Minnesota could illy bear." [30]

No Minnesotans, however, felt the crisis as keenly as did the citizens of Minneapolis and St. Anthony. Day by day throughout October crews battled the Mississippi, only to have the river defy again
and again "the most herculean efforts . . . of a thousand men." At
the end of the month they claimed a temporary victory over the
current which ripped the limestone sheath to pieces even as they
worked, but they knew that the staggering task of repairing the damage and preventing a recurrence of the catastrophe still lay before
them.[31]

In these first weeks, Minneapolis and St. Anthony men worked as
one, for the compelling necessity to save the falls transcended other
considerations. Forgotten were the attitudes that had thwarted previous efforts. When the crisis broke, the citizens immediately held a
mass meeting, chaired by Dorilus Morrison, to form the Union Committee for Falls Preservation. Recognizing that all segments of the
two communities must share the responsibility, the committee raised
approximately $22,000 by assessing the Minneapolis Mill and St. An-
thony companies 40 per cent of the sum, the governments of Minne-

apolis and St. Anthony 38 per cent, the tunnel proprietors 15 per cent, and Farnham and Lovejoy and Averill, Carpenter, and Company—two manufacturers on Hennepin Island—7 per cent.[32]

The amount the committee apportioned to Eastman and his associates aroused few objections, although the *Tribune* admitted that the tunnel builders' assessment might seem small. The "principle of aid from the two cities, and the water power companies is right," it maintained on October 8, 1869. "The bad issue of the tunnel enterprise we regard as less a fault than a misfortune. . . . Had the tunnel scheme resulted in no misfortune, but have been the means of covering the Islands with mills," it reminded the city, "Mr. Eastman would have been highly lauded where he is now dispraised if not denounced."

The St. Anthony company was in a less generous mood. Although it contributed to the union committee's fund, it insisted that the tunnel proprietors assume responsibility for the damage. Eastman responded by protesting against the 1867 agreements; he demanded that the company reconvey the water rights and accused it of error in choosing the place where the tunnel should be built. The battle between the two antagonists waxed so hot that the *Tribune* appealed for peace. Let bygones be bygones, it advised on April 16, 1870, and "by a regular council of war, come together to work in unison against the further encroachments of the Father of Waters." The journal observed that if the antagonists continued their fight, "like Kilkenny cats, there will be nothing left of them but their tails."[33]

The waters were too troubled to be calmed by so small a vial of oil, and litigants besieged the Minnesota courts with cases that sprang from the collapse of the tunnel. Eastman and Merriam brought suit in 1870 to regain the water rights they had relinquished in the 1867 compromise. The district court found for the company and the state supreme court upheld this decision. In 1870, too, the St. Anthony company sued for $150,000 in damages, alleging that Eastman and his associates were negligent in construction and that they "wantonly abandoned" the tunnel after the collapse. The district court dismissed the case and refused the company's motion for a new trial. The organization then appealed to the Minnesota Supreme Court, which upheld the lower court's judgment. To further complicate matters, a firm owning the Island mill brought suit against the tunnel proprietors for damages to its property on Hennepin Island, and the Hennepin County District Court awarded it a judgment of $7,200. The bitterness engendered by the battling antagonists lingered, and over twenty years later the St. Anthony Falls Water Power Company would have good reason to remember William W. Eastman when it again faced him in a court of justice.[34]

While the dissension was raging, the organizations concerned with falls' preservation began their work. Turning again to the eastern seaboard, the union committee in 1870 engaged James B. Francis, a well-known Lowell engineer, to formulate a comprehensive plan for preserving the falls. After studying the desolate scene, Francis proposed that the apron — upon which work had ceased when the tunnel collapsed — be completed, that the tunnel be sealed, and that low dams be built above the falls to keep water over the limestone sheath at all times. Regarding apron construction as first in importance, the committee then decided to join the board of construction in completing it.[35]

In July, 1870, the board recalled J. T. Stevens, who had gone home to Maine when work on the apron stopped, and again the cities resounded with the ring of hammers and the shocks of blasting. By November the workmen had fitted the huge water slide against the cataract. The *Tribune* of November 15 reported that the falls "exhibit now the wonderful genius and power of man, and are shorn of their power for destruction to property and capital."[36]

Meanwhile the St. Anthony company, after appealing fruitlessly for help from Minneapolis Mill, began to repair the shattered tunnel area that lay so close to its property. Through the winter of 1869–70 and into the spring, men plugged the tunnel and built masonry walls around the damaged area. The work was interrupted in April when spring floods unleashed a great volume of water and battered the falls with ice and logs. The flood ripped out some of the new installations, tore away parts of Hennepin Island, shook the foundations of buildings, and sent the Summit mill and a warehouse crashing into the river. The company battled the new catastrophe valiantly, and by the fall of 1870 it had brought the situation under control.[37]

While the apron was being built and the tunnel plugging got under way, a fourth helper joined the three organizations engaged in preserving the Falls of St. Anthony. Aroused by the tunnel break, the United States Army Corps of Engineers in November, 1869, engaged Franklin Cook, an engineer who had been in the employ of Minneapolis Mill, to survey the damages and recommend action. His conclusions paralleled those reached by Francis, but Cook also proposed that the federal government aid the project. If the falls were to go out, he reasoned, it would cost at least $1,200,000 to build a dam which would preserve the navigability of the river above the cataract. He estimated that the government could protect the natural dam for an estimated $245,000, not only saving money but also providing "inestimable protection to manufacturers and those interested in the mill and water-power companies who have expended a large amount of capital in improving the water-power." [38]

The United States engineers accepted Cook's recommendations and the die was cast. The two communities again launched a campaign to secure Congressional appropriations. Yielding to the pressures, Congress in 1870 appropriated $50,000 to preserve the falls and maintain navigation. The government engineers then took over the tunnel-sealing project from the St. Anthony company. Their problems were compounded in 1871 when a new chasm opened in the east-side millpond. Cutting under the limestone, water flowed into the tunnel near the shattered area where the break had occurred two years before. To free the United States engineers from responsibility for the new work, the union committee, which had been concentrating on the apron, undertook to solve the problem. [39]

The millpond break convinced the government engineers that they could never save the falls by patching holes as they appeared. Investigating the sandstone formation upriver, they found many cavities which seeping water might turn into channels beneath the limestone. The only solution, they believed, was to build above the apron an underground dike — a massive wall that would penetrate the river bed deeper than any of the cavities and prevent the water from undercutting the protective limestone sheath. The great wall, they estimated, would cost $200,000. [40]

A federal board of engineers convening in Minneapolis in 1872 concurred in the plan for a dike. Since not enough money was available to build it, however, the board suggested that the temporary work on the tunnel be continued. It also allotted $37,500 to the union committee for work on the millpond break. Irritated by the demands for federal funds from communities whose businessmen had produced the conditions which were destroying the cataract, the board closed its report with a rebuke. It stated that it could not "too strongly condemn the practice, which prevails so commonly throughout the country, and of which the locality now under consideration affords a manifest instance, of erecting structures in and across the natural water-way of navigable streams by the authority of . . . States, or municipalities, and sometimes even without any authority whatever, and in all cases without any authority from Congress. The board therefore recommends," it continued, "that the attention of Congress be invited to this matter, with a view to such legislation as will cause these objectionable structures to be removed or altered, and to prevent their erection in the future." The time would come when the federal government would see fit to implement the board's recommendations and Congress would enact laws controlling the two water-power companies.[41]

The millpond break convinced the city governments that they, too, must contribute additional funds to finance a more comprehensive plan for saving the falls. Since they could not issue bonds until the legislature of 1872 passed enabling legislation, the two city councils proposed in 1871 that the citizens subscribe $100,000, accept city certificates for the amount, and exchange them later for bonds.[42]

This suggestion uncorked the resentment that had been gathering since the crisis first touched the citizens' pocketbooks, and they unburdened their feelings in meeting after meeting. As they had during the earlier movements to save the falls, they again denounced the water-power companies. Joel B. Bassett, the lumberman who was a leader in the opposition, vented his ire upon Minneapolis Mill. He objected, the Tribune reported on August 6, 1871, "to giving a dollar for the preservation of the falls so long as the water power was owned by a close[d] corporation. If the water power company desired a loan from the cities, he should not oppose it; but it looked to him just like the people were to be taxed to preserve the Falls, when those Falls were owned by the richest men in the city—men who could afford to advance all the money necessary to do the work, and never miss it." Expanding the area of complaint, other residents criticized the government engineers for failing to make the cataract secure and murmured against the city councils for exposing their citizens to monetary loss if the legislature failed to approve the bond issue.[43]

After thoroughly airing their disgust at being placed in such a position, Minneapolis and St. Anthony residents reluctantly provided the funds on the grounds that falls' preservation really amounted to "self preservation." With the money they subscribed the union committee shored up the millpond. The 1872 legislature then authorized Minneapolis to issue $84,500 in bonds and St. Anthony $15,000. The Minneapolis City Council on February 24 sanctioned the measure, and the St. Anthony voters on April 4 approved it. The action was to be the last contribution St. Anthony, as a separate entity, would make to the cataract which had been responsible for its birth, for on April 9, 1872, St. Anthony became a part of the city of Minneapolis.[44]

Perhaps emboldened by the fact that it now spoke for a community with a combined population of 24,296, the Minneapolis City Council on April 15, 1872, adopted a resolution asking legislative approval of another $50,000 in bonds. Joel Bassett, who was a member of the council, submitted a minority report objecting to the measure. The "benefits directly resulting from said expenditures inure to two private corporations over which the public have no control, and in which they have no direct interest," he pointed out. "It is true they [*the public*] have an indirect interest in securing said water power; so they have in every other improvement made in this city. Every block of buildings that is erected in this city adds to its worth, but it is not expected that the city will tax itself to aid every enterprise that threatens to suspend." The companies' owners, he continued, "tell us that they have the finest water power on the continent, which is undoubtedly true, and it really seems they could well afford to expend fifty thousand dollars to preserve and secure it." The council responded to Bassett's criticism on April 20 by amending the previous resolution to provide that its recommendation take effect only if the water-power companies deeded five hundred horsepower to the city of Minneapolis as compensation.[45]

At this point even the *Tribune*, long the companies' public defender, had enough. Departing from its previous line, it suggested that the newly united city buy both companies and place them under the jurisdiction of a board of public works which would aggressively develop the cataract to its maximum efficiency. It is wrong, the journal argued on May 2, 1872, to leave the falls which are "the prosperity of the city . . . in the hands of a few men, who can promote or retard it as they choose."[46]

A lull in the storm followed the *Tribune's* blast. In 1873 the legislature authorized the city to issue the additional bonds, and the companies offered the required concessions. A delay occurred, however, when wrangling over the quality of the concessions broke out in the Minneapolis City Council. Disgusted with the whole transaction, the council recommended that the voters reject the bond issue. They promptly did so, and it was evident even to the most ardent advocates of municipal support that the citizens were in no mood "to bond the city to save the Falls." The total sum the citizens, the companies, and the cities had contributed to falls' preservation since the trouble began was $334,000. The board of construction and the union committee then spent the funds remaining on hand as well as a few private contributions made after 1873, and the people washed their hands of the task of preserving the falls.[47]

The federal government took up the burden. A board of engineers, convening in Minneapolis in 1874, confirmed the plan for completion of the apron and the construction of a dike and low dams. This time Congress responded with generous appropriations. In 1876 the engineers finished the dike, which measured 40 feet deep and 1,850 feet long.[48]

The *Tribune* on November 20, 1876, greeted the dike's completion with an observation on what the crisis had meant to Minneapolis and with a salute to the future of the water-power city: "The final completion of the great sustaining wall . . . removes the only obstacle that has ever seriously threatened the onward progress of the city of Minneapolis, or retarded its realization of the Manifest Destiny which is to make it the great metropolis of the northwest. The city of Chicago is no more certainly to be the empire city of the middle continent, than Minneapolis to be the undisputed mistress of the upper Mississippi states." Gone was the danger which had "blanched the cheek of every owner of property in the city, and promised to transform the busy thoroughfares of a thriving manufacturing mart once more into the unpeopled prairie from which so recently it had sprung."

The government finished the work without fanfare. Between 1876 and 1880 it completed the apron abandoned by the board of construction, built two low dams above the falls to maintain a safe water level over the limestone sheath, and constructed a sluiceway to carry logs over the falls. To widen the river channel, it won an agreement from Minneapolis Mill to remove the row sawmills as soon as their leases expired. When the last timber was fitted into place, the government—which had spent $615,000 between 1870 and 1884 in order to ensure practically nonexistent navigation on the upper river—prepared to withdraw, leaving responsibility for the falls once more to the water-power companies.[49]

The crisis which endangered the cataract exposed paradoxes in the attitudes of Minneapolitans toward it. In the years before 1869, the city's inhabitants had never been confronted with a situation that forced them to analyze what the water power meant to the community. With the falls apparently secure in the river and with industries developing on the power, community leaders did not seriously question the role the falls played or would play in the city's evolution. Their response to the threat of the cataract's destruction was complex. Throughout the crisis and the ensuing conflict, most of them seemed wedded to the proposition that the cataract was essential to the city's existence and future growth, yet some balked at subsidizing two private corporations in the name of self-preservation. The extent to which the citizens identified community welfare with the water power would have been more sharply revealed had not the prospect of federal aid appeared as an alternative. Government intervention clouded the issue of whether Minneapolitans thought the water power important enough to pay handsomely for its preservation.

6.

The Troubled Decade of the 1870s

AT THE SAME TIME THAT MEN FOUGHT TO SAVE THE FALLS, the two companies labored to continue the development of the water power. For both organizations the 1870s were a troubled decade. To the burden of preserving the cataract were added problems created by the firms' histories. The St. Anthony company faced the challenge of stemming the tide of failure, and Minneapolis Mill experienced no less serious crises appearing in the wake of success. Events in a larger arena also complicated their problems. The nationwide panic of 1873 made it difficult for the owners to raise money, while local citizens, as their newly united city more than tripled in population, sponsored transportation schemes that conflicted with the companies' interests.[1]

The east-side company should have been in a position to avoid errors which time and again in the past had brought it to the brink of failure, for the new owners who took over in 1868 knew the situation well. Richard Chute, president and lone survivor of the group which had controlled the organization since its incorporation, was rich in experience — albeit most of it bad. Frederick Butterfield, who held Franklin Steele's shares as security for loans, had been in touch with the company's affairs throughout the 1860s. Among the twelve local men who had bought the Davis-Sanford-Gebhard interest were manufacturers schooled in the tradition that the water power, if developed, could support a great industrial district.

Before the new owners had time to orient themselves to their task, however, the St. Anthony company suffered a serious setback. On the evening of October 20, 1870, a workman in one of the sawmills on the east-side row decided to save a little time by filling a kerosene lamp while it was still lighted. The lamp exploded, the kerosene spread over the dry floor, and the mills were ablaze. Within an hour "the whole row of mills was a vast furnace of coals and charred timbers, great sections of which were dropping into the seething waters below." Firemen rushed to the scene, but so swiftly did the flames devour the old frame buildings that the men could only rescue adjoining blocks and prevent a general holocaust. The conflagration was "visible for miles around," according to the *St. Paul Daily Press* of October 21, 1870, and, in the short space of an hour, mills built at great cost to the east-side owners were completely destroyed. The row, now in ashes, mirrored the company's history. There Steele, Cushing, and Rantoul had begun the enterprise; there Arnold Taylor had laid plans for more mills; and there the petulant New Yorkers had centered their hopes for the company's success.[2]

When the smoke cleared, the firm found itself out of the lumber business for good. The sawmills, valued at $75,000, were not insured, and the dam against which they rested was so badly damaged that it had to be rebuilt. With the mills gone, the company did not have the resources to begin again. In 1871 it sold five sawmill sites with attached water power for $5,000 each, departing entirely from its early plan of leasing company-owned plants to operators. By the transaction it avoided rebuilding, but it also gave up an annual income of about $20,000 which through the years had been its chief sustenance.[3]

On the heels of this loss the water-power company faced another financial problem evolving from an earlier period. It will be recalled that in the 1860s William Gebhard and Thomas Davis had brought suit against the St. Anthony firm to recover money they had loaned to it, and the company's property was at last up for auction to satisfy the judgments. When the sales began in February, 1871, the St. Anthony stockholders allowed only city lots not necessary to the water-power development to go under the hammer. Butterfield, who went out from New York to attend the sales, then conferred with Chute on measures that could be taken to avoid a second auction, scheduled for March 13, at which property vital to the water power might be sold.[4] As the company's leaders deliberated, the *Tribune* of February 25, 1871, reported that the "air is full of rumors about the situation of this corporation." Ever optimistic, the journal went on to say there was "good ground for the hope that all hindrance to the prosperous growth and improvement dependent upon this company and its magnificent property will be early removed."

For a change, the *Tribune* was right when it announced good news about the organization. Butterfield offered to advance the corporation $80,000 if the other stockholders would match the amount. When the resident owners agreed to do so, the company stopped the second sale by settling the judgments still unsatisfied. The firm then paid its back taxes and had money left over for water-power development.[5]

At last, it seemed, the knot that had been strangling the company since the 1857 panic was loosened. The *Tribune* of March 4, 1871, remarked: "We confidently believe that this new departure will be instrumental in leading to a full development of the almost exhaustless Water Power on this side of the river. . . . The new arrangement . . . must at once lift the Water Power from the Slough of Despond in which it has heretofore continually floundered." Gone were the days, the journal believed, when the organization would neglect industrial development while it fought internal battles. "Choice sites for manufacturing purposes are in market," the newspaper reported on March 26, "together with valuable opportunities for leasing water powers, and with the harmony now effected in the company's affairs, and the good terms offered, they cannot fail of rapid development and use." With millsites and power owned by men who would use them and with the company ready to construct facilities for water distribution, the paper predicted that "the wealth of St. Anthony can now only be hinted at!"

More attuned to failure than success, the St. Anthony company embarked upon a new series of misadventures and ownership changes. In 1871 Steele, unable to pay his debts, forfeited his shares to Butterfield. By 1873 the latter had had enough of the company, and he offered to sell his interest to Richard and Samuel Chute. The brothers were unable to make the purchase, and Butterfield remained reluctantly in the firm. In 1875 the Chutes acquired the remainder of the locally held shares and became with Butterfield the sole owners.[6]

The desire of Butterfield and others to escape from the organization may have been partly due to the maze of lawsuits which enmeshed it in the 1870s. The action it had instituted against the tunnel proprietors in the 1860s and the two suits the proprietors had in turn filed against the company culminated in a standoff when the Minnesota Supreme Court in 1871, 1874, and 1878 rendered decisions adverse to each complainant. Since neither litigant prevailed in its contention against the other, they compromised their differences in 1878. The company granted Eastman the right to draw from a sawmill site on the dam 126.56 cubic feet per second, and to utilize the water by installing a wheel on the location. The corporation also authorized him to place in the St. Anthony millpond above the dam two towers which were to hold a wire rope carrying power from the water wheel to manufactories he planned to establish on lower Nicollet Island.[7]

Eastman promptly began the development of the island that a decade before had been stopped by the tunnel disaster. In 1878 he joined Asa B. Barton, a retired dry-goods merchant, and two of his original partners, John L. Merriam and Amherst H. Wilder, in organizing the Island Power Company. In 1879 the new firm constructed on lower Nicollet Island the towers as well as a building designed to house small industries. By the year's end J. R. Clark, a boxmaker, had moved into the structure; he was soon followed by manufacturers of sashes, doors, furniture, and feed.[8]

Extending his utilization of the island, Eastman in 1877–78 built across its upper section two rows of houses. He spared no effort to make these stone and brick residences, constructed at an estimated cost of five thousand dollars each, a combination of "elegance, comfort, convenience and good taste." In choosing this site, Eastman used the only location near the falls which was still attractive for fashionable dwellings. The western riverbank was congested with industries, and traffic rumbled over its busy streets. The eastern shore and Hennepin Island were less crowded, but the scattering of mills and manufacturing plants discouraged residential development.[9]

While the St. Anthony company was digesting the unpalatable results of Eastman's ambitions, controversies arose with other men who owned property affecting its riparian rights. The seeds of a new and bitter harvest also dated from an earlier day. They had been planted in 1854 when Steele, compromising a pre-emption dispute with Ira Kingsley, had allowed him to gain ownership of Hennepin Island's western shore. Kingsley deeded portions of his holding to others, and through a complex series of transactions, Farnham and Lovejoy, a sawmilling firm, came into possession of the property in 1858.[10]

Entrenched on Hennepin Island and interested in expanding their holdings at the falls, Farnham and Lovejoy launched an attack against the St. Anthony company, alleging that the water-power organization's dam, which diverted water into the eastern channel, diminished the flow on the island's western shore. Steele's unfortunate compromise with Kingsley fell with full force upon the company in 1876 when Farnham and Lovejoy brought suit, charging infringement of their riparian rights.[11]

Fighting to avert a decision that would compel the St. Anthony company to alter its dams, the corporation's attorneys advanced an argument dangerous to all riparian owners at the falls. Eager to deny Farnham and Lovejoy's contention that as a shore owner it had the privilege of using the normal flow of water past its land, the water-power company's counsel argued ambiguously that "the government" rather than the riparian owners had exclusive rights to water power on navigable streams. The St. Anthony company, they claimed, derived its right to the falls' power from the charter the Minnesota legislature had granted in 1856. Since Farnham and Lovejoy did not have such a charter, they concluded, it had no riparian privilege to protect.[12]

Fortunately for the company's long-term interests, the courts ruled for Farnham and Lovejoy. The district court in 1878 and the Minnesota Supreme Court in 1879 handed down clear-cut decisions that were to become an important part of the nation's riparian code. "The riparian owner," stated the supreme court, "may undoubtedly use, for any purpose, the water of a navigable stream passing or adjoining his land, for his own advantage, so long as he does not impede the navigation, in the absence of any counter claim by the state or United States as absolute proprietor." The court concluded that Farnham and Lovejoy "have a right to the natural flow of the water past their land, and any interference with this flow, to their injury, is a wrong for which they are entitled to an appropriate remedy." If the St. Anthony company had prevailed, the doctrine of riparian rights derived from English common law might have been weakened. The contention that the government had exclusive control over water power on navigable streams foreshadowed a position that both state and national legislative bodies would take in the years ahead. Some thirty years later the company was to offer in its own defense the judgment the court handed down against it in 1879.[13]

The lawsuits were not the only events which thwarted the company's progress. After the new management took over in 1868, it revived the canal project that had been abandoned a few years before when workmen encountered the large cave. The firm still wished to build a canal like Minneapolis Mill's great waterway in order to extend the range of water distribution. The east-side industrial district was stagnant, not because mill-building sites were in short supply, but because the makeshift system of water distribution limited use to nearby locations. Confined to an area scarcely a block square, the eastern district had grown little since the 1850s. In 1871 the company asked the St. Anthony City Council for permission to tunnel under Main Street. The council promptly refused the request on the grounds that the city would be obligated to maintain coverings on the street, and, reportedly, because it did not believe the company was financially sound enough to complete the project.[14]

After the union of St. Anthony and Minneapolis, the company renewed the request and kept it before the city council for several years. Councilmen and interested citizens, however, had numerous objections. Property owners who had already secured land from the company along the route of the proposed canal wanted assurances that they could get water power at a moderate rate. Demonstrating that the recent merger of the cities was an uneasy union, west-side councilmen also objected; they felt that increased water use by the St. Anthony company would decrease the amount available to Minneapolis Mill, and that the project might revitalize industry on the east side.[15]

So heated did the debate become that the *Tribune* on January 21, 1876, commented: "The large majority of the citizens favor the wisest plan in utilizing the East Side power. . . . 'Feverish debates' may do in national bodies but in local interests they are not of much consequence. 'Business' should be our town motto — and the same for all sides." Such pleas for civic unity did not deter the obstructionists, however, and the decade closed without council approval of the canal project.

Meanwhile, the company — accustomed to settling for less than it wanted — secured some return on its investment by granting Mannesseh P. Pettingill the right to use the completed portion of the tunnel and the cave as a resort. From 1875 until 1883 he carried passengers on flatboats into the cave at ten cents a head and sold water from the adjoining "Chalybeate Mineral Springs." [16]

The succession of setbacks strengthened Butterfield's resolution to rid himself of his share of the property. News of his intention to sell broke in Minneapolis on March 1, 1880, when he announced in the *Tribune* that the water power was "too large a non-productive piece of property to hold," that he was not disposed to undertake development himself, and that he did not intend to invest any more money in it. The Chutes then also decided to sell, and within the month the company was purchased for $425,000 by the principal stockholders of the St. Paul, Minneapolis, and Manitoba Railway Company, including James J. Hill of St. Paul.[17]

The departure of Richard Chute — the last of the original owners — signaled the end of an era marked by failure. Vitiated by poor management and internal contention, the company had missed the opportunity to foster on the east side a business complex which would have made it a profitable operation. Sawmilling was the only industry which prospered. Flour milling was still in its infancy, and the ironworks, carding mill, and other miscellaneous businesses contributed little to the firm's income.

Although James J. Hill, the local leader of the new owners, had a strong interest in water power, his primary concern was transportation. When he emigrated to Minnesota from Canada in 1856, he entered the forwarding and commission business on St. Paul's busy steamboat levee. With the dawn of the railroad age in the 1860s, he became an agent of the St. Paul and Pacific, and by 1879 he was one of the stockholders as well as general manager of that road's successor corporation, the St. Paul, Minneapolis, and Manitoba. It was the business of this railroad that drew him to the falls area, where he wished to bridge the Mississippi and build a new west-shore depot to improve the line's Minneapolis facilities. The St. Anthony company's property lay in his pathway, and from the hands of Butterfield and the Chutes he lifted the burden.[18]

Reports of the sale recognized the fact that Hill was primarily interested in a right of way rather than water power, but newspaper spokesmen chose to interpret the change of ownership as a good omen for the east side. They predicted that the St. Anthony company would have a bright future "under the control of that bold and dashing manager" and that the district would waken from its "Rip Van Winkle sleep."[19] The *St. Paul Daily Pioneer Press* of March 19, 1880, endorsed this view. The purchase, it observed, would "give to the East Side . . . an impetus which will work miraculous changes and improvements, and speedily line the east bank of the river with great mills and factories, rivalling in number and importance the mammoth mills and factories of the West Side, which alone have made Minneapolis famous."

The transaction injected a comic note into the war between Minneapolis and St. Paul, which was waged in these years by solemn adversaries. When the news that Hill had purchased half of the vaunted St. Anthony power spread through the capital city, its glee was unrestrained. "HERE SHE BOOMS. St. Paul Buys Out Minneapolis for $425,000," read a headline in the morning *St. Paul Daily Globe* of March 20, 1880. Stung by the jest, the *Tribune* replied on the evening of the same day that "The Globe has simply got the cart before the horse. The fact is, that the superior advantages of Minneapolis are irresistibly attracting St. Paul men of brains and capital. Before another decade passes away we shall doubtless witness a wholesale emigration of St. Paul's leading business men to this metropolis. They will receive a warm welcome."

Unlike the St. Anthony company, whose problems in the 1870s were caused primarily by mismanagement and ownership changes, Minneapolis Mill's proprietors continued to view harmoniously most questions that concerned the company's welfare. The principles guiding the two Washburns and Morrison remained the same as they had been in the pioneer period—to expand the water power as rapidly as possible and to use generous amounts of it for their own mills.

Although the two Washburns experienced bitter years during and after the panic of 1873, they managed to keep afloat their various milling enterprises and railroad ventures as well as Minneapolis Mill. For a few months in 1874 W. D. was forced to suspend his milling business, causing considerable concern in Minneapolis. Like many frontier businessmen, William, said his brother C. C., had overreached himself in his "haste to be rich." He had built mills, bought land, sponsored the Minneapolis and St. Louis Railroad, and invested heavily in the water-power company. C. C. backed him in these enterprises by endorsing his notes without security. When W. D.'s creditors pressed for satisfaction, his brother took over the properties temporarily and paid off the debts. Cadwallader, investing large sums in mill building, also felt the pinch. He called so often upon Algernon S. Washburn for funds that his brother in Maine warned, "You labor under a small delusion when you think I can pass 5000$ notes as easy as a chicken can swallow a grasshopper." [20]

Although the brothers had to scramble for cash and credit, Minneapolis Mill was not plagued by the serious financial exigencies which beset the St. Anthony firm during the 1870s. In a drive to increase income, Minneapolis Mill gradually raised the annual millpower rate between the late 1860s and 1876 from $500 to $1,200, and in 1876—the only year for which figures are available—the firm's gross receipts were $57,734.54. The company declared no dividends during the decade, but in 1880, in lieu of a cash distribution, it granted seventeen free millpowers to C. C. and five each to W. D. and Morrison. [21]

The company's greatest problems in this period stemmed from its success. Apparently convinced that the falls could furnish an unlimited amount of water, the organization had concentrated on attracting manufacturers rather than on securing maximum power from a given quantity of water. As new flour mills and sawmills absorbed an ever-increasing amount of water, the company found that the Mississippi's flow was not sufficient. Thus it had the unhappy choice of limiting additions to the manufacturing district or of assuming a new role in water management.

Boldly tackling the problem, Minneapolis Mill in the 1870s began implementing its authority to discipline the water use of its lessees. The firm's new attitude was evident in a letter written in 1871 to Joel Bassett, the sawmill operator who at the time was opposing the bonds for preserving the falls. Although there is no evidence that Bassett was singled out for severe treatment because of his attitude toward the bonds, the water-power firm ordered him to cease dumping wood refuse into the tunnel leading to his water wheel. In 1873 the company again made the new policy plain when it warned Gardner and Barber, a flour-milling firm, to use the leased water "under the greatest head reasonably attainable by the system of tunneling now in use at the Falls."[22]

Determined to enforce measures requisite for water economy, the organization in 1875 engaged Joseph P. Frizell, a Boston engineer, to study the amount of water the manufacturers were drawing and the head or fall at which they were using it. When his report revealed that the lessees were drawing far more water than they had purchased and that they were wastefully using it on a low head, the company inaugurated sweeping changes. In October it notified the lessees that they would be charged until July 1, 1876, at the rate of five hundred dollars a year for every millpower they used in excess of the number granted. If by that date they had not changed their installations to achieve a greater head, and consequently were still overdrawing the water allotted to them, the company served notice that it would charge them a thousand dollars per millpower annually for the excess.[23]

After so long neglecting its own rules for water economy, Minneapolis Mill found it no easy matter to police the lessees, and it took a firm tone to secure compliance. For example, on October 3, 1880, the company wrote the proprietors of the Galaxy flour mill, warning them that equipment for measuring water would be installed the next day. "If you desire," wrote a Minneapolis Mill official, "to have a representative to see that justice is done in the matter, please have him on hand."[24]

In its new zeal to conserve water, Minneapolis Mill took a dark look at the sawmills resting against the dam, for they, too, were operating wastefully on a low head. In 1866 it had encouraged the operators to increase the head by offering each of them a five-hundred-dollar allowance on rentals in exchange for improvements. After Frizell made his report, the firm made the changes mandatory by announcing that lumbermen who had not made the alterations would be charged for the water they wasted.[25]

The organization also appointed for the first time a trained engineer to fill the post of agent. Over the years the company had hired engineers to execute specific projects such as building dams and canals, but the day-to-day operations had been supervised by men trained in finance, business, or law. Now beset by new managerial problems, the firm in 1877 secured Henry H. Douglass as its first engineer-agent. He had earlier been employed by the federal government to work on preserving the falls, and he knew intimately Minneapolis Mill's plant and water-power practices.[26]

The company's success in attracting manufactures to its property, as well as the owners' far-reaching business interests, created still another crisis in the 1870s. So rapidly did milling develop along the canal that the district was sorely in need of railroad facilities to carry wheat to the mills and flour from them. C. C. Washburn took care of the needs of his own mills in the early 1870s by a private arrangement with the Minneapolis and St. Louis Railroad (of which W. D. Washburn was president).[27] The other millers, however, did not have adequate trackage to handle their wheat and flour.

In 1878 Joel Bassett incorporated the Minneapolis Eastern Railway Company to build a track between the mills and the river. The new company was sponsored by the Chicago, Milwaukee, and St. Paul as well as by the Chicago, St. Paul, and Minneapolis railroads, both of which wanted direct access to the mills. In order to build its line, Minneapolis Eastern had to secure a right of way from Minneapolis Mill. After first looking favorably on the proposal, the water-power company reversed itself on the grounds that the proposed line would destroy a sawmill site, cut off part of the gatehouse controlling the passage of water into the canal, and block possible future extension of the canal. Minneapolis Eastern then began eminent domain proceedings, and commissioners appointed by the Hennepin County District Court awarded Minneapolis Mill $36,000 for the right of way. Refusing to accept the decision, the company declared that it would undertake a legal battle to protect its property.[28]

In the midst of the furor over condemnation, Minneapolis Mill and the Minneapolis and St. Louis Railroad exploded a bombshell. Ignoring the plans of Minneapolis Eastern, they announced their intention to build an elevated trestle over the canal. At the same time the two firms undercut Minneapolis Eastern by offering to handle cars for the two Chicago railroads which sponsored it.[29]

The fat was then in the fire. Bassett accused C. C. Washburn of feathering his brother's nest rather than fostering the district's welfare. His pen sharpened by the campaign then raging between W. D. and Ignatius Donnelly for a seat in Congress (a contest in which he supported Donnelly), Bassett bitterly assailed the dominance of the Washburn brothers in the economic life of Minneapolis. "Is there no end to their avarice," he asked, "and [are] we bound hand and foot to the tail of their kite?" He complained that the brothers had already taken much from the city. "God in His infinite wisdom has made the rain and the sunshine, has made the rivers to flow through the country . . . for the use of man," he lamented, yet when the Mississippi reached Minneapolis the Washburns appropriated it. Not content with controlling a natural resource that should be shared by the community, he continued, the brothers had asked the city to help them exploit it. When the break in Eastman's tunnel threatened their water power, the city bonded itself to save the falls, and when W. D. sponsored the Minneapolis and St. Louis, the city again issued bonds to aid the enterprise. The new railroad proposal, Bassett maintained, was one more indignity heaped upon Minneapolis by two willful men acting in their own interests.

Strong words from Joel Bassett did not shake the Washburns, and Minneapolis Eastern gave way before their obdurance. The railway compromised its dispute with Minneapolis Mill late in 1878 by agreeing to pay $16,500 and to modify the proposed route, thus avoiding damage to the company's property. At the decade's close, Eastern was laying tracks along the river. The Minneapolis and St. Louis also proceeded with the blessings of Minneapolis Mill to complete the trestle over the canal. On November 20 cars propelled by water power, which was substituted for steam to eliminate the fire hazard, rolled over the Minneapolis and St. Louis tracks.[30]

The controversy with Bassett was a tempest in a teapot compared to another fight in which the company became embroiled during the troublesome 1870s. The issue was the construction of a lock and dam at Meeker Island, approximately half a mile below the falls, to bring navigation into the city and develop water power practically on the St. Paul–Minneapolis boundary. Converging in this proposal were the latent hopes of both cities, for St. Paul had long coveted water power, and Minneapolis had from the beginning looked forward to the day when the city would become a regular port of call for steamboats.[31]

The advent of railroads in the 1860s and 1870s did not diminish the zest of navigation advocates. Although an expanding rail network decreased the communities' dependence on the Mississippi and opened routes beyond the reach of the river, a substantial number of citizens believed that the growing communities needed water transportation as well as railroads. Water, the *Tribune* argued on April 19, 1870, remained the cheapest mode of transportation for bulk produce, the Mississippi was still the "great highway of the West," and Minneapolis was still "practically" the head of navigation on the river.

The seemingly innocent Meeker Island project, first suggested in 1857, caused conflicts in the Twin Cities in the 1870s. It set Minneapolis Mill for the first time against powerful navigation interests; it broke temporarily the tight triumvirate of Minneapolis Mill owners, for Dorilus Morrison found in navigation a principle important enough to divide him from the Washburns; it drew the Washburns and Richard Chute of the St. Anthony company together in common cause against a competing water power; and it set the Twin Cities one against the other, for Minneapolis' desire to deny St. Paul water power was equaled only by the capital city's avidity to deny the mill city navigation.

The trouble began in 1857 when Dorilus Morrison, Bradley B. Meeker, a former territorial judge who owned Meeker Island as well as lands on the east shore, and other Minneapolis men incorporated the Mississippi River Improvement and Manufacturing Company. The territorial legislature granted the company a fifteen-year charter and authorized it to build a lock and dam for improving navigation and creating water power.[32]

The new company began to execute the plan late in 1865 when it sent Congress a memorial requesting a land grant to help it finance the lock and dam. Buttressing the company's appeal, the Minnesota legislature forwarded early in 1866 a similar petition based entirely upon the contention that navigation must be brought to Minneapolis. Reviewing the efforts of St. Anthony and Minneapolis to help themselves, the petition maintained that the cities had succeeded well until the stringent times brought on by the 1857 panic and the Civil War forced them to abandon river improvements. As a result, said the legislators, twisting the facts somewhat, navigation "has receded some sixteen miles, to St. Paul, where all the freight destined to these cities . . . and the vast regions north and west dependent on them for their goods and groceries, must break bulk and be carried on cars or wagons to their destination." The petition argued, perhaps speciously, that the land grant was necessary because for some time the new organization would have virtually no income — the abundance of water power already available at the falls would deprive it of immediate sales and it was obliged under the terms of its charter to lock boats without charge.[33]

The Meeker group was aware that its proposal would probably arouse the antagonism of St. Paul as well as the opposition of the water-power companies entrenched at the falls. In the hope of allaying St. Paul's fears about the threat to its pre-eminent position at the head of navigation, the company in 1866 threw the capital city a sop by backing a memorial to Congress requesting that river improvements be made between St. Paul and St. Louis. As for the water-power companies, Judge Meeker wrote, "Their fear is *another* water power that might result *incidentally* from our effort to get Boats to the Falls of St. Anthony." [34]

Meeker hoped that Morrison could soothe his associates in Minneapolis Mill, but this apparently was not to be the case. In March, 1866, the judge warned Ignatius Donnelly, who had undertaken to carry a land-grant bill through the House, that he should beware of the Washburns and the "slippery" Richard Chute. Their chief strategy, which he termed *"Washburne through out,"* would be to block the land-grant bill, push through another measure providing for a river survey, and then control the surveyor's report. The Washburns' influence was particularly dangerous, Meeker told Donnelly, for their brother, Elihu B. Washburne, was in 1866 a member of Congress.[35]

Although it is not known what role the water-power companies played in the maneuver, part of Meeker's prediction was fulfilled. The land-grant bill which Donnelly introduced in 1866 was defeated, and Congress did provide funds for a survey. Outraged, Meeker denounced W. D. Washburn for opposing the land grant because "it *might* make water-power which that interesting family of patriots could not control." He had even more cause for alarm when the

United States Army Engineers selected as the man to make the survey Franklin Cook, an employee at various times of Minneapolis Mill. On this score, however, Meeker's fears were apparently groundless, for when Cook made his report in 1867, he recommended construction of the lock and dam.[36]

With the favorable report before it, Congress in 1868 passed a bill granting 200,000 acres of land to the state of Minnesota to finance the installations.[37] Minneapolitans who had long fought for navigation were delighted. "A dam and lock at Meeker's Island," said the *Tribune* of June 7, 1868, "will be of immense importance to Minneapolis, as it will make St. Anthony Falls in reality the Head of Navigation on the Mississippi, and transfer the commercial *prestige* of this upper country from St. Paul to the 'Magnet.' It will also give us another Water Power, just below the city limits, nearly equal in volume to that at the Falls, proportionately increasing our manufacturing facilities. With our city the head of navigation . . . and seventy-five per cent added to her already magnificent resources in point of manufacturing capacity, who will longer dispute that Minneapolis is the real 'Seat of Destiny' in the Northwest?"

Strangely the *Tribune* seems to have overlooked the fact that by this time St. Paulites controlled the Mississippi River Improvement and Manufacturing Company. It had been sold on February 7, 1867, to three St. Paul men—Horace Thompson, Dominic W. Ingersoll, and Russell Blakeley. Thus the capital city gained control of a water power in exchange for its support of a land-grant bill that would bring navigation to Minneapolis. The *St. Paul Daily Press* of April 23 heralded the event in extravagant language. "We believe," it stated, "there is no instance on this continent, or on the other, where a valuable water power is associated with a great commercial centre. Manufacturing towns, based on water power, are almost universally . . . inland places, at more or less distance from those great lines of water transit, which are the indispensable bases of great commercial centres. Such water powers are very often found in the close neighborhood of commercial cities, and the manufacturing towns built up thereon, are necessarily secondary and tributary to their commercial neighbors." When the St. Paul water power is developed, the *Daily Press* boasted on May 2, "we shall be able to compete 'with all the world and the rest of mankind.' "[38]

Some six months after Congress approved the land grant, a group of men headed by Morrison and other incorporators of the original company joined forces to grab a slice of the pie. On January 25, 1869, they organized the Mississippi River Slackwater Navigation Company. Although the new firm's avowed purpose was to build a lock and dam "at or near" Meeker Island, its real intent was to obtain the land grant which the state held in trust for the company which would build the installations. The new firm's bid failed, however, and on March 6 the legislature awarded the grant to the rival company, with the proviso that it complete the work within two years after it received the land.[39]

Defeated in their attempt to wrest from the St. Paul organization the grant that would enable it to develop the property, Minneapolis men interested in navigation then found an opportunity to regain control of the company. In 1870 the Mississippi River Improvement and Manufacturing Company asked Congress to remove the limitation in the 1868 law which required it to select no more than one section of land in any township. The firm needed the support of influential Minneapolitans in order to secure Congressional approval of this request. In exchange for such support, William S. King, a local Congressman acting for a group of Minneapolitans, demanded a controlling interest in the organization. Intent on securing the amendment from Congress, the St. Paulites agreed.[40]

Some Minneapolitans maintained that this highhanded maneuver was not blackmail but only simple justice. King, who had long been an advocate of navigation, declared that the 1868 law "was passed for the benefit of the community at the Falls, and with the intention of giving us facilities on the river equal to those enjoyed by St. Paul." He contended that "it was unnatural and unreasonable to make St. Paul men the custodians of such a trust, when it was well known that they would prefer to have the Mississippi run into a cave at Fort Snelling and disappear forever from sight, to having navigation brought to the Falls." [41]

From 1870 through 1873, while the bill was before Congress, citizens of Minneapolis spiritedly debated the pros and cons of the amendment. Altercations broke out in the Union Board of Trade, where contenders assailed one another in strong language. Supporting the measure were Dorilus Morrison, King, and other business leaders who saw in its generous provisions for selecting valuable public lands throughout the state the first real hope Minneapolis had ever had for winning navigation. Opposing it were the Washburns and Chute, who feared, as they had in 1866, the development of a competing water power. They were joined by a powerful combination of lumbermen and boom operators who enjoyed free use of the river for running logs and lumber, by citizens who feared the government's generosity to the company might impair the city's chances of securing additional funds for falls' preservation, and by men who maintained that river improvement was an obligation of the federal government not of a private corporation subsidized by the government.[42]

When the amendment was finally defeated in the 1872–73 session of Congress, the debates subsided. The men controlling the Mississippi River Improvement and Manufacturing Company did not build the lock and dam, and the land grant was not transferred to it. Fitfully, however, the subject of developing the Meeker Island water power turned up for reconsideration. In 1874 the St. Paul Chamber of Commerce appointed a committee to investigate the possibility of carrying water from Meeker Island to St. Paul through an aqueduct. At that time the *Tribune* declared that Minneapolis had all the water power it could use "and St. Paul is welcome to all that she can borrow from Meeker's dam." [43]

Five years later the subject was again considered as part of a proposal to consolidate Minneapolis and St. Paul into a single metropolis. A St. Paul man suggested that the Meeker development might weld the union, for "the creation of another water power vaster than that at the falls" would draw to the area "a dense population between the two places that would cement them into one great city." [44]

Neither plan came to fruition, and at the end of the decade the situation remained unchanged. St. Paul was without water power, Minneapolis was without navigation, and the water-power companies were secure in their control of the falls. Minneapolis still awaited a far distant day when boats would float through a series of government-built locks to a harbor in the heart of the city, while St. Paul, reluctantly conceding that it had been done out of the water power, put its faith in steam as the motive force for manufacturing.

Minneapolis Mill emerged from the fight with its reputation somewhat tarnished. The harmonious relationship among the three owners was so disturbed that at one point W. D. confided to a brother that his cousin Dorilus was a "sweet 'scented cuss.' " [45] More important, the conflict revealed the company's changing position in the city. Although it triumphed over powerful spokesmen for navigation, the fact that it had to wage the battle was significant. Throughout the pioneer period, its interests had been considered synonymous with those of Minneapolis. As water-power developers, mill builders, railroad promoters, and civic leaders, the owners had epitomized the hopes of the rising city on the western prairie. In the navigation battle they—with Richard Chute of the St. Anthony company—appeared as selfish men willing to sacrifice the city's navigation interests for their water-power monopoly. The criticism aroused by the struggles over preservation of the falls, over railroad facilities in the milling district, and over the Meeker Dam helped loosen the bonds between the community and the water-power firms in the 1870s. New attitudes were forming, not only toward the companies but toward the water power itself as the most influential factor in the city's growth.

7.

The Queen City of the Northwest

MINNEAPOLIS IN THE 1870S HAD GOOD REASON to congratulate itself. In little more than twenty years, the falls had vindicated the pioneers' faith that the water power would create a city. The Minneapolis Mill and the St. Anthony organizations, in spite of their ups and downs, had developed the cataract into a substantial source of power.[1] The industrial district, hugging the riverbanks close by the cataract, was in the 1870s the core of the city's economy, and all its major industries were compressed into a few blocks there. Stone flour mills towered in close ranks over the waterfall. Logs glutted the river for miles, and the high whine of saws filled the air. Wagons and railroad cars rumbled ceaselessly through the area, and thousands of workers found employment in its varied industries.

In terms of manufacturing growth, the falls in the 1870s produced the most notable results thus far in their history. The total value of products turned out in Minneapolis and St. Anthony in 1870 was $6,810,970. By 1880 the figure had more than quadrupled, and the consolidated city was producing goods worth $29,973,476. At least 75 per cent of this amount came from mills based on the water power. The two leading industries were lumbering and flour milling; in 1880 they employed 1,722 men, paid $962,911 in wages, and used materials valued at $20,710,619. Impressive as these statistics are, they do not measure the total importance of the water-power industries in the economic life of Minneapolis during this period. They do not reflect, for example, the many activities which were related to the mills at the falls—the manufacturing of water wheels, milling equipment, and flour barrels, the cutting, driving, and booming of logs, the outfitting of lumbermen, the trading and storage of wheat, and the transportation, sale, and marketing of raw materials and manufactured products. Nor do the figures take into account the hundreds of bankers, doctors, lawyers, teachers, merchants, millwrights, and others who were drawn to the community to provide the services needed by its growing population.[2]

In the 1870s the men who owned the water power and the mills clustering beside it had a status in Minneapolis similar to that of the falls. They not only dominated the city's trade associations and held significant amounts of stock in its banks, railroads, and other enterprises, but they also played prominent roles in its religious, social, charitable, and cultural organizations. William Washburn, Dorilus Morrison, Richard Chute, John S. and Charles A. Pillsbury, William Eastman, Joel Bassett, Sumner Farnham, George Brackett, John Crosby, George H. and John A. Christian, Charles M. Loring, George W. Crocker, William H. Dunwoody, and others whose mills were located at the falls wielded an influence in the city out of all proportion to their numbers. The careers of many of these men spanned the history of Minneapolis from the 1850s to the 1880s, while the careers of others who were relative latecomers extended into the twentieth century.

Most of these community leaders were flour millers, and the 1870s saw that industry expand dramatically at the falls. The value of its product rose from $1,125,215 in 1870 to $20,502,305 in 1880, when it comprised almost two-thirds of Minneapolis' entire value in manufactures. During the same period, flour production grew from 193,000 barrels annually to 2,051,840, and flour milling displaced lumbering as the city's leading industry.[3]

This unprecedented increase in production gave Minneapolis a new importance among the nation's milling centers. Throughout the 1870s, the city steadily crept up on St. Louis, which for years had held first place. "St. Louis," declared the *Tribune* of December 1, 1876, "must yield the palm of queen flour city of America . . . to Minneapolis, the young queen city of the northwest." As the gap narrowed still more in 1878, the *American Miller* predicted that "Minneapolis is destined to become the Budapest of America." The comparison with Europe's greatest flour city was warranted. In 1880, unable to keep pace with the northern giant, St. Louis yielded its crown—a crown Minneapolis was to wear for fifty years.[4]

Many factors made possible the concentration of flour mills in the city. Foremost among them initially was the abundance of cheap water power provided by the Falls of St. Anthony. But this alone would not have been enough to produce a great milling center if railroads had not opened fresh agricultural areas to wheatgrowers, provided connections between the mills and their markets, and offered generally favorable rates to the millers.

Minneapolitans had been avid railroad promoters in the 1850s and 1860s, and local newspapers, like those of many other western cities, had projected airy empires bound to the central city by railway routes. In reality, however, St. Paul took the lead in sponsoring and attracting lines, while Minneapolis, beginning with railroad connections established in the 1860s by the St. Paul and Pacific and the Milwaukee and St. Paul, shared somewhat unequally in the benefits. Sparked by a new commercial orientation and probably by their own long role as protestors against St. Paul's real and fancied railroad advantages, Minneapolitans in the 1870s became active promoters of lines owned or controlled in the city. They voted bonds for the Minneapolis and St. Louis, projected a system of relatively inexpensive, municipally sponsored narrow-gauge railroads designed to bring to Minneapolis the trade of northern and western Minnesota and portions of the Dakotas and Iowa, and laid the groundwork for a Minneapolis built and controlled line to Sault Ste. Marie.[5]

During that decade, too, the St. Paul and Pacific (which in 1879 became the St. Paul, Minneapolis, and Manitoba) reached into western Minnesota and northward to the Canadian boundary. The Northern Pacific, building west from Duluth to the Montana line, rolled its cars into the Twin Cities over the tracks of the St. Paul and Pacific. The Lake Superior and Mississippi reached Duluth from St. Paul, and Minneapolis secured a connection through the Minneapolis and Duluth Railroad. The Minneapolis and St. Louis stretched southward into the rich acres of Iowa, and the Minnesota Valley Railroad, arriving at Sioux City, established contact with tracks leading to the Southwest. At the end of the 1870s the major problems were the extension of three existing systems — the Northern Pacific, the St. Paul, Minneapolis and Manitoba, and the Chicago, Milwaukee, and St. Paul — to the west coast and the construction of the road to Sault Ste. Marie.[6]

As the tracks extended farther and farther into the hinterland, settlement flowed westward across Minnesota and on to the Rocky Mountains. During the decade, the state's population grew from 439,706 to 780,773, Dakota Territory's increased from 14,181 to 135,177, and Montana Territory's rose from 20,595 to 39,159. Breaking the tough sod of the virgin prairies, Minnesota wheat farmers more than doubled their harvest — from 17,660,467 bushels in 1869 to 39,399,068 in 1880 — and newly plowed acres in the Dakotas were eloquent harbingers of the future. Railroads hauled the golden harvest to the falls, and from the mills they carried flour to far-flung markets in the United States and Europe through connections with Chicago and Milwaukee as well as with Duluth, the Lake Superior port at the western end of the Great Lakes waterway.[7]

In the 1870s some Minneapolis business leaders became keenly aware of opportunities afforded by the emerging hinterland. There had been some wholesaling in the city since the 1850s, but the business was now promoted more aggressively. By 1877 Minneapolis wholesalers sold $8,034,000 worth of merchandise, as compared to $27,815,072 sold by St. Paul houses. Minneapolitans also established small livestock and meat-packing businesses which were touted as the beginnings of a great industry, and they made a start in grain marketing. With a larger wheat supply available than ever before, the millers at the falls moved to snatch it from competing Milwaukee and Chicago buyers. Regularizing a buying pool formed in the 1860s, they organized in 1876 the Minneapolis Millers Association. The group established rules for grading and pricing, sent buyers into the country, bought wheat by sample, and distributed the supply to the mills according to their production capacities.[8]

By 1878 the city's influence in the hinterland was becoming marked enough to be an irritant, as the Congressional campaign of that year demonstrated. William D. Washburn, miller, water-power owner, and railroad man, was the Republican candidate; Ignatius Donnelly, an agrarian spokesman whose zeal was heightened by an unsuccessful fling as a wheat farmer in western Minnesota's Stevens County, ran as a Democrat. Washburn represented the urban center; Donnelly was identified with its tributary area, and the campaign indicated that a gulf was developing between the two interests represented by the candidates. Although Washburn won the election, Donnelly filled the columns of the state's newspapers with invectives against the millers who, he said, dictated to Minnesota and Dakota farmers the prices they would receive for their wheat.[9]

The seat of power at the falls from which the millers exerted the influence to which Donnelly objected was three blocks long and little more than a block deep. The Minneapolis Mill Company's canal was the factor determining the size of the district. In 1869 the area was not congested, for only eight flour mills were scattered along the waterway. Between 1870 and 1876, however, ten new water-power mills were built, and almost every site within the range of the canal was utilized. In that period the structures were high and narrow, and it was not unusual for a mill with a sixty-by-eighty-foot base to rise six stories above the ground. Most of them were limestone buildings, and they had slate or gravel-topped roofs crowned with cupolas.[10]

Dominating the district was the Washburn A, Cadwallader's new mill. When he began its construction in 1873, he confided to a friend that he intended to have the "finest flouring mill in the world." If it was not the world's largest when it was completed in 1874, the structure certainly excelled any other mill at the falls, and "Cad" immodestly claimed that he was "making such flour as was never before seen on this continent." The Washburn A had forty-one run of stone (the next largest at the falls was the Pettit which had fifteen); its equipment included machinery manufactured in Austria; and its operators were trained in the techniques its owner had observed in Budapest, Prague, Paris, and Vienna.[11]

Visitors flocked to the canal for a look at the famous mill, and the A's commanding appearance fulfilled their expectations. Its limestone walls rose seven and a half stories; its powerful water wheels were located forty-five feet below street level; its base measured 100 by 138 feet. During its brief existence, the A clearly symbolized Washburn's confidence in water power, the dominance of flour in Minneapolis, and the city's drive toward milling supremacy.[12]

But the mill was destined to stand only four years. On May 2, 1878, it suddenly exploded, threatening the entire milling district. The explosion, which killed eighteen men, occurred without warning during the twilight hours, as the mill rumbled softly and filled the air with fragrant dust. So powerful was the blast that the roof rose hundreds of feet into the air, and stones from the shattered walls crashed into a house eight blocks away. The walls of nearby mills collapsed, and sheets of flame fanned by a "merciless north wind" swept through the district. Terrified, the "whole population" of the city poured into the streets, and St. Paulites, believing that an earthquake had taken place, hurried to the falls.[13]

For a time "confusion reigned supreme," but firemen gradually brought the flames under control. When morning dawned over the devastated area, an observer wrote that "Scarcely one stone stands upon another, as it was laid, in the big Washburn mill, and the chaotic pile of huge limestone rocks is interwoven with slivered timbers, shafts and broken machinery from which pours forth steam and water. The destruction of the Humboldt and Diamond mills is even more complete. The fire-seared walls of the Pettit, Zenith and Galaxy mills stand stark and burned, cleaned of their contents."

The explosion attracted nationwide attention. The *New York Graphic* of May 10, 1878, devoted its front page to illustrations of the scene, and other newspapers gave the disaster almost as much attention as they had extended to the Chicago fire seven years earlier. A month later, when the ruins were still smoking, crowds of visitors from near and far continued to gather at the falls to view "the terrible destruction."[14]

Various rumors "borne on the excited wings of consternation and despair" fixed responsibility for the explosion on gas, on recently installed steam boilers, on a cargo of nitroglycerin allegedly stored in nearby railroad cars, and on a lantern supposedly lowered into a wheat bin. However, John A. Christian (head of J. A. Christian and Company, the firm which operated the mill for Washburn) advanced the theory that flour dust caused the disaster, and his explanation later proved to be correct.[15]

The explosion of the Washburn A ranked with the tunnel break nine years earlier as a major catastrophe in the history of Minneapolis, for it leveled in a single night one-third of the city's milling capacity, as well as lumberyards, planing mills, a machine shop, a wheat-storage elevator, a railroad roundhouse, and a number of nearby residences. Minneapolitans did not, however, feel the same responsibility to repair the damage as they had when the tunnel collapsed; they seemed to feel that the mills were the responsibility of the owners who profited from them. Nevertheless 1878 was a year when the city's future hung in the balance. It was a question whether Minneapolis would recover from the blow and continue its drive for milling supremacy or whether the explosion would mark the point at which the industry so important to the city lost its impetus for growth.

The powerful fraternity of millers answered the question promptly. In a burst of energy "without a precedent" in the city's history, they immediately rebuilt the milling district. "Where but a few weeks ago was ruin and desolation," the *Tribune* reported on July 19, 1878, "now gigantic walls of solid masonry are reared up and are rapidly being fashioned into mills that will far surpass the structures blown into atoms by that terrible disaster." By the end of the year, seventeen mills were again in operation, among them the new Washburn A, Model, Excelsior, Northwestern, and Standard. By 1880 a total of twenty-two, new and old, were operating on the west side.[16]

Across the river, fire and the aftereffects of tunnel breaks threatened for a time to extinguish flour milling on the east side. Early in

the 1870s the industry vanished from its early stronghold on Hennepin Island. The Summit mill, it will be recalled, crashed into the
Mississippi in 1870 when the second tunnel break tore away part of
the foundation. The Island mill, which had been entirely remodeled
in 1869, burned in 1872, and the same fire destroyed the River or
Farmers mill. On the east shore, the St. Anthony mill burned
in 1871.[17]

While the east side lost four flour mills during the decade, it
acquired three new ones. In 1870–71 a small grist and jobbing mill
called the North Star was fitted up in a building once used for stores
and a foundry. Five years later the proprietors of the St. Anthony
mill (who had been operating on the west side since the 1871 fire)
erected a new mill, the Phoenix, on the east shore. Appropriately
risen from ashes, the Phoenix was constructed to endure. Four stories
high and fashioned of limestone, it was, said the *Tribune* of April 9,
1876, "a model of beauty, built on a foundation as solid as the everlasting hills." [18]

Even more impressive was the Pillsbury A mill begun on the east
side in 1880 by C. A. Pillsbury and Company. The limestone structure designed by LeRoy S. Buffington, a well-known architect of the
day, was completed in 1881. It stood on Main Street near the St. Anthony water-power company's dam. Seven stories high and measuring 115 by 175 feet at the base, it overshadowed the squat sawmills,
foundries, and other buildings clustered near it. The Pillsbury A
cost almost half a million dollars and contained two identical units
that gave it a capacity of four thousand barrels of flour a day. With
various additions made by its proud owners, the Pillsbury A was
soon to become the largest flour mill in the world.[19]

As the millers crowded the falls area with new structures, they
also determined to produce better flour. Competing with mills using
soft winter wheat, the Minneapolis men had been at a disadvantage
in the 1860s, for the flat-grinding process then in use made poorer
flour from northwestern spring wheat than could be produced from
winter wheat. Since the spring wheat kernels were very hard, the
millstones had to be run under great pressure and at high speed.
The flour produced under these conditions was discolored from heat,
speckled with particles from the husk or bran, and tended to spoil.
Even Minneapolitans preferred the white, better-keeping flour made
from winter wheat. Dorilus Morrison, for example, in 1871 asked
a steamboat owner to ship five barrels of the "best Brand St. Louis
Flour" for his personal use.[20]

Moreover, a nutritious layer of the spring wheat kernel next to the husk was so hard that the grinding only partially pulverized it, and it was then removed from the flour. This layer, with the bran, constituted the "middlings," as the millers called them, and they were frequently reground to make a low-grade but nourishing flour. To cope with the middlings problem a new process was developed in the 1860s by millers of southern Minnesota, and in the early 1870s the Minneapolis men began to adopt and improve upon it. The new process employed smoother millstones which were run at low speed, an innovation which prevented heat discoloration and minimized the crushing of the husk or bran that specked the flour. The middlings were separated from the flour, purified by the removal of the bran — through sieves and blowers — and reground into fine white flour. The machine which performed this operation became known as the "Middlings Purifier," and it revolutionized flour making. With its use, spring wheat yielded the "best bread-making flour of the world," and it quickly replaced winter wheat flour as a favorite in the market.[21]

In the late 1870s the millers further improved their methods when they began to substitute porcelain and later iron rollers for millstones. The rollers reduced the wheat to flour in graduated steps, increased the yield, generated less heat in grinding, used less power, and were easier to maintain than millstones. By 1880 this improved system was in common use at the falls, and the fine flour it produced helped Minneapolis win and hold its position as the nation's milling capital.[22]

In the wake of milling improvements and the erection of new structures came the beginnings of consolidation. Heavy capital outlays for buildings and machinery, the intricacies of buying wheat and selling flour, and other business problems encouraged this movement. In the 1850s and 1860s proprietorship of the mills had been dispersed among many owners. In 1869, for example, thirteen mills in Minneapolis and St. Anthony were operated by as many firms. Consolidation began in 1874 with the formation of C. A. Pillsbury and Company; by 1880 this firm was operating five of the twenty-five mills at the falls. The second large organization to emerge was Washburn, Crosby and Company, of which C. C. Washburn was a member. It was formed in 1879 and by the following year was running three mills. Together the two consolidated organizations controlled eight large mills which represented over half the city's production capacity.[23]

The trend toward consolidation which characterized flour milling during this period was not apparent in sawmilling, the city's second largest industry. In 1869 the eighteen mills manufacturing lumber at the falls were operated by eighteen different firms. By 1876—the last year in which all the water-power mills were operating—the situation had changed little, for the city's nineteen sawmills were run by eighteen different proprietors.[24]

In one respect flour and saw milling had a similar pattern. Though firm names changed frequently, the roster of individuals who were active in each industry remained fairly constant. In flour milling, for example, the Washburns, the Pillsburys, the Christians, George Brackett, and John Crosby were still important operators, while such men as Sumner Farnham, James A. Lovejoy, William Eastman, Joel Bassett, James McMullen, Levi Butler, Leonard Day, and John Martin remained in the lumber business year after year. Some of these men—Day, W. D. Washburn, and Eastman among them—were interested in both flour and saw milling, thus continuing a pattern begun early in the city's history.

Statistics indicate the prominent role sawmilling played in the economic life of Minneapolis. The industry was the city's largest employer, for it required more labor than did flour milling. In 1870 the annual value of its products stood at $1,733,011, and it ranked first among the city's industries in this respect. By 1880 the value of its products had risen to $2,740,848, but by that time flour milling had outstripped it and sawmilling fell to second place. During the same period, the total output of the city's sawmills grew from 90,734,595 board feet in 1869 to 179,585,182.[25]

The leading producers were the mills on the east-side row and Farnham and Lovejoy's establishment on Hennepin Island; in 1880 they contributed 94,977,182 board feet out of the industry's total of 179,585,182. The basis of this leadership was the new row built after the St. Anthony company sold the millsites following the 1870 fire. The five purchasers constructed mills which were far better planned than the old ones. Each owner allotted the first 50 feet of surface to the dam and bulkhead, the next 110 feet to the building, and another 110 feet to a platform for lumber piling and a roadway. Although the area was still congested, the movement of logs from millpond to saw, from saw to platform, and from platform to nearby yards proceeded smoothly.[26]

Typical of the new mills replacing the haphazard old structures was that of O. C. Merriman and Company. It was a frame building, about 52 feet wide by 110 feet deep. Its water wheel was located fifteen feet below the basement and five feet beneath the limestone sheath. Water entered the wheel from the millpond and exited beneath the falls through a tailrace four hundred feet long. Heavy shafting in the basement drove the machinery. The ground floor had several types of saws, among them two double circulars, one gang, one slab, six trimming, four edging, and one for cutting shingle blocks. On the upstream side, slips or conveyers extended down into the pond to draw logs into the mill. On the platform downstream, lumber, slabs, shingles, and laths were sorted and piled, ready to be hauled to the yards.[27]

The west-side sawmills also flourished early in the decade. The row mills at the dam, operated by changing proprietors, and Joel Bassett's establishment which was built nearby in 1867, were by 1876 producing approximately 53,000,000 board feet of lumber. In spite of the booming flour mills, the ceaseless movement of logs and lumber attracted notice, and the *Tribune* of January 1, 1875, described it as "one of the busiest sights that can be witnessed in our bustling city."[28]

Had it been left to develop naturally, the west-side industry should have enjoyed greater prosperity than ever before. In the 1870s the northern pineries tributary to the Mississippi still furnished all the logs the Minneapolis mills could use; railroads were extending the marketing area; and the water power—though Minneapolis Mill fretted about its efficient use—was still cheap and available. Nevertheless, other factors intervened to mark the beginning of the end of sawmilling on the west-side water power. Minneapolis Mill, which had granted the proprietors short-term rather than perpetual grants like those it made to the flour millers, decided rather abruptly in 1876 that the sawmills must go. The company's decision was influenced by the fact that the mills, even with improved installations, still used water wastefully at a time when the flour mills were demanding greater quantities. Moreover, the United States army engineers— completing in this year the great dike protecting the limestone sheath—warned the firm that by narrowing the river channel the sawmill row posed a constant threat to the falls' safety.[29]

Between 1876 and 1880 Minneapolis Mill, implementing a clause in the leases which permitted such action, bought all the sawmills. For a few years it derived additional revenue by leasing them on a short-term basis. Entering the lumber business as an operator for the first time, it also sawed for lumbermen and ran the mills with logs purchased from contractors. Until it razed the last two structures in 1887, Minneapolis Mill wholesaled lumber to yards in Minnesota, Wisconsin, Iowa, Dakota Territory, Nebraska, and Manitoba, Canada. But the water-power company's purchases cut west-side production, and by 1880 the center, consisting of six row mills and that of Bassett, was turning out only 52,000,000 board feet — almost 43,000,000 less than the east-side sawmills.

Another factor which contributed to the decline of sawmilling at the falls was steam power. As early as the 1850s and 1860s seven steam mills had operated at different times in the falls district. By the 1870s improvements in steam equipment enabled sawmill operators to reduce, or perhaps eliminate, the cost differential between steam and water power by building improved steam plants which burned wood refuse as fuel. Thus that decade saw the establishment of a new sawmilling district on the Mississippi River in north Minneapolis. Additional considerations influencing the movement away from the falls were the larger mill and yard space available at the new location, the removal of inflammable lumberyards from the heart of the city, the easy access to the boom, and the railroad trackage planned for the north Minneapolis area.[30]

Encouraged by these advantages and impelled by Minneapolis Mill's edict against sawmilling, several lumbermen abandoned the crowded district at the falls for the north Minneapolis site, where they were soon joined by others new to the business. The shift to steam gained momentum when Joseph Dean, P. G. Lamoreaux, the Minneapolis Lumber Company, and other operators built large mills. By 1880 the new center was turning out 32,608,000 board feet a year, or approximately 16 per cent of all the lumber produced in Minneapolis.[31]

The decade of the 1870s also witnessed a revival of the city's twenty-year-old ambition to become a textile center. The enthusiasm of spokesmen for cotton mills, which had been voiced as early as the 1850s, stemmed from several unrelated factors: a desire to imitate New England, a realization that such mills employed a great many people, and an awareness that the ratio of labor to value of product was generally higher than it was for either flour or saw milling. The enthusiasm also stemmed from a feeling of economic unity with the South which was especially strong in the years preceding the Civil War. Although northwestern trade was already oriented toward the East in the 1850s, the Mississippi River was a constant reminder of geographical affinity with the South. The *Express* of October 22, 1852, for example, informed its readers that the natural course of trade was between areas in different latitudes, and that northern and southern products should be exchanged without the interference of eastern middlemen. The persistence of this attitude was demonstrated by the *Tribune* in the 1860s and 1870s when it proposed that Minneapolis produce its own textiles and ship them to the South with other manufactured goods instead of buying textiles woven in New England from southern cotton. A significant index to the popular feeling that Minnesota and the South could serve each other by exchanging products was the plan first advanced in the 1850s for a "Falls to New Orleans" railroad, as well as the constant agitation over the years for improvements in the Mississippi's channel from Minneapolis to the Gulf of Mexico.[32]

During the fifties and sixties when sentiment for North-South trade was strongest, not a single cotton manufactory was established at the falls, but some Minneapolitans remained confident that the mills would come as a natural evolution of their city's economy. In 1866 when C. C. Washburn traveled east on a mission to bring a cotton mill to Minneapolis, an elated *Daily Press* correspondent predicted that "the hum of the spindle and the clash and clangor of modern enterprise" would soon "hush out forever the last sound of retreating barbarism." Washburn was unsuccessful, however, and it was not until 1870 that Dorilus Morrison and other local businessmen incorporated the Minneapolis Cotton Manufacturing Company. The new organization equipped a two-story building with twenty looms and began operations on the west side in March, 1870, when the first "load of cotton ever received in Minnesota" arrived from Memphis, Tennessee. A month later the *Tribune* of April 12 reported proudly that Minneapolis now had "the first and only machinery for the manufacture of cotton in the Northwest."[33]

The company, which Morrison took over entirely a few months after its incorporation, at first devoted itself exclusively to manufacturing seamless bags used for exporting flour. Bags were preferred to barrels for this purpose because they reduced freight costs, lowered the risk of leakage, and had a resale value at the terminal market. By the end of 1870 the mill was producing seven hundred bags a day. Two years later the proprietor added machinery to fabricate white and colored duck for tents, wagon covers, and awnings, and at the same time built a dyehouse as an annex to the mill. In 1873 the expanded plant turned out 241,000 bags, 40,000 yards of duck, and 200 tents and wagon covers, but three years later the enterprise was obviously flagging. Morrison leased the business to Honcomp and Cummings (a Chicago firm), the mill moved three times, and in 1881 it closed.[34]

Efforts to found a cotton industry on the east side were even less successful. A group of citizens in 1870 petitioned the St. Anthony City Council to grant a subsidy to an organization called the Northwestern Cotton Company, which planned to build a mill. The council agreed to do so, but the mill was not built. The following year a citizen presented a paper before the Union Board of Trade pointing out the economic advantages the community would reap from cotton mills. And again and again the local press and the board vainly urged businessmen to expand the industry from the nucleus formed by Morrison's mill.[35]

Although there is no certainty about why cotton milling languished in Minneapolis while it throve in New England cities, the failure was probably due to the same factors which dictated the industry's general lack of progress in the West. It has been suggested that textile plants profited from proximity to the eastern seaboard, a location which facilitated the importation of dyes, chemicals, new patterns, and long-staple cotton. The New England area, too, had a large force of trained operatives, an ideal climate for textile manufacturing, and a concentration of establishments that made possible specialization in fabrics and processes. Against these advantages, the *Tribune*, for example, called attention to the allegedly higher cost of transporting raw materials to eastern mills and the certain higher cost of carrying the manufactured product to western markets, but these differentials were not sufficient to be determining factors.[36]

The falls community was similarly unsuccessful in its efforts to found a woolen industry modeled on the mills at Lowell. The lone carding plant, which had been established on the east side in 1861 by David Lewis, went out of business about 1870. The Minneapolis Woolen Mill on the west side closed in 1875, and the carding mill nearby remained only a small operation. The outlook seemed even bleaker when the North Star Woolen Mill, begun in 1864 by W. W. Eastman and Paris Gibson, went into bankruptcy in 1876.[37]

Since the North Star mill employed many persons and had earned a fine reputation for its products, several Minneapolitans tried to save it. When their efforts failed, Minneapolis Mill stepped in and purchased the property—a rescue operation the *Tribune* of January 12, 1877, felt was "of more consequence to Minneapolis than the result of half-a-dozen presidential elections." Between 1877 and 1880 the water-power company engaged managers to operate the mill. Among them were Paris Gibson (a member of the woolen firm that failed), James C. Tuttle, and William G. Northup.[38]

Under their direction, North Star's production boomed, and it was to continue as an important Minneapolis industry until the 1940s. The company manufactured scarves, flannels, cassimeres, and yarns, but the real source of its growth was blankets. North Star began to specialize in them in 1869, using such brand names as Mountaineer, Royal Rose, Cardinal, Red River, Itasca, and the Falls of St. Anthony. In recognition of their fine quality, the Philadelphia Centennial Exposition awarded them its highest prize in 1876. The mill sold blankets widely at both retail and wholesale, but its best known customer was the Pullman Palace Car Company of Chicago, which used them in America and in Europe. The Northwest was a very strong market; orders came from Minnesota, Wisconsin, Michigan, Iowa, Dakota and Montana territories, and to a lesser extent from more distant points in Illinois, Indiana, Ohio, Missouri, Kentucky, Nebraska, Colorado, and Wyoming. Beyond the Northwest, Chicago, St. Louis, and New York City served as the chief distributing points. As North Star's production increased, Minnesota farmers could not furnish enough high-quality wool to supply its needs. In 1875 Paris Gibson claimed that the mill had purchased most of the state's clip, and still the supply was not sufficient. To augment it, the firm bought wool in Wisconsin, Colorado, Montana, New Mexico, and Texas.[39]

The success of North Star was not typical, and the fate of other miscellaneous industries at the falls was scarcely encouraging to water-power enthusiasts. The North Star Iron Works, hampered in its expansion plans by congestion near the falls, switched to steam and moved in 1869 or 1870 from the east side to a location beyond the reach of water power. Impelled by the same need for space, the Monitor Plow Works migrated in 1875 from the west side to the city's outskirts, where its owners built a steam-powered plant on a twenty-acre tract; and at the decade's end the Minnesota Iron Works, which had been purchased by O. A. Pray and Company, also left the crowded milling center. Joining the withdrawal from the falls was a furniture manufacturer, who moved in 1872 to a new steam-powered plant away from the St. Anthony shore.[40] Interest in the paper mill, founded on Hennepin Island in 1859, declined when its owners built a plant in Appleton, Wisconsin, in 1878. It closed after a fire four years later, leaving the Minneapolis Paper Mill, which had been established on the west side in 1866, as the sole remnant of this pioneer effort at the falls.[41]

Such changes were indicative of several trends that would have a profound effect upon future patterns of water-power usage as well as business development in Minneapolis. It was becoming apparent that the amounts of land and water power available in the falls district were limited, that the flour mills—expanding beyond the expectations of the most exuberant optimist—were crowding out other types of manufacturing, and that the growing use of steam power gave operators greater flexibility in choosing locations for their plants.

The movement toward steam in part reflected a national trend and in part the expansion of industries requiring more power. In 1870 steam provided 51.82 per cent and water power 48.18 per cent of the total power used in manufacturing in the United States. Ten years later steam accounted for 64.07 per cent, while water power fell to 35.93 per cent. In Minnesota the ratio in 1870 stood at 64.82 for water and 35.18 for steam; by 1880 it was 53.25 and 46.75 respectively, a gain of 11.5 per cent for steam. Although statistics for Minneapolis are not available, it is known that almost every new plant established in the city during the 1870s used steam rather than water power.[42]

Other trends toward wholesaling and the development of trade with the hinterland indicated that Minneapolis' future economic life would be less dependent upon industry at the falls. The *Tribune* of March 22, 1879, for example, asked its readers to remember that "no purely manufacturing city in this country ever attains metropolitan proportions." Minneapolis, the paper said, must awaken and add trade to its industry. During this period questions about the city's destiny which had earlier been asked only infrequently became more persistent. Was the future growth of the city really dependent upon manufacturing? What of commerce? Could the water power be increased enough to support growing manufactures? Or would steam reduce the falls to a minor place in the city's economy?

The emergence of a new attitude toward the water power was typified by a story in the *Tribune* of December 2, 1878. "Citizens who stand by in stolid idleness and point to the Falls of St. Anthony as the beginning and end of the needs of a great city are stagnant fools," the journal lectured. "The falls are merely one of the agencies which, properly subordinated, make for success in the long and persistent struggle for metropolitan supremacy. Minneapolis, cooped up with a Chinese wall around her falls, will be like a mummy of a human body without veins leading to its heart . . . or arteries radiating from it to build the body up."

Residents of Minneapolis in the 1870s did not fully recognize that water power as the prime factor in the city's economy was at its zenith. The expansion of flour milling during this decade kept attention focused on the cataract, and most of the industries which left the falls remained in the city. Indeed, the condition of Minneapolis — grown from straggling twin villages into the Queen City of the Northwest — seemed a vindication of faith in water power. When the results of the 1880 census were published, Minneapolis ranked first in flour production, third in sawed lumber, and twentieth among all the nation's cities in the total value of its manufactured products. The number of its inhabitants had also increased during the decade from 18,079 to 46,887, making it the thirty-eighth largest city in the nation.[43]

The new Queen of the Northwest had no peer west of Chicago. It had surpassed St. Paul in population by more than four thousand persons, and no contenders had emerged on the plains rising to the Rockies. Portland, Seattle, and Tacoma on the Pacific slope were still small towns. On the Mississippi, it was exceeded in population only by New Orleans and St. Louis, and in the entire trans-Mississippi West only by San Francisco and Kansas City. In the years ahead, as Minneapolis maintained its place in the front ranks of western cities, its reliance upon water power would diminish while its increased demands upon the falls would present the owners with a host of new challenges.[44]

8.

Stretching the Power

IN THE 1880s THE CITY which had once resembled a New England town took on an appearance to match its new importance. Constructed during the decade were such massive edifices as the Minneapolis Exposition Building, the Boston Block, and the Post Office, while plans were made for the combined courthouse and city hall that is still a Minneapolis landmark — a pink "granite palace" covering a full block and costing when completed in 1906 about three and a half million dollars. As the new buildings were erected, the *Tribune* of May 6, 1882, observed, "Houses which have long been landmarks in the older parts of the city, are, by dozens, on wheels and trundling off to remote sections of the city." Concerned with other values, the citizens also organized the Minneapolis Society of Fine Arts and the Minneapolis Club, built a new public library, and laid out an extensive park system. Remnants of more uncertain years remained in a defensive attitude toward older urban centers, the militancy with which "culture" was sought, and a youthful braggadocio, but the city, proudly and affirmatively, was achieving its own identity.[1]

It did so in an age when as many changes took place at the falls as in the city's general profile. Minneapolitans paused to comment upon their debt to water power in 1880 when they commemorated the two-hundredth anniversary of Hennepin's discovery of the Falls of St. Anthony. A great parade marched from the cataract to the University of Minnesota, where orators narrated the city's history. One speaker recalled that Hennepin had been the "first white man who ever saw and heard the throbbings of that mighty artery of power which now gives life to thousands of people. . . . The wildest dreamer of two hundred years ago could not have foretold of the wondrous changes which would be worked upon the scene."[2]

And there were more changes to come. The age of electricity was dawning, an age that would eventually convert the falls into a hydro-electric site diffusing their energy throughout the city, lighting homes, offices, and streets, powering manufactories, and propelling streetcars. Before that event took place, however, the water-power companies, pressed by the opportunities hydroelectricity afforded and by the flour millers' increased needs, would at long last face the problem of developing the cataract to its full capacity.

A trend begun in the 1870s — the movement of industry out of the crowded falls district — accelerated in the 1880s. During those years, sawmilling, which at one time had been almost totally dependent upon water power, was virtually extinguished at the cataract. At the decade's close only two lumbermen were using the falls' power — James McMullen on the east side and Joel Bassett across the river. The industry's migration to north Minneapolis was speeded in 1887 by the razing of the west-side sawmills and by a fire which destroyed the east-side row. By 1889 eleven steam-powered mills were operating in the new district, and within the next ten years their production would make Minneapolis the nation's greatest sawmilling center. Other manufactories joined the exodus from the falls, and by 1889 the flour millers had the area almost to themselves.[3]

Although the departing plants released a substantial amount of water, the millers quickly absorbed it and called for more. Flour production rose from 2,051,840 barrels in 1880 to 6,088,865 in 1889. Far exceeding the output of St. Louis, New York City, and Milwaukee — the next ranking centers — the mills retained for Minneapolis its position as the nation's flour capital. The value of their product accounted for the largest single unit of Minneapolis' total of almost $83,000,000.[4]

The tripling of flour production at the falls was achieved by expanding the capacities of existing mills rather than by building new ones. As the decade opened twenty-five mills had a daily capacity of about 25,000 barrels, while in 1889 only twenty-two mills could produce over 36,000 barrels. During the latter year, Pillsbury A, which was the largest mill at the cataract and reputedly the second largest in the world, could turn out 7,000 barrels a day. In view of the presence of this giant in the city, the *Northwest Magazine* found it hard to acknowledge that "a town in such an out-of-the-way place as Hungary, and with such an unconscionable name as Buda-Pesth, should have the impertinence to build a larger mill" than the A. Greater operating efficiency was also achieved during the decade by further consolidation in the milling industry. By 1889 three companies controlled approximately 60 per cent of the total production capacity, while twelve operators controlled the remaining 40 per cent.[5]

These trends had a direct effect upon developments at the falls. Even with the water released by departing industries, the cataract could not supply enough power to operate the busy flour mills continuously. The booming industry in the 1880s steadily encroached upon the available supply, and the water-power companies, overwhelmed by the millers' demands, well knew they had a tiger by the tail.

Minneapolis Mill and the St. Anthony firm entered the decade resolved to meet these new requirements. The framework in which they made the effort was different from that in which they had operated in the 1870s, for the managements of both organizations were strengthened. On the east side James J. Hill was in charge. Across the river Minneapolis Mill, abandoning its former practice, placed operations in the hands of a manager who was not a stockholder. The firms' determination to extract maximum profits and utility from the cataract was to lead them down numerous new avenues.

With the exit of Richard and Samuel Chute from its management, the St. Anthony company was reorganized by Hill. He became the majority stockholder and the firm's president by 1882. Joining him as a stockholder was Richard B. Angus, and serving as officers and members of the board were Edward Sawyer, George Stephen, Donald A. Smith, and Norman W. Kittson, all of whom were Hill associates in the St. Paul, Minneapolis, and Manitoba Railway Company.[6]

None of the new owners or officers participated directly in management, a situation quite different from that which had existed in the years of Richard Chute and Franklin Steele. Hill vested direct supervision of the water power in a succession of agents, the most outstanding of whom was John T. Fanning, a skilled engineer. Unlike earlier absentee owners, however, Hill kept a sharp eye on matters both large and small. For example, the directors in 1882 amended the bylaws to transfer authority for leasing and selling property from the agent to the president, and the agent communicated with Hill on problems as trivial as installation repairs, occupancy of company land by squatters, and arrangements for granting water.[7]

The decade also brought changes in the management of the Minneapolis Mill Company. C. C. Washburn, who had been a stockholder since 1856 and the company's president since 1865, died in 1882. He bequeathed his stock in the firm to the Washburn Memorial Orphan

Asylum, which was constructed in Minneapolis in 1886. Dorilus Morrison and W. D. Washburn were named to the asylum's board, and representatives of Cadwallader's estate served on the governing body of Minneapolis Mill. Morrison succeeded C. C. as the company's president, and W. D., who served as United States Congressman from 1880 to 1885 and again in 1889, was represented by his business associate, William D. Hale. Thus the triumvirate of owners who had so long presided over Minneapolis Mill's affairs was broken.[8]

Although the owners did not know it at the time, the Minneapolis Mill Company's leadership vacuum would be filled by a newcomer who was to leave his mark on the Falls of St. Anthony. He was William de la Barre, a gifted Austrian engineer trained in the Vienna Polytechnic College, who entered the company's service in 1883. After emigrating to the United States in 1867, he was employed for ten years by Morris, Tasker and Company of Philadelphia, where he gained experience in building steam, gas, and waterworks machinery. He was drawn to Minneapolis in 1878 by news of the explosion of the Washburn A mill, for he wished to demonstrate a machine designed to prevent the recurrence of such a calamity. C. C. Washburn, who was intrigued by the able and charming Viennese gentleman, detained him in the city to supervise the construction of his new flour mill, and in 1883 he was hired by Minneapolis Mill as engineer and agent after the death of Henry H. Douglass.[9]

In the year of De la Barre's appointment, W. D. Washburn commented to Hale that with assistance from more experienced members of the firm, "he will probably get along nicely." And he did. As engineer he plotted the installations that stretched the power, and as agent he negotiated satisfactory solutions of water-shortage problems with the lessees. In 1888 he was elected to fill the post of treasurer in addition to those of engineer and agent. De la Barre's dominant role in company affairs represented a sharp break with the past, but the challenging new age required the talents of imaginative management. The company had found the man who could do the job.[10]

The most immediate problem De la Barre faced was an acute water shortage, a situation which had been developing over the years and of which both Minneapolis Mill and the St. Anthony company had ample warning. When it had experienced curtailed supplies in the preceding decade, the St. Anthony company had felt for the first time the inequities resulting from the intensive development on the west side. Although the firm was using far less than half the river's flow, its officers saw the water needed to sustain the feeble east-side industries draining into the waterways of Minneapolis Mill. So short was the supply in 1878 that a St. Paul wag feared the mill owners might "be compelled to open the flood gates of Orth's brewery and run their machines with beer." [11]

Minneapolis Mill also drifted into the crisis. From 1858 to 1869 it had granted 56½ millpowers. During this period the company easily furnished water to its lessees without giving marked attention to the head on which it was used, the continuity of river flow, or the freedom with which manufacturers overdrew their allotted amounts. Water economy measures were first taken in the 1870s when the firm responded to the growth of milling by leasing 36 additional mill-powers.[12]

The efforts to discipline lessees were inadequate, however, and a severe water shortage developed in 1879. The Mississippi's flow was particularly low that year, and to meet what he regarded as an emergency the company's engineer ordered the millers to reduce their operating day from twenty-four to sixteen hours. At this the *St. Paul Globe* remarked that "for a year past the boasted water power at St. Anthony Falls has proved entirely insufficient to transact the business of the mills already erected there, and it is idle to talk of increasing the milling capacity of Minneapolis with water as the reliance for motive power." [13]

Although it was well aware that a water shortage existed, Minneapolis Mill granted another 41 millpowers in the 1880s. By then the organization was in serious trouble. Most of the leases, carrying a total of 133½ millpowers by 1889, were perpetual. Furthermore, the early ones, which produced the least revenue, carried the highest priorities and had first claim on the water supply. In times of low flow, when the company was unable to supply enough water, it not only lost the large income from the low-priority lessees, but was forced to pay them rebates. With its income at times reduced, the aggressive company was indeed caught in a web of its own weaving.[14]

When De la Barre began his career with the organization in 1883, he immediately sought to remedy the situation. Since there was a wide gap between the millers' requirements and the company's ability to provide water on a year-round basis, he encouraged the millers to install steam engines to provide auxiliary power.[15] At the same time, he turned his attention to increasing the head, improving the distribution facilities, and tightening up water management.

Two factors induced the millers to accept steam as a stand-by power source. The first and most immediate was a prolonged drought in the mid-1880s that caused a more severe water shortage than the millers had ever before experienced. The second was an improvement in steam engines which made them better adapted to produce the steady motion required in flour milling. Between 1884 and 1889 the Washburn A, B, and C, Pillsbury A and B, Galaxy, Pettit, Columbia, Crown Roller, Standard, Anchor, Humboldt, Palisade, Phoenix, and Northwestern mills were equipped with auxiliary engines. By the end of the decade only seven flour mills were still completely dependent upon the fickle cataract.[16]

Impressed with the efficiency of steam and disgusted with interruptions in their operations, several millers spoke out against water power. After adding steam engines to his mill, one prominent operator declared that "water power can 'go to thunder.'" Others pointed out that the difference in power costs then prevailing in Minneapolis (three cents more per barrel of flour for steam) and the initial expense of installing steam plants were more than offset by production losses when there was no water. "I heard a Minneapolis miller say," a *Northwestern Miller* reporter wrote in 1881, "that if he had been able to run his mill to its full capacity, when troubled with low water last winter, he could have saved enough to have bought a complete outfit to run his mill by steam."[17]

If De la Barre had not moved quickly to improve the water situation, the millers at this point might have completed the conversion to steam. By acting decisively the engineer changed the entire concept of water use at the falls. In the pioneer years the men managing the company had rarely thought in terms of economical use or of extracting the maximum amount of power from the available water. In that era they strove only to attract more industries to the falls, and their success created the problem to which De la Barre now turned his attention.

As his first step, the engineer in 1884 asked the millers for their support and co-operation. Loath to forgo cheap water power in spite of its disadvantages, they responded to the overture by appointing a committee to treat with him. In 1885 the two parties agreed to increase the head and fall available: De la Barre undertook to deepen the canal and lower the tailraces under his jurisdiction, while the millers promised to lower their wheel pits, tailraces, and headraces.[18]

Before the year ended, De la Barre had deepened the canal from 14 to 20 feet and lengthened it from 600 to 950 feet. The expansion increased its flowage capacity from 30 to 40 per cent and raised the water level to produce more power by bringing water to the lessees' wheels at a greater head. The engineer satisfied the second part of his bargain by building between 1887 and 1892 a capacious tailrace along the western shore to carry away the water which the mills discharged through fifteen lateral races. By increasing the fall the new installation reportedly gave the millers an opportunity to secure 30 per cent more power from the same volume of water.[19]

Most of the mill owners kept their part of the bargain by adapting their installations to utilize the new head and fall. The millers, however, were individualists, and De la Barre learned to his sorrow that treating with their committee did not automatically solve his problems. When a few refused to make the changes agreed upon, the engineer had to force compliance by charging them for the difference between the amount of water they would have used had they made the improvements and the amount they were actually drawing.[20]

An even more serious problem for De la Barre was the millers' general disregard of the water-power company's regulations. Accustomed to casual administration, the millers usually took the amount of water they needed whenever it was available, ignoring both their obligations to Minneapolis Mill and the relative rights of others. To these practices De la Barre called a halt. He systematically measured the amount of water drawn, enforced clauses in certain leases limiting its use to sixteen hours a day, and sent offenders bills for the excess they drew.[21]

Even with the exercise of tact, which he had in abundance, De la Barre found it difficult to keep peace and at the same time enforce regulations after years of neglect. The lessees complained about the accuracy of his measurements, the punitive charges for excess water, the company's slow expansion of the power, and of favoritism in its distribution. They implemented their complaints by refusing to pay rents and by appointing protest committees to confer with the engineer.[22]

In such situations De la Barre carefully explained the reasons for his actions. When gentle persuasion failed, however, he either shut off the lessees' water supply or instituted suits against them. A letter written to a flour-milling firm which had been drawing almost double the amount of water it was paying for demonstrates the diffuse diplomacy abounding in his communications. "Contrary to my duty and orders," he wrote, "I have allowed you to run the mill, depending somewhat upon the assurances of a member of your firm that an adjustment of our claims would be made . . . and as I did not wish to be arbitrary, or ugly towards your firm, I have allowed matters to drift along until it has reached a point where I must call a peremptory halt, as I find to my regret and sorrow that I have been too lenient altogether, and that the mill must be shut down and a suit commenced to stop the mill from any further appropriation of water power, without pay to this company." [23]

In his efforts to secure the maximum amount of power from the water available, De la Barre tried to create a community of interest at the falls. He urged the owners of Minneapolis Mill to push improvements rapidly, for, as he wrote in 1885, the "millers are getting ugly." Toward the millers he showed great consideration, warning them of impending low water conditions, giving them technical advice on power requirements, and urging them to keep peace with one another. [24]

In their turn, the millers at times co-operated, sharing the water during periods of low flow. Their favorite device was the water pool, which was first used at the falls in the late 1870s and was employed extensively during the next decade. Whenever the company served notice that there was not enough water for all and that it would invoke priorities, the millers banded together to limit their usage with least injury to themselves. Since one mill was frequently run by several millpowers bearing different priorities, the pool managers manipulated the system to enable each operator to use all of them together. Thus each mill could command its full water power but for limited periods of time. [25]

The pool members made various types of schedules for sharing water. Since continuous operation was desirable in flour milling, they tried to prevent frequent stopping, starting, and shifting back and forth between water and steam. At times they allocated water to a mill every other week, or for three or four consecutive days. As steam capacity increased, they often relinquished water to mills which had no engines or which had steam plants inadequate for full production. The recipients then compensated those who relinquished the water. [26]

The pools had one unfortunate feature. Instead of dissolving them by common consent, individual millers often resumed taking water without notice. The withdrawal of one miller from a pool then opened what the *Northwestern Miller* called a "go-as-you-please" race for the water. The resulting chaos disrupted the whole distribution system, for the sudden drain lowered the level in the canal and decreased the head at all the mills. Then every manufacturer suffered from lack of power until the company intervened to restore order. [27]

On the east side the St. Anthony company had a somewhat similar problem with the lumbermen. During the 1870s it had paid little attention to the amount of water the sawmills used, for it could easily supply them. The situation began to change late in the decade when the water supply was low, and it became acute in the 1880s as the drought continued and the Pillsbury A leased large amounts. The new flour mill installed steam engines for auxiliary power, but the sawmills did not. And contrary to orders from the company, the lumbermen continued their old habits of taking the water they needed without regard for the amount specified in their grants.[28]

The water-power company in 1884 put an end to this practice by taking legal action against the five sawmilling firms. When the district court upheld the company, four of the firms appealed to the Minnesota Supreme Court, which in 1886 sustained the lower court's judgment. The decision obligated the lumbermen to pay for any water used in excess of their grants, but at times there was none available for them to buy. The operators then made arrangements with Pillsbury A's owners to release water by running its steam plant; for this concession they paid the mill's owners seventy-five dollars a day. This situation continued until 1887, when the sawmill row was destroyed by fire.[29]

The *Mississippi Valley Lumberman,* which was outspoken in its defense of the sawmill men, charged in 1885 that the St. Anthony firm had created the water shortage by its negligence. "The East side mill ponds are now simply sand bars," it maintained, "and the deepening of the canal on the west side will expedite the converting of the whole east side channel into good town lots unless the Water Power Company would open their hearts to the extent of clearing out the old channel."[30]

The St. Anthony company was aware that its failure to build and maintain adequate facilities for water distribution had caused inequities in the division of the river's flow, and during the 1880s it tried to correct the situation. In 1887 it cleared and deepened the east-side channel—as the *Lumberman* had suggested—and from 1886 to 1889 it renovated the dam which extended into the western channel.[31]

When plans for these improvements were announced in 1886, the *Northwestern Miller* of July 9 remarked that the west-side firm "will resist any such move, and if undertaken, the matter will undoubtedly become deeply involved in litigation." So keen was the competition for the available water that upon completion of the project, the west-side millers—seemingly ignorant of the inequities existing between the two water-power organizations and eager to protect their own interests—protested sharply. Backed by the millers, Minneapolis Mill in 1886–87 was ready to contest the St. Anthony company's right to increase the amount of water it was drawing. At about the same time it was rumored that Hill was preparing to bring suit against the west-side firm in order to secure his company's rightful share of the flow. Nothing came of these threats, however, and levels in the millponds continued to rise and fall as one firm or the other drew water.[32]

The St. Anthony company took further steps to extend its water-distribution facilities and husband the precious supply. The main feature of its plan for new installations was the revival of the canal project begun in the 1860s and defeated in the next decade by the conflict between the east- and west-side representatives on the city council. In 1881 the council authorized the canal's construction, provided the work was completed within two years. The company then faltered in its purpose. Pressed by a commitment to have an ample water supply ready for the Pillsbury A mill early in 1881, it substituted for the water course that was to run along the east bank to a point below the falls a short canal leading from the river to the mill.[33]

If the longer canal had been built, the water-shortage crisis would have been more serious than it was. The east-side industrial district was little changed in extent and density from the 1850s, for water-power use was still limited to the row, to Hennepin and Nicollet islands, and to a few sites on Main Street within a block of the dam. Nevertheless the addition of the Pillsbury A mill in 1880–81 cut so deeply into the available water supply that the burning of the row sawmills in 1887 was viewed by some as a blessing.[34] The longer canal, accompanied by a campaign to attract more mills, would have extended the east-side area, and the showdown between the water-power companies which was threatened in 1887 might have become a reality.

The St. Anthony company knew that part of its problem in controlling the east-side water supply stemmed from the fact that many years earlier valuable rights had been alienated, and in this decade the organization began to repossess some of them. Hill started the program in 1880 by purchasing from William W. Eastman three unused millsites on the dam at a cost of $42,500. Two years later the firm acquired Farnham and Lovejoy's interest in Hennepin, Cataract, and Spirit islands for $150,000, a purchase that threw the water-power company into direct conflict with the city.[35]

The conflict developed because the paper mill of Averill, Russell, and Carpenter, adjoining the Farnham and Lovejoy property on Hennepin Island, burned in 1882, and a year later the paper firm sold its property to the city for conversion into a pumping station. This was not the city's first foray into the acquisition of pumping stations. As early as 1867 it had leased three millpowers of water on the west side, fitted up a pump house, and laid miles of water mains under the streets. Now it needed additional facilities, and in 1885 it began drawing water from the river at the rate of 3,500,000 gallons a day. The new station and the old pump house on the west side provided the entire public water supply for a city of 129,200 persons.[36]

Concerned about the water loss, the St. Anthony company in 1886 contended that the city had no water rights under its deed from Averill, Russell, and Carpenter because the property was inland and not riparian. The city maintained that it did have such privileges, since in 1865 Farnham and Lovejoy had conveyed to a predecessor firm of Averill, Russell, and Carpenter water sufficient to run the paper mill, and the city had inherited this right.[37]

The contest focused attention for the first time on the respective rights of private business and the public to the water at the falls. The company's agent maintained that the municipality, representing the public, had no superior rights, and the city engineer countered by questioning the authority of a private corporation over the river "that God Almighty made." The controversy did not long remain in the realm of theory. The mayor, a direct actionist, reportedly stated that he would settle the matter by ordering the police to remove a gate the company had installed to keep the flow from the waterworks. Other city officials suggested dynamite as the proper solution.[38]

In this atmosphere the company brought suit against the city in Hennepin County District Court. Before it was concluded, the litigation thoroughly examined the riparian rights attached to the Hennepin Island property as well as the tortured lines of ownership evolving from the division of the island made by Ira Kingsley and Franklin Steele in 1854. After hearing the evidence, the court ruled that the city's claim to water was valid, and that the water-power company had inherited from Farnham and Lovejoy the obligation to honor the commitment. The St. Anthony firm then carried the case to the Minnesota Supreme Court, which in 1889 upheld the lower court's judgment.[39]

Although each water-power firm had special problems during this troubled decade, they also had areas of common interest. One of these was preserving the Falls of St. Anthony. The burden was placed squarely upon them in the 1880s, for both the city and the United States government withdrew their support. De la Barre took the lead, seeking conferences with the St. Anthony company on ways and means. Under his leadership the two firms maintained the installations that had been built to hold the cataract in place, and together they tried to keep the channel free.[40]

Their new role as protectors of the falls brought the water-power organizations into conflict with the boom companies, for in these years millions of logs were passing over the cataract on their journey from the northern pineries to sawmills farther down the Mississippi. Although the United States government had built a sluice to carry them through the installations which preserved the cataract, the logs frequently broke free and tumbled pell-mell over the apron. The water-power firms worked with the boom companies in an effort to control the situation, but the problem was not fully solved until the second decade of the twentieth century when the great drives ceased.[41]

Another threat to the falls came in 1885 when the city announced a plan for replacing the ten-year-old Suspension Bridge, which occupied a site immediately above the cataract. The pillars of a proposed new stone arch bridge would penetrate the fragile limestone sheath, and De la Barre feared that the falls would be damaged. To forestall this "public calamity," as he called it, he rallied the companies and the lessees to oppose the project. They protested to various city officers, and they also asked the federal government to intervene on the grounds that the installations preserving the cataract would be injured. After these measures failed, they secured an injunction restraining the city from building the bridge. The city then modified the proposed design, and the companies withdrew their objections.[42]

The two firms had another common problem, the solution of which would have important effects upon their development. Throughout their first quarter century, they had given little thought to the cataract's ultimate potential. Charles Bigelow, the engineer engaged by Minneapolis Mill when it began operations in 1857, had stated categorically that the falls "would rival in extent the largest improved Water Power in the World." This concept of great potential lingered during the years the companies were building their installations. Minnesota's commissioner of statistics in 1862 stated that the cataract's potential was 120,000 horsepower; in 1870 James B. Francis, an experienced hydraulic engineer, set the figure at 100,000. The press published these figures many times, and the idea that the cataract's potential was virtually unlimited was apparently accepted both by the companies and the public.[43]

During their first thirty years, the water-power firms developed very little of this alleged capacity. In the mid-1880s it was reported that 10,000 horsepower were in use on the west side and 3,000 on the east. Yet with even so small a portion of the supposed potential tapped, the companies, as we have seen, had difficulty in securing enough water to supply the mills. By this time it was apparent that something had gone wrong with the engineers' predictions.[44]

An obvious explanation for the difference between the estimated potential and the number of horsepower actually developed lay in the way the companies had managed the water power. The estimators had based their figures on the use of water at a full head of fifty feet in efficient water wheels, as well as on the re-use of the flow at another plant below the falls near Meeker Island. But the companies had allowed the lessees to use the water on heads averaging only thirty-six feet and, despite improvements in design, on water wheels that were often outmoded and inefficient. Furthermore the firms made no attempt to employ the flow below the falls, and when other organizations had tried to do so during the Meeker Dam controversy, they had blocked the project. Although the companies had begun to rectify some of the errors in water management, any marked improvement would have required a much more thorough overhauling of both the distribution facilities and the installations for developing the power.[45]

An unrecognized but more important reason for the miscalculation was lack of knowledge about the Mississippi's flow. Until the acute water shortage forced a consideration of the problem, everyone concerned seemed to assume that the flow was fairly constant. The prognosticators who placed the potential at 100,000 to 120,000 horsepower predicated their figures on high water conditions, and the companies during their first twenty years of operation had learned only the most obvious fluctuations of the erratic Mississippi. They knew the winter river with its blanket of ice which diminished the flow and cut off the northern pineries from the sawmills. And they knew its wild springtime floods which hurled walls of water and ice at the dams. But until the mid-1870s the companies did not chart the day-by-day variations in flow, and even then they did not use the information to mold policy.[46]

Abandoning the casual attitude of previous managers, De la Barre began in the 1880s to study the Mississippi intensively. In the long years of personal observation, record keeping, and research that followed, he learned its characteristics so well that he became known as the "Sage of the River." As he pored over flow records kept by Minneapolis Mill and reports on the river made by the United States engineers, he came to realize that "water and weather are 'powerful onsartin.'" The amount of flow at the falls depended upon rainfall and other conditions in a drainage area of 19,585 square miles, with an average annual precipitation of twenty-five inches. The amount of water that reached the Mississippi fluctuated, and the rate of evaporation, the thaws and freezes, and the formation of ice and snow barriers all influenced the quantity arriving at the falls.[47]

Ignoring the extreme conditions existing in times of flood and drought, De la Barre figured the probable flow in specific terms. He determined that the average monthly cubic-foot-per-second flow was as follows:

JANUARY	2,000	JULY	7,311
FEBRUARY	2,000	AUGUST	4,422
MARCH	3,000	SEPTEMBER	4,936
APRIL	13,636	OCTOBER	6,245
MAY	14,534	NOVEMBER	4,681
JUNE	11,855	DECEMBER	2,500

By depending upon steam auxiliaries to fill the gaps when needed, he estimated that the water-power companies could safely lease 6,000 cubic feet per month on a year-round basis.[48]

Although 6,000 cubic feet of water used at full head should have yielded over 20,000 horsepower, two factors prevented the companies from obtaining this amount in the 1880s. The first was the failure of the firms and their lessees to utilize fully the entire fifty-foot drop available at the falls. In 1889—even after the improvements initiated by De la Barre were completed—only an average of thirty-six feet was employed. Years were to pass before the entire amount was used, and until that time the power potential was substantially limited. The second factor was the erratic character of the river, which often failed to conform to predictions based on past performance. The highest known peak in the 1880s was 73,000 cubic feet, and the all-time low was 500. Action to improve this situation was forthcoming in the 1880s when men set themselves to the task of evening the flow that varied from day to day, month to month, and year to year.[49]

Those who studied the upper Mississippi and its drainage area noted that two natural regulators tempered the direct action of climatic conditions upon its water flow. The first was the wide expanse of swampy land around the headwaters, where roots and matted growth released moisture gradually. The swamps' beneficial effect in moderating drainage was negated somewhat by the high evaporation rate (about eighteen inches annually), because the water was spread thinly over a great area. Moreover, in the winter, when the river most needed contributions from the drainage basin, the frozen swamps cut off the flow.[50]

The second regulator—and the one which was to bring the federal government back into partnership with the companies in protecting the water supply at the falls—consisted of the lakes near the headwaters. Located on or near the Mississippi between its source in Lake Itasca and the Crow Wing River 388 miles below, these lakes formed a series of natural reservoirs tempering flow. In seasons of high precipitation, their basins filled. When diminished precipitation and drainage lowered the river level, the lakes contributed additional water. The natural reservoirs operated even in winter, for water continued to escape into the river beneath their frozen surfaces.[51]

Long before the companies faced a critical water shortage, the idea of converting lakes into reservoirs had occurred to men concerned with navigation, flood control, and water power. From the late 1850s on, Charles Ellet, a noted Pennsylvania civil engineer, and others promoted plans for controlling the lower Mississippi by building reservoirs on the Ohio River and at other strategic locations. Thomas M. Griffith, the engineer who had designed and supervised the construction of the first Minneapolis Suspension Bridge, applied the concept directly to the upper Mississippi in 1861. By 1870 enthusiasm for converting the headwaters lakes into reservoirs had become so intense that some of the benefits predicted for them were termed "extravagant and impossible."[52]

United States army engineers were also interested in the reservoirs as a means of preventing floods and improving navigation during low water periods, and in 1866 they began to examine the lakes and the drainage area. Their surveys, carried out over the next fourteen years, yielded new information on climate, topography, vegetation, and geology. They analyzed the use made of the river for log driving, navigation, and water power, assessing the probable effects the reservoirs would have on each of these interests. In survey after survey, their conclusions were the same: headwaters reservoirs could and should be built.[53]

The engineers recommended that sites be selected on the stretch of river between present-day Bemidji and Brainerd. The specific locations suggested were Winnibigoshish, Mud, Leech, Pokegama, and Gull lakes, and the Vermillion and Pine rivers. Since the area above Gull Lake, the lowest site, encompassed almost one-fourth of the entire drainage district north of the falls, the engineers predicted that the reservoirs would greatly increase control over the river and improve navigation as far south as Lake Pepin.[54]

The water-power companies took a keen interest in the reservoir movement from the beginning. When the first survey got under way in 1866, General Warren, the United States engineer stationed at St. Paul, commented that the "mill people already have their attention directed to the large lakes about the sources of the Mississippi as a means of increasing their power." In co-operation with the government, the companies in 1869 sent Franklin Cook upriver to investigate the possibility of using reservoirs to control the floods threatening the falls. William D. Washburn in the same year acquired land near Pokegama to make sure that flowage rights would be available when the government was ready to act.[55]

Washburn furthered the project in other ways. Throughout his career in Congress his sponsorship was so ardent that he became known as the "father of the reservoir system." He spoke out for federal appropriations, and in the public press he refuted the arguments of those who attacked the project. So intimately was he identified with the reservoirs that one newspaper reporter erroneously credited him with originating the idea for their establishment. Washburn himself was not modest about his contribution. Exaggerating his role somewhat, he wrote in 1905: "*I* am almost entirely responsible for the conception and building [of] this system of Reservoirs, as all the early appropriations were secured by me when in the House of Reps. in the early 80s."[56]

As the engineers and water-power companies thumped for the reservoirs, the movement gained strong support from other interests—from the city of Minneapolis, desiring as it had in earlier decades free access to the river both above and below the falls; from cities and states in the Mississippi Valley who saw in headwaters control a means of minimizing flood damage; and from antirailroad men, who firmly believed that a flourishing steamboat traffic would serve to regulate freight rates.

Minneapolitans predicted that the reservoirs would revive and extend navigation above the falls, where a limited steamboat traffic had been carried on since the 1850s. With settlement in northern

Minnesota growing and the city's appetite for commerce increasing, Minneapolis saw itself as the foot of navigation on the upper Mississippi, the marketing and transshipping point for a new commercial empire. The *Tribune* of December 5, 1879, commented: "Minneapolis will one day see not only the steamers of the lower Mississippi landing regularly at the foot of our Falls, but also an independent fleet of river craft plying *above* the Falls and penetrating northward almost to the very sources of the Mississippi."

When they discussed the reservoirs, men living along the river, north and south, felt a kinship as inhabitants of the Mississippi Valley. They hoped the system would encompass the St. Croix, Chippewa, Wisconsin, and other tributaries as well as the headwaters. A Louisiana engineer speculated in 1880 that thus controlled the "mighty river" would be "bound hand and foot, and its arms pinioned by tiny ties at each of the sources of its life, and the great giant rendered harmless to the people below. I have seen in my mind's eye dams and locks at all its sources, and connected by telegraph with stations below, so that when we might want additional water for navigable purposes, we should only touch the telegraph knob, and such gates . . . would rise and give us the required water."[57]

Although communities downriver often gave local Mississippi River improvements a higher priority than the headwaters project, they nevertheless offered it strong support. A river improvement convention, meeting in 1879 at Quincy, Illinois, for example, adopted a resolution endorsing the reservoirs, and the Hannibal, Missouri, Common Council in 1880 sent Congress a memorial backing them.[58]

Up and down the river there was considerable sectional interest in the reservoirs as a means of breaking the railroad monopoly. An editorial in the *Mississippi Valley Lumberman* of 1877 stated: "With these huge reservoirs, which nature has provided . . . and the Southern bars let down, this great national highway, extending from the Northern to the Southern border, becomes at once available for all the commerce of the West, as the great safety valve and natural protector of the interests of the West against the rapacity and extortion of railroad combinations, as well as conspiracies of eastern combinations to rob the producers of the West." The *Tribune* declared that the reservoirs would revive the Mississippi "as a great commercial highway, through which the extortions of railroad pools may be perpetually held in check, and the great agricultural interests of the central west given adequate protection." In urging the headwaters project upon Congress, the Hannibal council also maintained that

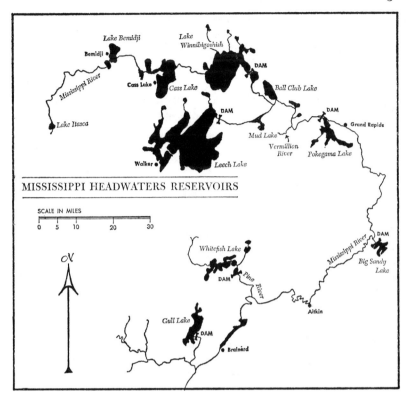

MISSISSIPPI HEADWATERS RESERVOIRS

improved water transportation would deter the railroads' "unreasonable exactions," which were strangling the Mississippi Valley.[59]

Since the proposed reservoirs affected so many different interests on the upper Mississippi, it is not surprising that some opposition arose. Objections came from lumbermen who had long enjoyed almost a monopoly of the river above the falls for log driving. They feared that the reservoirs, by impounding spring flood waters, would deprive them of water when they most needed it to move the winter's cut down the Mississippi from the northern pineries.[60]

For a time, too, some citizens of St. Paul joined the opposition. They feared that the reservoir system, like falls' preservation, was only another attempt to secure government aid for the water-power companies under the guise of navigation improvement. In the Minnesota legislature, Representative James Smith, Jr., of St. Paul attempted to defeat a memorial urging Congress to make appropriations for the system, and in 1881 the St. Paul Board of Trade passed resolutions condemning the project. These actions aroused the editorial wrath of the *Tribune*. It called the St. Paul board "a collection of picayunish peddlers whose jealousy of Minneapolis is so blind that they are willing to deprive St. Paul of the benefit which that place must reap from the system, in order that Minneapolis may not secure its advantages. In an equally contemptible spirit some members of the legislature oppose the resolutions asking congress to make the appropriation. It is to be hoped there are large men enough in the assemblage at St. Paul to suppress this miserably narrow and petty hostility." [61]

In spite of such protests, Congress in 1880 began to make appropriations and plans for building the reservoir system, and four of six proposed regulating dams were completed during the decade on Winnibigoshish, Leech, and Pokegama lakes, and on the Pine River. The design for converting the lakes into reservoirs was simple. Dams with sills and gates were built at the lake outlets to control the water levels. The opening and closing of the gates was managed by the United States Army Corps of Engineers headquartered in St. Paul. Since the system was intended chiefly as an aid to navigation, the engineers impounded water in winter and early spring and released it to raise the water level in late summer and fall.[62]

When the reservoirs began to operate, conflicts arose between the government engineers and the loggers above the falls. The *Mississippi Valley Lumberman* reported in 1884 that the engineers shut down the dams "at the very critical moment when all the great log drives had been forced out of the small streams into the main river." The engineers complained that the lumbermen closed their own dams after the drives had passed even though the additional water was needed for navigation, and they made what the loggers regarded as an ominous suggestion — that the government should assume jurisdiction over all dams affecting river flow.[63]

The water-power companies, on the other hand, were outspoken in their praise of the system. They recognized that the engineers were obligated to time the release of water to aid navigation rather than to meet water-power requirements. Although the reservoir gates were closed during the winter when the firms were most troubled by low flow, they welcomed the additional water released in late summer and fall. It was estimated that the reservoirs contributed as much as 40 per cent of the total water volume at the falls in August and 50 per cent in October and November.[64]

De la Barre and the government engineers in St. Paul established a harmonious relationship that rarely faltered in succeeding years. He advised them on procedures for disseminating information on reservoir management helpful to water-power interests, and they reciprocated by manipulating water releases to conform to his companies' needs whenever possible. In addition the engineers at St. Anthony and those in St. Paul exchanged technical data on conditions in the drainage area which affected river flow.[65]

Although the water management measures instituted in the 1880s somewhat increased the power the falls produced, Minneapolis Mill and, to a lesser extent, the St. Anthony company realized at last that the cataract's potential was not unlimited. The reservoirs helped even out the flow; the head and fall had been increased from a mere eight feet when Franklin Steele built his first sawmill to an average of thirty-six feet in 1889; and the companies stringently disciplined the manufacturers in water use. Responsible spokesmen during the decade reduced the estimate of the falls' total potential—above and below the cataract—from 120,000 horsepower to 35,000. Although the Falls of St. Anthony might not drive the "mills of a continent," they still exceeded the estimated potentials of the New England sites at Holyoke, Lowell, and Lawrence, Massachusetts, Manchester, New Hampshire, and Lewiston, Maine.[66]

Nevertheless, with the growth of steam-powered manufactories and commerce, the cataract in the 1880s declined in importance as an economic influence molding the development of Minneapolis. This change in status was symbolized during the decade by the disappearance of the sketch of the falls from the masthead of the city's leading newspaper, the *Tribune,* and by that journal's decreasing emphasis upon news of the water power. By 1890 Minneapolis had ceased to be a city dependent upon water power for its existence and growth.

The companies at the falls found their problems magnified in the next decade. They learned that, whether they willed or not, their fortunes were intertwined and their major problems could be solved only if they acted together. They found that further progress depended upon new techniques which would adapt their operations to the river's uneven flow, and they contemplated the substantially increased output to be obtained from the wasted water below the falls. Had their managers been omniscient, they might have read a partial answer to their problems in hydroelectricity, an industry that came to the cataract in 1882 and that in time would transform the face of the falls.

9.

Portent of Things to Come

THE FIRST HYDROELECTRIC CENTRAL STATION to begin operations in the United States was built at the Falls of St. Anthony in 1882. Constructed by the Minnesota Brush Electric Company, the tiny station was a landmark in water-power history. From the days of primitive man when the force of falling water was used to grind grain on the Nile, the Euphrates, and other rivers, water wheels had been employed in mills located close by power sources.[1] Although techniques and machinery had been vastly improved during succeeding centuries, the basic application of direct water power remained unchanged. The employment of water power for the creation of a nondirect form of energy — hydroelectricity — ushered in a revolution, for electric power could be transmitted to industrial plants far from waterfalls where it could be utilized to light homes and factories and to propel railways. These expanding uses were to give water power a new importance in the nation.

In the years following 1882 the Falls of St. Anthony felt the full impact of these technological changes. The transformation to hydroelectricity was inaugurated when the Minnesota Brush Electric Company leased water from Minneapolis Mill to operate the pioneer station; it was accelerated in the next two decades as the water-power organizations themselves built hydroelectric plants; and it culminated in the absorption of the firms by a public utilities corporation. The transformation retained for the cataract an important but different place in the business life of Minneapolis. By solving many of the problems which plagued the firms in the 1880s, hydroelectricity also opened the way for maximum development of the falls' potential.

Although the phenomenon of electricity had been known and experimented with by Alessandro Volta, Michael Faraday, and many others, the break-through in technology that made its use commercially feasible did not occur until the 1870s. Among the innovations was the development of arc lighting, in which Charles F. Brush of Cleveland played a prominent role. The source of current for arc lighting was a dynamo or generator. Illumination was produced by arcing current across a small gap between the ends of two pieces of carbon housed in a lamp. Many improvements were made in the generators, lamps, and carbons by Brush and others. The Brush system was best adapted for illuminating large areas like streets and halls because of the high candle power of the arc lamps. In 1879 Thomas A. Edison was granted a patent on an incandescent lamp designed primarily for interior lighting. It produced illumination by transmitting current through a carbon filament housed in a vacuum.[2]

Business organizations quickly took the inventions of Brush, Edison, and others out of the laboratory. Arc lamps were installed in the Wanamaker store in Philadelphia in 1878 and on the streets of San Francisco in 1879; electricity was employed to power Edison's manufacturing plant as well as an experimental railway in Menlo Park, New Jersey, in the early 1880s; and a steam-powered central station to provide incandescent lighting was opened by Edison in New York City in 1882.[3]

In 1879 an electrical illumination system powered by a steam engine was installed at the Lake Elmo amusement park a few miles east of St. Paul. Other isolated lighting plants (as distinguished from central stations which served many structures) were soon placed in a few Minneapolis homes, factories, and mills. The one attracting the most marked attention was a Brush plant installed in the Pillsbury A mill at the falls in 1881. "The sixteen lights . . . ," reported the *Mississippi Valley Lumberman,* "present a beautiful appearance and make the mill lighter than it is at noonday." The writer claimed that the A was the first mill in the world to use the light, "but it is undoubtedly only a question of time when it will be used in all the mills." By 1882 the *Tribune* was predicting that electricity would soon replace gas and steam for lighting and powering manufactures.[4]

Even though the lights of Pillsbury A glowed through windows overlooking the falls, Minneapolitans apparently gave little thought to the cataract as a major source for electric light and power. In 1871 the magazine *Scientific American* published a St. Anthony citizen's suggestion for generating electricity at the falls and transmitting it to "manufacturers at a distance."[5] A correspondent in the *Tribune,* identifying himself as "Dynamo," hinted on January 28, 1882, that he would soon discuss "the idea of supplying power over the State from an abundant water power at our door." But such comments were rare. Local attitudes toward the cataract were oriented toward the past, and even the water-power managers at this point failed to make the correlation between electricity and water power that in retrospect seems obvious.

The pioneer central station came to the falls as a casual business venture established by Minneapolitans who incorporated the Minnesota Electric Light and Electric Motive Power Company in 1881. Among the stockholders were men who had been active in fostering other enterprises at the falls — William Washburn, Joel Bassett, Sumner Farnham, James Lovejoy, Otis A. Pray, Loren Fletcher, and C. M. Loring. These lumbermen, millers, and foundry owners were joined by other Minneapolis business and professional men, representing wholesaling, banking, real estate, law, and journalism.[6]

On July 15, 1882, the new firm changed its long and awkward name to the Minnesota Brush Electric Company. The move was a logical one, since four months earlier the Minneapolis organization had entered into an agreement with the Brush Electric Company of Cleveland which established a close relationship between the two concerns. The Cleveland firm, organized in 1876 by Charles Brush, manufactured electrical equipment which it marketed through organizations like the Minneapolis company. The local groups raised the capital. Then in exchange for exclusive rights to use, sell, or rent Brush equipment, they usually assigned to Cleveland Brush about one-third of their capital stock. Although the arrangement with the Minneapolis firm was typical in most other respects, the amount of capital stock transferred was 48 per cent.[7]

As soon as the agreement with the Cleveland firm was concluded, Minnesota Brush began preparations for establishing its central station. It leased from Dorilus Morrison the Upton Island site and the water formerly used by the cotton mill, and it secured an additional water grant from Minneapolis Mill. The new company then constructed a small frame building and installed five Brush arc-light machines, which were connected to a water wheel by means of a line shaft. The machines, which had belts running to the shaft, could be connected or disconnected by means of clutches. Overhead wires were strung to saloons and shops on Washington Avenue, a few blocks from the falls. Four circuits were arranged to carry the current from arc-light machines to lamps in the customers' buildings. All the circuits were set to go on at dusk. The first was scheduled to turn off the lamps at 9:15 P.M., the second at 11:15, the third at 12:10, and the fourth to burn all night. Charges for the first type of service were set at 33 ⅓ cents per lamp per night, for the second 45 cents, for the third 60 cents, and for the fourth $1.00. [8]

The company turned on the lights for the first time during the evening of September 5, 1882, and thereby earned its place in history. The Minneapolis station became the first in the nation by only twenty-five days, for a completed hydroelectric station at Appleton, Wisconsin, was awaiting permission from Thomas Edison to begin operations. The Appleton plant became the country's second when it started generating electricity on September 30. [9]

Contemporary Minneapolitans were unaware of the distinction the local station won by so narrow a margin. On September 6 the *Tribune* announced merely that the "electric lights were used in the business houses for the first time last evening." It sandwiched the meager notice between advertisements for Lydia E. Pinkham's Vegetable Compound and Brown's Iron Bitters. Less cavalier in its news placement but no less cryptic, the *St. Paul and Minneapolis Pioneer Press* reported on the same day: "One circuit of the Brush light was tested yesterday and worked perfectly."

The few shops and saloons on Washington Avenue did not constitute a substantial enough market to make operations profitable, and Minnesota Brush expended a great deal of effort to secure more customers. Although it was the only electric company operating a central station in the city, it had an energetic competitor in the Minneapolis Gas Light Company. In the late 1870s this firm had begun a concentrated campaign to increase gas consumption by reducing its prices. It had a street-lighting contract with the city of Minneapolis, and hundreds of homes, offices, shops, and industrial plants had installed gas lamps. Minneapolis Gas was not about to yield any portion of its market without a struggle. In fact, news of the electric company's organization in 1881 prompted the aggressive gas firm to announce that it, too, could furnish electricity (produced by gas motors) whenever the demand was great enough to justify the move. [10]

An even more formidable obstacle in the path of Minnesota Brush was the public's attitude toward electricity. Although Minneapolitans seemed enthusiastic about the idea of electricity as the wonder of the age, they feared that wires strung through the streets would endanger life and property, and they also had doubts about the reliability of the lamps. The *Tribune* of March 1, 1882, reported a

fire in Philadelphia caused by overhead wires and commented on
September 12 that if the wires in Minneapolis caused a "misfortune
to person or property no general surprise will be occasioned." Unfortunately for the company, its early ventures confirmed some of the
public's suspicions. The arc lights were unreliable, largely because
the firm was short of power. As soon as the lights went on in 1882,
it became all too evident that the water power was not adequate to
provide steady service. Although a company official hastened to assure
them that the lamps "will burn better when we get our arrangements
complete," Minneapolitans' suspicions were heightened by the flick-
ering, faltering lights. Determined to secure more power, Minnesota
Brush negotiated with Minneapolis Mill in 1883 and 1884 for additional water, but the discussions came to nought, and the electric
company looked elsewhere for a solution. Thomas S. King, a Minneapolis journalist who was secretary of the new firm, attempted to
allay the public's fears by stating forcefully that the transmission of
electricity through insulated wires was perfectly safe, but there is no
doubt that the poor service, compounded by the people's fears,
helped delay the general acceptance of electricity in the city.[11]

The specter of danger and the opposition of Minneapolis Gas converged in an issue which had confronted the company even before
it began generating electricity. In order to place poles and wires on
Minneapolis streets, the firm was obliged to secure an enabling ordinance from the city. The legal pathway at first seemed smooth, for
on February 1, 1882, the council adopted the ordinance which the
company requested and transmitted it to the mayor for his signature.
There it hit a snag, for Alonzo C. Rand, who was mayor of Minneapolis in 1882, was also president of the gas company. He vetoed the
ordinance on the grounds that he had "absolute knowledge of the
great danger both to life and property in training wires on poles to
conduct such powerful electric currents as are required for the purposes of lighting or power."[12]

Conscious of the delicate position he occupied as mayor and president of the gas company, Rand cited similar vetoes by the mayors of
Chicago and Detroit. He quoted Detroit's Mayor W. G. Thompson
as saying that a "magazine of nitro-glycerine in the centre of the
city would . . . be a less prolific source of danger than the aerial
system of transmitting powerful currents of electricity in use by the
Brush company," and that "in undertaking to utilize electricity as a
means of lighting, they are as yet dealing with a factor of unknown
quality; the question is still largely experimental in its nature, and I

should prefer the experiment to be carried on elsewhere than with the lives and property of the citizens of Detroit."[13]

Thomas King of Minnesota Brush was too good a strategist to ignore Rand's vulnerable position. As soon as the veto message appeared in the *Tribune,* King lashed back at his adversary: "That reminds me that vetoes are ripe now and should be gathered in—by gaslight exclusively. No well-regulated family should be without a veto—and a gas meter. Gas is only $4 per thousand, now, and the gas company, being mayor, has an exclusive franchise . . . which doubtless explains the extreme reluctance with which Mayor Rand allowed one Thompson, of Detroit . . . to veto the ordinance under which certain gentlemen proposed to risk a considerable amount of capital in the general introduction of the electric light in Minneapolis. All the first-class cities of the country have it, and are happy. Even Fergus Falls is about to introduce it, and it seemed as though an enterprising city like this should not be without it. As a matter of fact, but for an opposition the source of which seems to be revealed by the discovery of the African in the gas-house wood pile, forty lights would have been burning in various business houses of our city, before the holidays. . . . If our citizens prefer darkness at $4 per thousand to brilliancy for half the money," he added, "why, darkness is abroad in the land, and they can just help themselves. On the other hand, if they are willing to let this company put a large amount of money into an experimental enterprise which may or may not repay its originators, but which is certain to take at least two dollars' worth of starch out of the price of gas . . . why, all of Minneapolis (save the gas company) may be happy yet."[14]

The *Tribune* on February 17, 1882, suggested a compromise. The paper pointed out that Mayor Rand, knowing he could not prevent the use of electricity in Minneapolis, had stated that he did not oppose a system using underground transmission. It recommended that action be postponed for thirty days to see if any electric company would undertake such a solution. If none volunteered to do so within that time, the city council should then adopt an ordinance permitting overhead wires to be used under careful restrictions and reserving to itself the right to require removal whenever "the public welfare requires it."

Mayor Rand was not again put to the test. He did not run for re-election, and in April, 1882, Albert A. Ames became mayor. On May 10, 1882, the council enacted an ordinance granting the electric company permission to erect the poles, wires, and other fixtures necessary to conduct its business. Incorporating the idea recommended by the *Tribune*, the ordinance gave the council authority to order the wires removed and permitted it to make further provisions for the protection of life and property if necessary. Five days later Mayor Ames approved the measure. Four years were to pass before the city ordered Minnesota Brush to put its wire underground, and not until 1890 did the company heed the command.[15]

"Bright as the Sun," the *Tribune* entitled its story of May 12, 1882, congratulating the city upon the passage of the ordinance. Reviewing the company's preparations for giving "the advantage of continuous daylight" to customers, the journal predicted ready acceptance of the new illumination. "Quite a large number of firms are already prepared or preparing to introduce the new light into their stores and warehouses," it stated, "and several private residences are receiving wires."

The company's managers knew, however, that passage of the ordinance and contracts for illuminating buildings would not automatically ensure success. To put the organization on a sound business basis and to further the acceptance of electricity, they felt that the Minneapolis Gas firm's monopoly of street lighting must be broken. Early in 1882, while the ordinance was still under debate, the new organization made plans to demonstrate the effectiveness of electric street lighting by building on Bridge Square in the heart of the city's business district near the falls a high tower, called a "mast," which would carry a number of lights. The parent company had provided a precedent for the venture by erecting such a structure in Cleveland. Acclaiming the Ohio project, the *Tribune* of March 25, 1882, remarked that a mast would indeed be useful in Minneapolis "when the moon fails to appear as advertised, which she often does."[16]

The mast, 257 feet high and bearing eight arc lamps, shed its first light upon Bridge Square on February 28, 1883. Hundreds of spectators crowded the area and cheered when the lights went on. The experiment was pronounced a success. The city, according to the *Tribune* of March 1, was enveloped in a "halo" that "seemed in the distance indescribably beautiful." "With half a dozen more masts judiciously placed," the *Tribune* proclaimed, "the city would be lighted in a manner which would shame gas lamps."

A few days later the company pressed its advantage by inviting members of the city council and a few private citizens to witness a demonstration. All the gas lamps in the Bridge Square area were turned off, and at eleven o'clock the party set out in carriages to inspect the effectiveness of electricity. Members of the party, who claimed they could see the faces of their watches a few blocks from the mast, praised the new lights effusively.[17]

As brilliant light illuminated Bridge Square and the surrounding area, the *Tribune* of March 18 asked rhetorically: Who could oppose lighting the city with electricity? The answer it gave was the gas company, of course, cautious aldermen perhaps, and others. " 'I don't think the light is a bit nice,' said a young lady who was riding with her beau; 'tisn't a bit better than riding by daylight.' . . . 'Spoils our business, pard,' said an evil looking man with his slouch hat drawn over his eyes; 'we'll have to skip out for other parts.' "

Once the mast had proved successful, the council took up the vexing problem of whether it could or should contract for electric lighting on the city's streets. In response to a request from Minnesota Brush, it instructed the committee on gas to test the comparative merits of the mast and the 114 gas lamps located in the vicinity. After touring the area at midnight first by gaslight and then by the light of the mast, the committee reported that electricity gave stronger and clearer illumination.[18]

Immediately after the committee submitted its report to the council, a motion was made that the city enter into a contract with Minnesota Brush to furnish street lighting. The motion was referred to the committee on gas and to the city attorney with instructions "to ascertain whether there is any thing in the franchise of the Minneapolis Gas Light Company that will prohibit the city from entering into such a contract." On June 6 the committee and the attorney recommended that the contract be made, and, at the same time, that the city protect the gas company from as much loss as possible. The council then authorized a one-year contract with Minnesota Brush. Before the close of 1883 the company was operating eight lamps on posts as well as the mast, and it had petitioned the city to permit a substantial expansion.[19]

The gas company, stubbornly resisting the inroads of electric lights, continued to burn its lamps in areas also illuminated by electricity. At this, the council effected a settlement which provided that the gas company would turn out its lights in the areas served by electricity and that the city would permit gas lamps to burn elsewhere.[20]

At the end of 1884 Minnesota Brush could report very little progress in extending street lighting, for only nine lamps were burning in addition to the mast. It blamed this lack of progress on the hostility of its rival. "The Gas Company," Thomas King complained, "have not yet publically renounced their alleged belief that 'in six days God created the heavens and this particular portion of the earth' for the exclusive benefit of the Gas Company, although concessions made . . . in order to obtain a renewal of their contract with the city leads to the inference that they at least have their doubts upon that point."[21]

A year later the tide turned. Although the companies waged many a war over the lighting of specific streets and at times stubbornly illuminated the same thoroughfares, the success of Minnesota Brush was assured. In March, 1885, the council granted the company permission to light experimentally four of the city's main avenues. The firm built the circuits at its own expense, and the city agreed to pay seventy cents a lamp per night for a period of three or four months. So marked was the improvement over "darkness by gaslight" that the council on July 20 authorized a two-year contract at a minimum charge of two hundred dollars a lamp per year. By the close of 1885, 232 lamps, including those on the mast, were burning on Minneapolis streets, and by the end of 1886 the number had increased to 261. A year later the city approved a five-year contract, and by 1888 the number of lights had increased to 463. Although some gas lamps cast their glow over Minneapolis streets until 1924, electricity had definitely come to stay.[22]

While the company devoted its major attention to wresting the street-lighting business from Minneapolis Gas, it also pursued other markets. From the beginning it aspired to light homes, public buildings, stores, factories, and hotels, and by 1887 it had installed 270 lights in such places. By that year, too, the company had begun to sell electric motors for use in propelling printing presses, sewing machines, elevators, and other equipment requiring small amounts of power. Although some people alleged that the motors were dangerous, the company maintained that no one had been injured and that no one was likely to be unless "intent on committing suicide." Buyers purchased the units outright, and the company charged them for the energy furnished. By the end of 1889 the organization had thirty-four motors in operation, and it had only begun to exploit the potential market.[23]

Almost from the beginning Minnesota Brush encountered competition from other electric firms. The United States Electric Lighting Company of New York, which offered both arc and incandescent lighting, opened an office in Minneapolis in 1882 and began selling isolated plants. By 1884 the firm had replaced the Brush system in the

Pillsbury A mill, and it numbered among its customers the Washburn A as well as sawmills and other businesses. In 1882 the Safety Electric Light Company was also organized to sell isolated plants.[24]

Minnesota Brush's most aggressive competitor, however, was the Edison Light and Power Company, incorporated in 1888. It built a central steam-powered station in downtown Minneapolis. Soon it was providing incandescent lighting through ten miles of underground cable and was selling electric motors as well. Although Minnesota Brush easily held its own in the street-lighting business, the Edison company proved a formidable competitor in the field of interior lighting. Incandescent lamps were vastly superior indoors because the light was smaller and did not flicker. When Cleveland Brush failed to keep pace with other firms in developing an incandescent system, Minnesota Brush—forbidden by its agreement with the parent company to buy the equipment of other firms—found itself in an untenable position.[25]

To meet this problem and to satisfy the demand for incandescent lighting, Cleveland Brush purchased rights to lamps developed by Sir Joseph Swan. These were connected to Brush-made storage batteries, which were charged by the regular arc circuits running from a central station. The local firm acquired a franchise for the Brush-Swan system in 1883. When the batteries began to arrive in January, 1884, company officials were jubilant about the prospects. "Orders are in for a considerable number of these batteries," King reported, "and a number of the finest residences and public buildings in the city, have already been wired or are to be wired. . . . Citizens who have ordered batteries are impatiently awaiting their arrival, and it is evident to me that the demand . . . will be beyond our capacity to supply for many months to come."[26]

These high hopes were destroyed within the year. As it turned out, the batteries were difficult to keep properly charged, the acid spilled, the cases disintegrated, and the lights were short-lived. King wrote in January, 1885, that the failure of the batteries "was a disastrous thing, and it would have been greatly to our advantage never to have experimented with them." The company protested strongly to Cleveland Brush about the inadequacies of the system and complained that the fiasco discredited it in the city. Edison and United States Electric, King pointed out, snatched "part of the business right under our noses," while the parent company was "dilly-dallying and considering whether or not they can enable us to meet competitors on equal terms."[27]

The local firm's disgust with the Brush-Swan batteries accentuated the resentment it had felt against the Cleveland company since the first year of their association. In November, 1882, it had requested that the parent company reduce both the amount of capital stock it held and the prices it charged for equipment. The concessions, Minnesota Brush argued, were a "vital necessity" if it was to operate on a "safe commercial basis" in Minneapolis and sell equipment outside the city. Although the Cleveland organization lowered equipment prices somewhat, it did not reduce its capital stock holding.[28]

To resolve the conflict with Cleveland Brush, the Minnesota company in 1887 opened negotiations to repossess its stock, and the following year it purchased the parent firm's holdings for fifty cents on the dollar. Now free to deal with other organizations, Minnesota Brush in 1889 secured from the Westinghouse Electric Company the right to use its incandescent system. The emancipated organization, resolving to exert every "reasonable effort" to keep out all "systems or kinds of electric lighting" other than "those owned and controlled by this company," then set out to meet the competition of the Edison organization.[29]

In the midst of the Swan battery fiasco, the company's problem with water power came to a head. Three questions vexed the organization. The low flow prevailing from 1882 to 1884 prevented it from securing all of the small amount of water it had leased; Minneapolis Mill, planning improvements in the installations near Upton Island, announced that it was going to cancel the lease; and the electric company's expanding business required a larger building as well as a great deal more power.[30]

Although Minneapolis Mill offered to provide a building site and sixteen millpowers at the dam (which the sawmills were then abandoning) and the Chute brothers offered a location on the east side, Minnesota Brush had concluded by 1884 that "water power alone could not be relied upon." Committed to furnishing its customers with steady light whether the water was high or low, the company was frequently embarrassed by the necessity of closing down its plant. It could turn to steam auxiliaries as the flour mills had done, but the cost of a new building, water, and coal, combined with the fact that Minneapolis Mill would grant only a thirty-three-year lease, drove the organization temporarily from the falls.[31]

It moved to an upriver site at Third Avenue North, where a group of its stockholders organized the West Side Power Company and constructed a building with a steam-power plant fueled by sawdust and later by coal. West Side Power leased the new facilities to Minnesota Brush, and on October 1, 1884, the company began operations at the new location.[32]

After Minnesota Brush rejected its offer, Minneapolis Mill tried to interest other electrical organizations in a thirty-three-year lease. Negotiations with the Union Light Company—a firm organized for business by 1883—and with the United States Electric Lighting Company, failed. Not until the next decade did an electric firm return to the cataract, and then it located on the property of the St. Anthony company.[33]

Nevertheless the water-power firms gained a great deal from the events that occurred in this turbulent decade. Although Minnesota Brush remained at the falls only two years, a local precedent had been created for the use of water power in generating electricity. A market had been established despite public fears of electricity and despite the opposition of Minneapolis Gas. Burdened as they were with other problems, the water-power companies were not ready in the 1880s to assume leadership in fostering electrical firms or to enter the field themselves. Events transpiring in 1889 would soon put them in a position to do both, and when that time came their enterprises would rest on a firm local foundation built by Minnesota Brush.

10.

Hydroelectricity Comes of Age

ECONOMIC FACTORS COUPLED WITH technological improvements made possible the conversion of the Falls of St. Anthony into a hydroelectric site between 1889 and 1908. The initial step in the process was the unification of the falls under a single management. Since the first dam had been placed across the river in 1857, the power of the falls had been shared by two dissimilar business organizations. Men responsible for the preservation and development of the cataract had long advocated unification as a solution to many of their problems.[1] In 1889 the way was opened when the Minneapolis Mill and St. Anthony companies were purchased by a single firm, the Pillsbury-Washburn Flour Mills Company, Limited. The new owners introduced innovations at the falls that more than doubled the power output and made possible the sustenance of the milling industry as well as the conversion of the cataract into a major hydroelectric site.

The firm, which was an example of the general movement toward milling consolidation, was formed in 1889 by members of the Washburn Mill Company, C. A. Pillsbury and Company, and a group of British capitalists. Pillsbury-Washburn was the first of the nation's large milling corporations; it included, in addition to the water-power companies, five flour mills controlling almost a third of the city's production capacity and two grain elevator companies having large terminal facilities in Minneapolis as well as a line of country elevators.[2]

The change in ownership of the water-power companies aroused little concern in the local press, and the general reaction was one of approval. The *Tribune,* for example, asserted on January 22, 1890, that divided control of the water power had been a disadvantage in the past. "Now," it commented, "the great Pillsbury-Washburn company has united the parts and can properly guard and utilize the full power that nature offers." Only the *Northwestern Miller* expressed concern. It hoped that Pillsbury-Washburn would not be unfair to lessees who were its competitors in flour milling at the falls.[3]

The ease with which the press accepted the water-power companies' loss of independent status was probably due largely to the city's emancipation from the falls. Minneapolis was growing at a spectacular rate; its population climbed from 164,738 in 1890 to 301,408 in 1910. As trade expanded the city became an important wholesaling center as well as the nation's largest primary wheat market. Concerned about broadening the industrial base, business leaders encouraged the manufacture of linseed oil, farm machinery, and other products in areas away from the falls, while the steam mills in north Minneapolis turned out mammoth piles of lumber that made the city from 1899 to 1905 the nation's leading sawmill center. The cataract played no role in these developments, and thus the fate of the two companies was no longer a vital matter. Moreover, Minneapolis Mill had long been owned by flour millers. Thus its tie with the new firm did not represent a radical change.[4]

The passage of the old St. Anthony company apparently gave little cause for regret. James J. Hill's achievements in developing the water power were limited to consolidating the firm's property, improving its installations, and systematizing its leases. During the years of his presidency, he did not take positive action to promote industry. Coincidentally manufacturing on the east side actually declined. The lumber industry, the paper mill, and other miscellaneous manufactories had virtually disappeared, and only one flour mill — the Pillsbury A — and a small foundry had been added. Hill's chief contributions to the city during these years lay in the field of transportation rather than in water-power development. The railroad with which he was associated opened a great hinterland to wheat farmers who marketed their product in Minneapolis. Hill left behind him extensive trackage in the city, a union depot constructed above the property of Minneapolis Mill, and a magnificent stone arch bridge across the river at the falls. Negotiating with C. C. Washburn for a right of way along the western shore in 1881, Hill had announced that the bridge would cost about half a million dollars and would be "the finest structure of the kind on the Continent." The bridge, completed in 1883, and the depot, finished in 1885 and later rebuilt, remain as enduring monuments to Hill's contributions.[5]

Pillsbury-Washburn achieved unification of the falls by centralizing the management of the water-power companies rather than by mergers. Unwilling to disrupt the legal status of the leases already granted or to relinquish the 1856 charters which gave the firms legislative sanction for placing dams in the Mississippi, it retained the Minneapolis Mill and St. Anthony companies as separate corporations. It unified their management by appointing William de la Barre as agent, engineer, and treasurer of both organizations. Representatives of Pillsbury-Washburn served as officers and directors. An even stronger bond was created in 1899 when De la Barre was elected to the board of Pillsbury-Washburn.[6]

De la Barre's promotion to a key management position in the unified companies unleashed his great talents. Already seasoned by experience with Minneapolis Mill, he now gathered information on a wide variety of topics, including turbine design and hydroelectric equipment. In 1903, for example, he visited Europe to examine "the most modern Water Power and Electric Plants on that continent." Aware that owners of sites at Coon Rapids, St. Cloud, Little Falls, and other points on the Mississippi above the falls were beginning to develop their water power, he analyzed each site in terms of the effect it would have upon his operation.[7]

The engineer's abilities were not limited to technical mastery of water power and electricity. De la Barre's managerial skill and his dedication to his employers' interests won their confidence. The trust they placed in him was to be an important factor in the future development of the falls, for the new owners were far too involved in other enterprises to give the water-power companies much attention. Whenever it was financially possible to do so, they accepted De la Barre's recommendations, and they praised him lavishly for his accomplishments. An English stockholder wrote in 1907, for example, that "when we are all dead and forgotten, your monument will remain in the shape of the grand work you have erected on the old dam." [8]

As De la Barre's reputation grew, men from many parts of the nation consulted him. Engineers sought his advice on technical problems, and businessmen placed before him questions involving the financial feasibility of proposed water-power projects. His answers demonstrated a wide-ranging intellect, an unwearied delight in learning, as well as common sense and humility.[9] Charles H. Bigelow, James B. Francis, Joseph P. Frizell, and other men trained on the eastern seaboard had given the pioneer enterprise at the falls expert guidance. Now William de la Barre, a European-turned-Westerner, repaid the debt which the companies owed to earlier eastern experts by disseminating a store of knowledge gleaned at the Falls of St. Anthony.

No task the engineer undertook during these years was more diffi-cult than preserving the falls, for the river lost none of its violence. Floods, logs, and blocks of ice, some weighing over forty tons, still battered the dams, ripping loose the apron and eroding chunks of the limestone sheath. Representing a unified management at last unhampered by quibbling between the companies, De la Barre was free to deploy their combined resources. "We keep up eternal atten-tion and vigilance," he wrote a London stockholder in 1898, "and permit nothing to get away from us that human skill can stay." Sup-ported by ample funds from Pillsbury-Washburn, he repaired the apron, which was damaged by floods in 1891 and 1894, and in the latter year he built at its eastern end a spillway costing $105,000 to carry flood waters over the falls and three hundred feet beyond their foot. When floods in 1897 washed 10,000 tons of limestone from the ledge, he added a second spillway at a cost of $150,000.[10]

The lumbermen were a constant annoyance to De la Barre in his efforts to preserve the cataract and keep the river channel free of obstructions. To minimize the dangers posed when they drove logs over the falls, he built a sluice through Hennepin Island in 1898, and in the following year he redesigned the slide which the United States government had constructed in 1879 at the apron's western end. When operators of the steam-powered mills in north Minneapolis, a short distance above the falls, constricted the channel and clogged the millponds by dumping wood refuse into the river, he protested energetically but vainly against the encroachments.[11]

Managing the cataract as a single power source, he expanded the program begun in the 1880s to improve installations, conserve water, and extract more power from it. He replaced the leaky dam aban-doned by the sawmills on the west side, and he completed the tail-race. He pressed manufacturers to improve their own facilities until the average head and fall reached forty-five feet, almost the maximum available at the falls. He kept up millpond levels to secure maxi-mum power from the available water, limited lessees to the quantities stated in their grants, encouraged the formation of pools, and estab-lished schedules for synchronizing water and steam use.[12]

His pathway was not always smooth, for the operators of the flour mills, the city waterworks, the two sawmills, the woolen mill, and the remaining foundries usually placed their immediate self-interest above the common welfare. It was particularly difficult for De la Barre to convince them that a diminished head meant decreased power. Again and again he lectured the lessees on this point, until his letters took on the tone of an exasperated schoolmaster. In 1901, for example, he wrote: "Whenever you reduce the head, you reduce the efficiency of the water wheels. . . . The lower the head of water at your wheels, the greater the volume of water that has to pass through them to yield a given amount of power. This is an hydraulic law which your operators . . . cannot change no matter how much they try." To a manufacturer who was urging him to release water before he was ready, he stated emphatically in 1897 that "we know our business and propose to attend to it and will open the head gates as soon as it is safe and prudent to do so and not before." Chiding the complainant, he added that "if you would take the trouble to come down to the canal platform yourself and view the situation, you would not write such nonsense." [13]

De la Barre also gave considerable thought to the leasing arrangements which Minneapolis Mill had inaugurated in 1857, and he devised an innovation which was to make possible the greater use of hydroelectricity at the falls. It will be recalled that the water grants made in earlier years were perpetual, and that, because the flow of the Mississippi varied greatly, the companies had been forced to limit the permanent leases to six thousand cubic feet, the amount of water that could usually be depended upon during a large part of the year. Whenever the flow exceeded this amount, the water ran wasted over the dam. In 1890 De la Barre began to sell this uncommitted or "surplus" water to manufacturers at the rate of five dollars a day per mill-power. The new system proved very profitable. During a twelve months' period in 1896–97, gross income from this source was $60,017. By 1909 De la Barre reported that in the preceding four years the companies' regular leases had yielded an annual average of $79,866, while the surplus had grossed $92,250.[14]

This scheme for using surplus water, coupled with technological improvements in hydroelectricity and changing conditions, made possible additional hydroelectric plants at the falls in the 1890s. During this period many old water-power users were leaving the cataract; sawmilling was gone, and by 1908 only the North Star Woolen Mill and the industries housed in the Island Power Company's building remained.[15] Flour milling was still centered in the falls district, but during these years its reliance upon water power decreased. As the millers' production grew from 6,088,865 barrels in 1889 to 13,694,895 in 1908, they increased their steam-power reserves as well as their use of water. The *Mississippi Valley Lumberman* on July 2, 1890, predicted that the flour industry would soon go the way of sawmilling by seeking a new location where steam would provide more reliable power, land values were lower, and railroad trackage more abundant. By 1908 it seemed that the prophecy might be fulfilled, for there were two fewer flour mills near the falls, while three new steam-powered ones had appeared outside the district.[16]

The advent of long-distance transmission of hydroelectric power in the 1890s further encouraged De la Barre to concentrate upon this emerging industry. Because it was now possible to use electricity far from the generating location, businessmen throughout the nation were taking a new look at water power. The most dramatic development was the mammoth hydroelectric plant at Niagara Falls, and the most interesting in Minnesota was an installation on the St. Louis River near Duluth that in time would supersede St. Anthony as the state's most productive water power.[17]

De la Barre made his first move to obtain a hydroelectric plant at the falls in 1894, when he offered twenty millpowers of surplus water to the Minneapolis General Electric Company, a corporate successor of Minnesota Brush, the pioneer firm which had moved from the falls ten years earlier. The company accepted De la Barre's proposal, leasing the water for thirty years at three dollars a day for each mill-power, two dollars less than the amount charged the millers. It completed its arrangements by renting three vacant east-side sawmill sites and their attached 10.4 millpowers, with an option to buy the properties at the end of five years. In 1894–95 the company built near the falls its Main Street Station, capable of generating a total of 8,000 horsepower, 3,000 of which was produced by water power.[18]

Steadily improving its power, Minneapolis General Electric gradually absorbed all the water once used by the east-side sawmills. In 1899 the firm bought the properties it had leased in 1894, and, at the turn of the century, it leased two more sites once occupied by the McMullen sawmill. The consolidation was completed in 1909 when the organization purchased the water rights and property of the Island Power Company.[19]

De la Barre found Minneapolis General Electric a dynamic organization. Two years before it came to the falls, it had absorbed a related group of companies, including Minnesota Brush, West Side Power, and Minneapolis Electric Light and Power. At the same time it bought the franchises and properties of the Edison Light and Power Company of Minneapolis, which had been Minnesota Brush's early competitor. In 1899 the process of consolidation continued when newly formed Minneapolis General Electric of New Jersey purchased the stock of the local firm. The New Jersey corporation, moreover, was but one link in the chain, for it in turn was controlled by Stone and Webster, a Boston firm which specialized in financing electrical companies and providing them with engineering services.[20]

The tendency of electrical firms to merge into large and complex business structures was to have far-reaching effects upon the development of water power. For example, in 1906 when De la Barre offered Minneapolis General Electric additional surplus water, the firm replied that it planned to transmit electricity to the city from subsidiaries owned by Stone and Webster at St. Croix Falls, Wisconsin, over fifty miles distant. The transmission project, which was completed in 1907, recalled events of sixty years earlier when two other Massachusetts men, Caleb Cushing and Robert Rantoul, held interests in the water powers at St. Croix and St. Anthony. Although long-distance transmission was unknown in the 1840s, these men had viewed the two power sites as part of a plan to control the natural resources of the Northwest. Through the medium of electricity and a new form of business organization, Stone and Webster combined power sources in a fashion little dreamed of in the mid-nineteenth century. Energy from the falls at Minneapolis and on the St. Croix flowed into the same pool, furnishing light and power to the mill city under the aegis of the Boston firm.[21]

In addition to attracting Minneapolis General Electric to the falls, De la Barre planned to build hydroelectric plants on the properties owned by the Minneapolis Mill and St. Anthony companies. In 1890 these firms were at last ready to develop the power below the cataract which had been unused throughout their histories. But their plans encountered opposition from a revival of the pioneer scheme to develop the Meeker Island area below the falls. In the 1880s a group of Minneapolis men, who had acquired control of the old Mississippi River Improvement and Manufacturing Company, again tried to enlist federal aid to build installations which would provide both water power and navigation facilities. Although the hostility between St. Paul and Minneapolis had not abated, the *Northwest Magazine* optimistically predicted in 1888 that this time the plan would command the full support of the Twin Cities, for "all progressive people in both see that they constitute . . . a single powerful center of trade, transportation, population and civilization."[22]

Nothing much came of the Meeker Island plan until 1890 when Thomas Lowry, an exuberant Minneapolitan who controlled the Minneapolis Street Railway Company, became interested in the site as a source of power for his streetcar system. Intent on abandoning horse-drawn cars, he began converting to electricity the Minneapolis system as well as that of St. Paul, which his firm had acquired in 1886. At first steam plants furnished the power he needed, but he saw in the Meeker water-power site a means of lowering his operating costs.[23]

Lowry's interest in the Meeker Island power was shared by Henry Villard, a New York financier well known in the Northwest for his promotion of the Northern Pacific Railroad. Villard was already involved in the street railway company's affairs, and his interest was sharpened by his association with the Edison General Electric Company, which at this time aspired to control central stations throughout the nation. When he announced his intention of working with Lowry in investigating the Meeker Island proposition, Twin Citians responded enthusiastically. Lowry was pleased with the reaction, for, he warned, "if Mr. Villard thinks that any old time jealousy is to be revived he will not waste a minute nor a cent on the undertaking." [24]

The investigation, which was conducted by one of Villard's representatives and a United States army engineer stationed at St. Paul, resulted in a recommendation that conflicted with De la Barre's plans and disrupted the short-lived harmony between the Twin Cities. The two men concluded in March, 1890, that the Meeker Island site was not the best place to build the dam. Instead they advocated a location a few miles downriver near Fort Snelling which would provide more water power as well as an "everlasting solution of the navigation problem." Since the proposed site for the hydroelectric station attached to the dam would be well within the St. Paul city limits instead of on the boundary line, Minneapolitans objected on the grounds that it would be a "perfect absurdity" to support a scheme giving so substantial a resource to its neighbor.[25]

At precisely the same time, De la Barre and Charles A. Pillsbury, chairman of Pillsbury-Washburn's local management committee, announced plans for developing the water power below the falls within the limits of the properties owned by the Minneapolis Mill and St. Anthony companies. They asserted that either of the proposed dams would ruin their power site by backing up the water, and they made it clear that they would take legal action to defend their riparian rights. When it was suggested that Villard and Lowry might quiet their objections by purchasing the water-power companies' shorelands below the falls, Pillsbury answered that "it would take a pretty large sum of money to make the purchase; too large, probably, to make the investment profitable." In the face of these problems and their disappointment with the estimated power available, Villard and Lowry abandoned the venture in 1890.[26]

De la Barre lost no time in taking advantage of the abdication. In 1890 he persuaded Pillsbury-Washburn to engage a board of engineers to confer with him on the best means of utilizing the twenty-foot drop within the water-power companies' property below the falls. When the board approved the project, he worked out the construction details for a dam (without locks for navigation) as well as for a powerhouse.[27]

The "Lower Dam," begun in 1895 and completed in 1897, was so bold an undertaking that it was promptly dubbed "De la Barre's Folly." The total cost of the installation was $953,332 — a substantial investment for even so strong a corporation as Pillsbury-Washburn. Built 2,200 feet below the falls, the huge dam stretched across the Mississippi at an angle that diverted the river's flow toward the eastern shore. The power station, which was located on the dam's eastern end, was equipped to convert 10,000 horsepower into electricity.

Although De la Barre entertained a number of proposals for leasing the new plant to manufacturers, his objective from the beginning had been rental to Lowry. The Twin City Rapid Transit Company, as the street railway organization had been called since 1891, was indeed a good prospect, for it was still using steam plants to generate electricity. Since the new hydro plant would save the firm an estimated $100,000 a year in power costs, Lowry readily assented. Learning a lesson from the rigidity of the old Minneapolis Mill leasing system, De la Barre limited the contract to forty years and scaled the charges to variable production. For each of the first 6,000 horsepower, the constant and dependable amount, the annual rental was $23; for the next 3,000 that would usually be available, $10; and for any amount over 9,000, nothing.[28]

Completion of the Lower Dam aroused considerable enthusiasm in Minneapolis. At a ceremony on March 20, 1897, marking the event, Charles Pillsbury declared that the installation represented "one of the greatest engineering feats of the present century," and the workmen saluted De la Barre with cheers that "would have moved anything but the dam." A writer in the *Electrical Engineer* commented that the achievement was "in scope and character second only, perhaps, to the hydraulic work which has made the waters of Niagara the servant of a vast territory." Looking into the future, a local newspaper reporter compared the development to the discovery of an inexhaustible coal mine, "for its power will continue so long as the ages roll and the power of gravitation endures."[29]

Not everyone, however, was enthusiastic about the enterprise. Opposition came from a group of men who were interested in a twelve-acre tract situated on the west side below the new dam. When the surveys for the dam began, Dr. A. H. Hedderly, one of the owners, warned De la Barre that by diverting the flow toward the eastern shore, the installation would destroy the power potential of the property across the river. De la Barre, convinced that the flow would return to its normal position in the channel before it reached the Hedderly property and that the tract's power potential was negligible in any event, was not deeply concerned. Charles Pillsbury offered the Hedderly group five thousand dollars to quiet objections, but its members refused the settlement.[30]

In 1897 Hedderly, William W. Eastman (who owned an interest in the tract), and the Minnesota Loan and Trust Company, acting for a group of easterners who had bought mortgage bonds secured on the property, brought suit against the water-power companies for removal of the dam. They maintained that their objective was to clear the way for water-power development. De la Barre and Pillsbury, however, believed that the Hedderly group was employing the suit as a strategy to exact a blackmail price for the land and that Eastman was actuated by "his love for strife, and his chronic desire to litigate with the St. Anthony Falls Water Power Co."[31]

The companies decided to contest the suit rather than seek a compromise, and De la Barre led the Pillsbury-Washburn organization in a spirited fight to save an investment of almost a million dollars. With the help of consulting engineers, he brought into the Hennepin County District Court an imposing array of facts about the river, the relative rights of riparian owners, and the Lower Dam's effect upon these rights. The testimony marshaled by both sides during the five-week trial filled almost two thousand printed pages, and observers commented on the extreme complexity of the issues at stake. The court unequivocally sustained De la Barre's contention that the Hedderly tract had no water-power potential and that, in any event, the flow returned to its normal position before reaching the property. The Hedderly group then appealed to the Minnesota Supreme Court, which in 1901 sustained the lower court's decision.[32]

When the results were announced, De la Barre was elated. Casting aside the reserve that usually characterized his business letters, he wrote: "I bought two good sized flags a few hours after we got the good news and one was placed on the East Side of the lower dam and the other on the west side and there they have been spread to the breeze ever since. I wish I could have bought a giant rooster, who could crow every five minutes, we should have placed him on top of our dam and kept him crowing." [33]

Not long after the victory a third hydroelectric facility was added to Minneapolis General Electric's east-side plant and the Lower Dam station. Pillsbury-Washburn gave De la Barre permission to construct a new plant on Hennepin Island, which was built between 1906 and 1908 at a cost of $317,265. It drew water from the St. Anthony mill-pond through a 350-foot canal and returned it to the river below the falls via a long tailrace. [34]

Designed to operate entirely on surplus water, the new station, which had a generating capacity of 12,000 horsepower, demonstrated the practical effects of De la Barre's creative management. By inaugurating the surplus system, he had found a way to utilize the flow which was available only part of the year. The reservoirs and his measures for conserving water had increased the surplus which was available, and his decision to allot most of the excess to hydroelectric plants rather than to flour mills had given a new direction to the development of the cataract. The idea of operating a hydroelectric plant on surplus water was in itself an innovation. "There were, to be sure," wrote a Minneapolis hydraulic engineer in 1917, "many water power developments having an excess of generating capacity way beyond the limits of permanent power available, but this plant . . . stands almost alone as being deliberately conceived and built to utilize only such power as is available during times of high water." [35]

Before the plant was completed, both Twin City Rapid Transit and Minneapolis General Electric indicated an interest in leasing it. De la Barre knew that either organization would make an ideal customer, for each had steam-power reserves which could be used when surplus water was not available. Since the street railway firm at the time was entertaining the idea of securing additional power from a hydroelectric station on the St. Louis River near Duluth, its managers quibbled with De la Barre over terms. He settled the issue on October 1, 1907, by leasing the plant to Minneapolis General Electric for a twenty-five-year period at an annual rental of $75,000. To protect the water-power firms from competition, he included in the contract a clause prohibiting Minneapolis General Electric from selling electricity to the companies' lessees without written permission. Minneapolis General Electric promptly sublet the plant to Twin

City Rapid Transit, and by December, 1907, the streetcar firm was utilizing all the newly installed hydroelectric power at the falls.[36]

Even in a city of almost 300,000 people largely concerned with other matters, the new Hennepin Island plant created a stir. When the station went into operation in 1908, a local newspaper congratulated Pillsbury-Washburn on completing the "big harness for St. Anthony Falls." The journal accurately commented that unless "some engineering genius of the future" devised a plan for using the peak points of the Mississippi's flow "the last chapter in the history of the St. Anthony Falls water power development may now be written."[37]

Although the developed capacity of the falls was doubtless disappointing to those who remembered the earlier estimates of 120,000 horsepower, substantial progress had been made. In the 1880s the installed turbine capacity had been only 13,000 horsepower. With the construction of three hydroelectric plants, careful water management, and the employment of surplus water, the total installed capacity reached 55,068 in 1908. Of this, the hydro plants possessed about 25,000 and the flour mills 24,000, while the remainder was controlled by the North Star Woolen Mill Company, the city of Minneapolis, and others.[38]

During this period of hydroelectric development, the water-power companies had to cope with two projects which would have diminished the flow of water at the falls. One of these was initiated by the city of St. Paul, which in 1890 began drawing water for public consumption from a tributary of the Mississippi above the falls; the second originated with citizens of northern Minnesota, who in 1905 attempted to persuade the United States government either to abandon the reservoirs or modify their operation. Although the water-power companies had often experienced crises involving the water supply, the new tests involved broader questions. Were the firms' rights to the natural flow at the falls superior to the claims of a municipality owning riparian lands above the cataract? Would the United States government, which had contributed to the water power by protecting the falls and by building the reservoirs, yield to northern Minnesotans concerned with other interests?

The conflict with St. Paul marked the companies' second encounter with a unit of government over the priorities of public and private rights. This time the issue was more clearly drawn than it had been in the contest between the St. Anthony Falls company and the city of Minneapolis in 1888 over the Hennepin Island pumping station. The difficulty began in 1881 when the St. Paul Board of Water Commissioners acquired title to riparian lands on Baldwin Lake north of the city. Through the lake flowed Rice Creek, which emptied into the Mississippi about eight miles above the falls. In 1890 the board began pumping from Baldwin Lake into Pleasant Lake (now within North Oaks); from there it drained water into the city system for public consumption. After use, the water was returned to the Mississippi below the falls, thus depriving the power companies of as much as ten million gallons (or 1.55 millpowers) a day.[39]

The two companies in 1893 instituted separate but identical suits against the St. Paul board in Hennepin County District Court, charging that the board had deprived them of property by diverting the water. In the two actions, which were tried simultaneously, the companies requested that St. Paul compensate them for the water withdrawn and that the board be restrained from using more than it paid for. The board answered that it possessed riparian rights through its ownership of land bordering Baldwin Lake, that a municipality as a branch of state government had the right to use water for public purposes, and that the public purposes had precedence over private claims. In a statement sharply challenging the concept of riparian rights hitherto widely accepted in the nation, the board maintained that the "state merely permitted the plaintiffs to use the bed of the Mississippi river with its incidental privileges until it saw fit to limit those privileges by using them for itself." Upon the board's motion, the district court dismissed the cases. Although the companies moved for a new trial, their requests were not granted. They appealed to the Minnesota Supreme Court late in 1893, but it upheld the lower court's order.[40]

The companies considered the decision an unwelcome "innovation in riparian law." It was, they maintained, "contrary to the accepted law of the property rights of riparian owners," and "erroneous on other grounds which arise under the Constitution of the United States," for it deprived them of "private property" without compensation. Under a writ of error, the companies then carried the case to the United States Supreme Court, which in 1897 upheld the Minnesota court.[41]

The decision, often cited in later years as an important ruling, said in part that the "question as to the nature and extent of the rights of riparian owners upon navigable waters, including the right to the continued flowage of the stream, is one to be decided by the courts of the state as a matter of local law, subject to the right of congress to regulate public navigation and commerce; and a decision by a state supreme court sustaining the power of the state, through its municipalities, to take water from a stream for municipal uses without making compensation to riparian owners below, who have been using the flow for water power, is not a taking of private property without compensation, contrary to the federal constitution." Although the companies lost the case, they defended themselves against further government encroachment in subsequent years by continuing to argue that their riparian rights constituted inalienable property rights.

The second area of conflict involved the headwaters reservoirs which had been constructed in the 1880s. De la Barre often commented on the benefits the system bestowed upon the falls enterprise. "What would we do now," he asked W. D. Washburn during a drought in 1894, "if it were not for your reservoirs? They have been opened up August 1st, and inside of two weeks we will have plenty of water, whether it rains or not." The system, enlarged by the construction of a fifth reservoir at Sandy Lake in 1895, opened the way for a great expansion of water power on the Mississippi between Pokegama, 329 river miles above the falls, and St. Paul. According to the calculations of government engineers, the annual gain to all the water-power owners would eventually reach half a million dollars a year. The major purpose of improving navigation, they believed, was also being fulfilled, for the contribution to the water level at St. Paul was approximately a foot during three months of low water, with gradually diminishing effects farther downstream.[42]

Although the government did not ask the companies to help support the reservoirs, the Minneapolis organizations felt their stake in the system was so great that they continued to aid the enterprise. They urged the construction of a sixth reservoir at Gull Lake and contributed funds to purchase flowage rights, for they believed that this addition would improve the flow at the falls more than any of the five already built. In 1900 John S. Pillsbury, president of the St. Anthony company, donated to the federal government 1,000 acres of flowage land he had purchased at Gull Lake, and in 1910 the companies gave another 995 acres.[43]

Not all the interests on the upper Mississippi were as happy with the reservoirs as the water-power companies. Lumbermen and the United States engineers operating the system continued to squabble over the timing of water releases. In the engineers' judgment the lumbermen showed bad grace in their protests, for year by year as they removed the forest cover they made the control system more necessary. Major William A. Jones, a government engineer in charge of the system, summed up the situation in 1896 when he said that Minnesota needed either more forests or more reservoirs to halt the decline in stream flow.[44]

Settlers, moving into the upper Mississippi area which had been only sparsely inhabited when the first reservoirs were built, added their protests to those of the loggers. North of Little Falls the flourishing communities of Brainerd, Grand Rapids, and Aitkin had emerged, each with industries, small agricultural hinterlands, and articulate newspapers. Brainerd, which in the 1870s had been a raw frontier village, was by 1900 the chief town, with a population of 7,524, while Grand Rapids had 1,428, and Aitkin, 1,719.[45]

The growth of the region complicated the engineers' problems. In addition to adjusting the operation of the reservoirs to the needs of navigation, water power, and log driving, they now had to consider the interests of farmers who had settled near the Mississippi as well as saw and paper mill operators located on the river above Minneapolis. "It is impossible," lamented the chief engineer in St. Paul, "to so manage the reservoirs as to suit all concerned, because each party minimizes or ignores entirely the interests of all the others."[46]

Agitation against the system reached a peak early in 1905 when a flood washed over the Aitkin area. Its residents blamed the engineers for keeping the reservoirs too full and called the system "one of the biggest nuisances ever foisted on the state." Although the engineers pointed out that flood damage would have been even more extensive if the reservoirs had not held back some of the water, the critics did not relinquish their charge in the face of logic.[47]

The outraged communities found an ally in Duluth. As the western end of the Great Lakes waterway and the eastern terminus of the Northern Pacific Railroad, growing Duluth aspired to displace the Twin Cities as the state's leading urban center. In 1880 its inhabitants had numbered only 3,483. It grew rapidly in the next two decades. By 1890 it had 33,115 people and in 1900, 52,969. Duluth's leaders believed that the city's transportation advantages would win the trade of northern Minnesota as well as meter through its harbor immense tonnages of east-bound iron ore and wheat.[48]

In the St. Louis River, which took its rise near the Mississippi drainage basin and flowed into Lake Superior at the city's doorstep, Duluth had a potential water power that further spurred its ambitions, and the city's newspaper spokesmen now stepped forward to lead the fight for elimination of the reservoir system. The *Duluth*

News-Tribune, centering its fire on the Falls of St. Anthony, claimed that the government engineers favored the interests of Minneapolis. If selfish millers and water-power owners at the cataract were willing to flood out the upper country to get a little more power, they would have to answer to Duluth.[49]

But the falls had a champion ready to carry the war to the enemy — De la Barre. Duluth, he declared, was fighting the reservoirs not to protect a stricken countryside it claimed as a hinterland, but to further a scheme for diverting water from the Mississippi drainage basin so that the water-power potential of the St. Louis River would be increased. On July 25, 1905, he reported to Major George McC. Derby, the engineer in charge of the reservoirs, that the Great Northern Power Company of Duluth was making surveys between the Mississippi and St. Louis basins. "Can it be possible, Major," he asked, "that there is a scheme on foot to divert water from the Mississippi River into the St. Louis River to improve the flowage?" Derby replied on July 26 that the "project . . . is news to me, but Duluth is an enterprising place and liable to divert its way anything Minneapolis and St. Paul can conveniently spare."[50]

To W. D. Washburn, De la Barre did not pose the proposition as a question. He stated categorically that the Great Northern Power Company was making surveys "with the idea of having a canal between the Mississippi and St. Louis Rivers for the divertion [sic] of water from the Mississippi for the purpose of increased flowage for their proposed water power development on the St. Louis River. What a scheme that would make if it could be carried out."[51]

"I need not tell you," he confided to Washburn, "what a terrible blow to our company's interests the abandonment of these reservoirs would be. I calculate that the revenue of the water power companies is likely to be diminished to the extent of $60,000 per annum in favorable years; in dry seasons it may be double that amount." Summarizing the extent of the opposition polarized under Duluth's leadership, he warned that the danger was great. "You of all men," he stated, "can appreciate what would happen if the U. S. Government would fall in with the idea of these scheming rascals and be brought around to abandon the reservoir system which has cost the government over $1,300,000."[52]

De la Barre led the fight to save the reservoirs from what he called a "conspiracy" by "an aggregation of men of influence and means." Sounding the alarm, he rallied support from Congressmen, river improvement groups, and water-power and mill owners on the Mississippi from the headwaters south to Rock Island, Illinois. In his counterattack he defended the government engineers, terming the criticism of them "simply vicious and utterly indefensible. I have been a close observer," he stated, "of the management of the reservoir system for many years, and in all that time the highest intelligence has been shown, as well as a determination to insure an absolutely 'square deal' between conflicting interests." [53]

After conferring with Major Derby, he urged a public hearing before a federal board of engineers to force the real issue into the open. In August the three members of the board toured the reservoir district to interview critics and survey the damage. When it convened in St. Paul in September, both friends and foes of the system crowded the hearing room. At De la Barre's side were Rome G. Brown, the water-power companies' knowledgeable counsel; John T. Fanning, a former engineer of the St. Anthony company and a hydraulics expert of recognized stature; William A. Meese, representing the Upper Mississippi Improvement Association and water-power interests at Moline and Rock Island; and several representatives of navigation, power, and manufacturing interests above the cataract from Coon Rapids to Little Falls. Speaking for the opposition were delegates from Duluth, Walker, Aitkin, Grand Rapids, Cass Lake, and the Chippewa Indians at Leech Lake.[54]

In view of the opinions expressed before the hearing, the arguments presented by opposition spokesmen were rather tame. They did not ask for abandonment of the reservoirs, but merely for a change in their management. For years, they contended, the system had been manipulated to benefit the Minneapolis water power and navigation pressures below the falls. "All we ask," said A. G. Bernard of Cass Lake, "is that the growing interests of . . . [northern Minnesota] should have their share of protection and not be subject to what we consider the mismanagement of the dams." C. S. Kathan of Aitkin stated that he had never heard of any proposal to abandon the reservoirs, and when quotations from the *Duluth News-Tribune* were cited, he declared that he was not responsible for "that paper." [55]

Most surprising was the mild statement presented by Herbert V. Eva, the sole spokesman from Duluth. He maintained that the city's commercial club, of which he was secretary, was interested in the matter only because "the territory affected is more or less immediately tributary to Duluth." He urged that the United States engineers in St. Paul give more attention to the needs of the upper Mississippi country, but he also complimented them on the job they had done in the past. Although he was not questioned directly about the alleged plan for diverting water from the Mississippi drainage area, he reiterated that Duluth was interested only in the region's trade.[56] Puzzled, the *Minneapolis Journal* remarked on September 13 that the "representative from Duluth, where the principal hue and cry has arisen, roared 'gently as any sucking dove' today."

De la Barre was probably correct when he stated that personal contact at the hearing produced more amicable feelings among the dissident parties. Although the comments made by northern Minnesota representatives about the Twin Cities' interests were at times intemperate, they also sounded a conciliatory note in their arguments. Jacob S. Gole, of Grand Rapids, for example, stated that the people he represented were not hostile to Minneapolis and St. Paul. "If they prosper," he commented, "we are going to prosper, and we want to join hands with them, and want to get such regulations as will be fair and just to everybody." Twin Citians, too, seemed amenable to changes that would help the northern communities. Rome Brown's view was that the confrontation in St. Paul resulted not from irreconcilable conflicts but "simply because of a newspaper sensation."[57]

After hearing the evidence, the board issued a report endorsing the reservoir system and the way in which it had been operated. The establishment of the reservoirs at a time when settlement was not far advanced and construction costs were low, the board said, was "a measure of great foresight and wisdom." It concluded, however, that the multiplication of interests now touched by the system increased the engineers' responsibility to disseminate widely information about its operation and to show all parties every consideration consistent with the primary purpose of improving navigation.[58]

The hearing and report, of course, did not effect a permanent solution of the problem. Immediately after the St. Paul sessions a few northern Minnesotans contended that the Twin Citians had been favored. The *Itasca County Independent*, a Grand Rapids journal, called the proceedings a "fore-ordained farce." "It was called a hearing," the editor said on September 16, "and in one respect it was. The distinguished military gentlemen could hear the twin cities interests, but no adder could come near them in deafness when other interests strove to be audible." Although its distant counsels were ignored during the hearing, the *Duluth News-Tribune* continued to agitate for the abandonment of the system. "Perhaps the time is not far distant," it prophesied on September 18, 1905, "when the waters of the Mississippi will flow unvexed in the channel prepared by the Almighty."

In the succeeding sixty years, many new conflicts arose over the reservoirs. The cessation of log drives, changed navigation needs, new requirements of hydroelectric and manufacturing plants along the river, increasing water consumption in the Twin Cities, and the emergence of northern Minnesota as a recreational area created constant pressures for adaptations. Never again, however, did the regional cleavage become so marked, and never again were the interests of the Minneapolis water power in the system so seriously threatened.[59]

Despite the difficulties they experienced during the period, the companies enjoyed unprecedented prosperity in the years from 1889 to 1908. Hydroelectricity had emerged from a tentative and struggling venture into equal status with flour milling as a user of the cataract's power. And by utilization of the surplus, careful water management, and hydroelectricity, the capacity of the falls had been increased from 13,000 to 55,068 horsepower in two decades. The results of this progress were reflected in the companies' incomes. In 1885 the gross receipts of the St. Anthony company had been $19,973.28 and those of Minneapolis Mill in the fiscal year 1887–88 totaled $66,084.69. In the fiscal year 1908–09 their combined gross income was $465,704.49.[60] Guided by the talented De la Barre and tied to a flour milling firm with large capital resources, the water-power companies at last achieved the objectives which had eluded them for years.

11.

The End of an Era

THE TWENTIETH CENTURY, which had opened so auspiciously for the water-power companies, was to mark the end of an era at the Falls of St. Anthony — an era in which water had been used directly to power the wheels of the mills that lined the Mississippi's banks. It was an era that opened in 1821–23 with the construction of mills on the west bank by soldiers from Fort Snelling. Since 1848, when Franklin Steele's sawmill began to operate, water wheels had been used continuously at the Falls of St. Anthony. Now almost a hundred and forty years later it was ending. By 1960 the cataract was to be completely converted to hydroelectricity and the last water wheel was to turn no more.

During the years from 1908 to 1965 the corporate destinies of the water-power firms were altered by a series of events which reflected a changing time, a changing business climate, a changing technology, and a changing attitude toward the waterfall that built a city. Some of these events had their origins in the distant past; others were culminations of movements which began early in the twentieth century. All, however, had two characteristics in common: They stemmed from situations beyond the water-power companies' control, and they were resolved, for the most part, without reference to the firms' welfare.

The period began with a crisis that catapulted Minneapolis Mill and the St. Anthony company into a maze of troubles. Pillsbury-Washburn, the organization which had provided the capital necessary to build hydroelectric plants at the falls, collapsed in 1908. Although the directors had been concerned about the dwindling profits from flour milling, the immediate cause of the debacle was the failure of a wheat-speculation venture secretly undertaken by members of the local management committee. Shocked by the sudden disclosure that Pillsbury-Washburn owed over a million dollars it could not pay, a London director confided to De la Barre that the "murder is out at last and a nice mess we are in." [1]

Plans to liquidate the debt and salvage Pillsbury-Washburn were fashioned by court-appointed receivers, a creditors' committee, and by De la Barre as the personal representative of the English directors. Willy-nilly the water-power firms were deeply involved in these plans, for they remained under Pillsbury-Washburn management, while the mills were leased to the newly incorporated Pillsbury Flour Mills Company. Mortgage bonds were issued with the water-power properties and the mills offered as security. Income from the water power and from the lease to Pillsbury Flour Mills was to be paid to the First Trust and Savings Bank of Chicago as trustee. First Trust was then to meet the interest on the bonds and accumulate a fund to retire them. [2]

De la Barre found the new arrangement a trying one, for it forced the water-power companies to pay First Trust most of their net earnings. After five years of this situation, he wrote in 1913 that the "famous scheme of reorganization" loaded the firms "down to the neck with obligations to pay . . . nearly one thousand dollars a day for every day in the year. This money has to be earned and in times of drouth . . . it became necessary to save or hang on to every blessed dollar that came within reach." [3]

The disposition of the companies' revenues from 1909 to 1923 illustrates the problem De la Barre described. The annual gross income derived from leases of the Lower Dam and Hennepin Island hydro plants, perpetual grants to flour mills, and the sale of surplus water fluctuated from a low of $388,748 to a high of $499,852. For the entire period it amounted to $6,059,116. Of this sum $4,165,995 went to First Trust, $697,539 was spent for repairs and maintenance, $509,592 for taxes, $365,024 for salaries and wages, and the remainder for office expense, insurance, and legal fees. [4]

The companies' closely balanced financial condition affected their operations in several ways: It endangered preservation of the cataract, thwarted plans for expanding hydroelectricity at the falls, delayed improvements in plant efficiency, and prevented the extension of operations upriver. De la Barre felt that the most serious effect was the neglect of the installations to preserve the falls. Deeply concerned about the destructive forces constantly threatening the water power, he reminded his employers that failure to make repairs might result in disaster. He was not always successful in making them understand the urgency of the problem, and they often disregarded his requests. They did, however, permit him to establish a small emergency fund which he regarded as a "sheet anchor to the companies' existence." In 1912 and 1916 they also provided money for rebuilding parts of the apron and improving the design of its eastern end.[5]

Other developments not connected with Pillsbury-Washburn aided De la Barre in preserving the cataract. In 1912 the federal government completed at Gull Lake the sixth reservoir, which it was believed would help control destructive floods. At De la Barre's request, the city in the following year redesigned a proposed bridge above the falls that would have imperiled the limestone sheath. In the second decade of the twentieth century, dwindling log supplies in the pinery tributary to Minneapolis brought to an end the great drives that had battered the falls and forced the closing of the sawmills that had spewed refuse into the channel.[6]

But no outside events came to the engineer's rescue as his plans to expand hydroelectricity at the falls foundered on the shoals of Pillsbury-Washburn's financial problems. De la Barre had viewed the completion of the Hennepin Island plant in 1908 as only one step in the conversion to hydroelectricity. On three occasions in 1909, 1912, and 1913 he proposed that the water-power firms repossess the grants made to the millers, build another hydroelectric station, and furnish current to the flour mills. When Pillsbury-Washburn vetoed the plan because of its cost and the millers showed an aversion to change, De la Barre reluctantly concluded that "the time was not ripe for such an undertaking." Scaling down his aspirations, he suggested in 1920 that Pillsbury-Washburn spend at least $300,000 in renovating the existing plants. "My version is," he wrote in support of this plan, "that improvements and additions will have to be made in the near future to enable the companies to hold their place and to meet their obligations." Although he assured the owners that the investment would yield a return of 15 to 18 per cent, the parent firm also rejected this proposal.[7]

During the years the companies were chained to Pillsbury-Washburn, De la Barre was disappointed in another suggestion to enlarge the firms' commitment to hydroelectricity. He well knew that on the Mississippi River above the falls were potentially important water-power sites at Coon Rapids, Sartell, Sauk Rapids, St. Cloud, Little Falls, Grand Rapids, Brainerd, and Bemidji. De la Barre believed that the Minneapolis companies should acquire some of these sites for hydroelectric development, but Pillsbury-Washburn's difficulties forced him to abandon the plan. It was a "sad retrospect," he wrote in 1920 as he considered the wasted opportunity. "If the net earnings of these companies could have been applied, for the last twenty years, only to the acquirement of waterpower sites and the development thereof, our revenue today would most likely exceed one and one-half million dollars per annum and we would now really be *some* waterpower company."[8]

But these were internal problems. On the larger stage beyond the companies' control attitudes toward the use of such natural resources as water power were undergoing a profound change. Throughout most of the nineteenth century, companies like those at the falls had operated with little government control in a legal framework favorable to private water-power development. Although the federal government had the authority to regulate navigable waters and the state of Minnesota held title to the beds of such waters within its boundaries, both governments had been generous. The United States, through its interest in navigation, had spent more than two million dollars to protect the falls and build the reservoirs that contributed so largely to the companies' welfare. Under the charters granted in 1856, the state had empowered the firms to dam the river, and the Minnesota courts had often sustained them in controversies over riparian rights.[9]

In the late nineteenth century, federal and state governments, ending a long period of *laissez faire*, began to examine intensively the current use and potential development of the nation's water-power resources. Two factors quickened their interest. From the ferment of the conservation movement arose questions concerning the public's interest in water power as a natural resource and in its enhanced value as a means of saving coal reserves. Drawing government attention, too, was the development of hydroelectricity. When long-distance transmission came into common use early in the twentieth century, public utility groups integrated power sources into large systems which distributed energy widely. Both federal and state governments then became interested in controlling monopoly growth and in weighing the remuneration due the public for the use of a natural resource by private enterprise.[10]

The federal government led the way. Between 1890 and 1910 Congress enacted a series of laws that had ominous overtones in the opinion of the water-power companies' managers at the falls. The legislation required the consent of Congress and the war department for building dams in navigable rivers, obligated individuals or firms developing new sites to secure permits from the government, and levied charges against permit holders for administrative and head-waters improvement costs. After a decade of controversy over further legislation, Congress in 1920 created the Federal Power Commission, which was authorized to grant permits and regulate many of the licensees' operations.[11]

Since the laws were not retroactive and the Minneapolis companies sold water rather than power, they were not immediately affected. Nevertheless, they viewed the legislation as a dangerous trend toward government control which might eventually impair their charter rights and assess them for the benefits they received from the reservoirs. Rome Brown, the firms' legal counsel, made their position clear during hearings before the National Waterways Commission in 1911. He labored particularly to distinguish between the government's power to reserve specific rights at the time it sold public land and its limited authority over privileges attached to riparian land already in private ownership. Brown maintained that conservation, which he defined as "the reserving of that which one has," was "legal and proper," but that "the attempted appropriation of any beneficial use, or the proceeds or advantage thereof, from another, which has passed to the latter in private ownership, is not conservation; it is confiscation."[12]

The state of Minnesota was no less interested than the federal government in exerting control over water-power sites within its boundaries. The legislature took a step in this direction in 1909 when it instructed the Minnesota Drainage Commission to make recommendations. The commission proposed a bill which required any firm planning new water-power developments to apply for state permits. Successful applicants would be granted a franchise for a specified number of years; renewal would be subject to current state laws, and, in the case of public utilities, to rate reviews. In addition an annual tax would be levied on the power created from the water grants.[13]

In 1911, less than a year after the drainage commission made its report, Representative Lewis C. Spooner of Morris, Minnesota, introduced a bill that not only included most of the commission's recommendations but contained a retroactive clause as well. The Spooner Bill seriously disturbed the Minneapolis companies, for they believed that its retroactive provision would make them leaseholders of the state, subject to additional taxation and to ejection when their permits expired. Sounding the alarm, De la Barre summoned to a conference in St. Paul representatives of Minnesota water-power interests on the Mississippi, St. Louis, and Red Lake rivers. The group appointed a committee to watch the bill's progress through the legislature and to present its case at the hearings.[14]

During the ensuing debate which raged in the legislature and in the public press, Brown, as the leading spokesman for the water-power group, applied to Minnesota the distinction he had sought to make on a national scale. He argued that Minnesota had adopted a code which made a riparian owner's right to use water flowing past his land a part of his property. He conceded that, like the federal government, the state had authority to regulate water powers attached to land it still owned, but he maintained that the clause which extended control to sites in private ownership was unconstitutional because it confiscated property without due process of law.[15]

As the leaders of the opposition and the owners of the largest water-power installation in the state, the Minneapolis companies took the brunt of criticism during the hearings. Spooner declared that the firms and other "predatory water-power corporations" were "fattening upon the investment of no capital other than that contributed out of the funds of the people, with the natural energy and the beneficial use of the whole Mississippi river and the reservoirs . . . improvements which have cost the people millions." James H. Davidson, chairman of the state waterways commission, asserted in the *Tribune* of April 5, 1911, that the "St. Anthony Falls Waterpower company has the Mississippi river shackled as much as that stately stream ever was when Confederate guns bristled from the walls of Vicksburg."[16]

The Spooner Bill passed the House by a vote of 84 to 28 and went to the Senate, where it also seemed to have strong support. Then the tide turned. In a hearing before the general legislation committee, opponents made a determined effort to force consideration of the bill's constitutionality on the grounds Brown had suggested. Swayed by their argument, the committee referred the bill to the attorney general for an opinion, and on April 13 Assistant Attorney General Lyndon A. Smith ruled that "the ownership of waterpowers and the right to the beneficial use of the same is a property right which is beyond the control of the legislature."[17]

Although the 1911 legislature adjourned without taking further action, the question of the state's control over water power was far from settled. In 1923 the Minneapolis firms were again alarmed when new measures including the same features they had regarded as objectionable in the Spooner Bill were introduced in the legislature. Although the bills were defeated, the companies realized that some type of water regulation was inevitable. It came with a law enacted in 1937, but the absence of a retroactive clause exempted the organizations at the falls from the controls established.[18]

By that time the water-power companies had a new owner — the Northern States Power Company. It bought the firms in 1923 from Pillsbury Flour Mills, which had acquired them earlier that year from Pillsbury-Washburn. The purchase price was three million dollars. Thus, after years of association with flour millers, Minneapolis Mill and the St. Anthony company became part of an organization dedicated to generating electricity.[19]

Acquisition of the water-power firms by Northern States was part of a trend toward consolidation which was prevalent among companies furnishing electric light and power. The emergence of Northern States itself typified the trend. Preliminaries began in 1912 when the Consumers Power Company, a firm which was controlled by H. M. Byllesby and Company of Chicago, acquired Minneapolis General Electric. Through Consumers Power the Main Street Station at the falls, built by Minneapolis General Electric in 1894, became part of a large system that included plants at St. Paul, Stillwater, Faribault, Mankato, and Coon Rapids, Minnesota, and at St. Croix Falls, Wisconsin. In 1916 the organization adopted the more descriptive name of Northern States Power Company.[20]

The sphere of Northern States continued to widen after it bought the water-power firms. The organization not only supplied the needs of Minneapolis, but in 1925 eliminated its only competitor in the capital city by purchasing the St. Paul Gas Light Company. In addition Northern States furnished light and power to over five hundred other communities in Minnesota, North and South Dakota, Wisconsin, Illinois, and Iowa.[21]

The Minneapolis cataract was an important part of the Northern States system. It was the most productive power source among the nineteen hydroelectric developments that furnished 50 per cent of the firm's total generating capacity. In other respects, however, the falls suffered a relative decline in status. By the 1920s they ranked second in Minnesota to a plant on the St. Louis River at Thomson; on the Mississippi they were dwarfed by an installation at Keokuk, Iowa. Nationally the Falls of St. Anthony were outranked by many developments, such as those at Niagara Falls and at sites on the Pacific slope, where new technology had made it possible to harness water falling several hundred feet.[22]

The position of the water-power firms within the new organization resembled their old relationship to Pillsbury-Washburn. Because of their charters, the legal status of the leases, and their character as distributors of water rather than power, they retained for a time their corporate identities. Technically, however, they were subsidiaries of the Northern States Securities Corporation, which in turn was a subsidiary of the Northern States Power Company.[23]

As the guard changed, De la Barre continued as president of the water-power firms, a position to which he had been elected in 1921. When he moved into the Northern States organization, his past contributions did not go unrecognized, for the new owners joined with the old in paying tribute to him as the "master mind and the guiding hand which have brought these Companies and their great enterprise to their present enormous development and success."[24]

De la Barre remained active in the firms' management until 1936, when he died at the age of eighty-six.[25] With failing eyesight but unfailing intellect, he had lived to train a new generation of engineers. To practical men intent on doing their jobs well, he transmitted skills necessary to keep the complex maze of installations functioning. To men graced with historical feeling, he gave a sense of continuity, for he had clasped hands with pioneers — old when he was young — who had arrived in Minneapolis in the mid-nineteenth century, and with men — young when he was old — who lived into the mid-twentieth.

De la Barre did not live to see the complete conversion of the Falls of St. Anthony to hydroelectricity under the control of Northern States. When the organization bought the properties, roughly half of the cataract's capacity was still used by the flour mills in the form of direct water power. The rest was used by three hydroelectric plants, but two of them — those at the Lower Dam and on Hennepin Island — were in the hands of the Twin City Rapid Transit Company, whose leases still had some years to run. Only the small output of the Main Street Station could be added to the 163,000 horsepower generated by the Northern States system to provide electricity for the Twin Cities.[26]

Although Northern States made no deliberate effort to convert the water power used by the flour mills into electricity, the conversion gradually took place as the milling industry declined. After World War I several factors combined to topple flour milling in Minneapolis. Most important among them was the so-called "milling-in-bond" privilege made possible when Congress passed the Dingley Tariff in 1897. Under this arrangement millers in the United States were permitted to import Canadian wheat duty free if the flour made from this wheat was exported. If the millers paid the duty, they could collect rebates from the government. Minneapolis millers experimented with milling-in-bond early in the twentieth century, but their competitors in Buffalo, New York, were more favorably located to profit from the privilege. This factor, coupled with the decline in the quantity and quality of spring wheat, changes in distribution and consumption patterns, and altered freight rate structures, led Minneapolis millers to build new mills in Buffalo and elsewhere. As a result, the local industry began to decline after 1916.[27]

The trend was not clear at the beginning of the twentieth century, for production climbed from 13,694,895 barrels in 1908 to 18,541,650 in 1916. Output then fell sharply to 10,797,194 barrels by 1930, while Buffalo, the city's most vigorous milling rival, raised its production to 11,076,301. In 1930 Buffalo became the nation's flour-milling center, seizing the crown that Minneapolis had worn for fifty years. And in the years that followed flour production in Minneapolis continued to fall, reaching 5,471,456 barrels in 1960.[28]

The decline of milling had a physical impact upon the falls district, destroying the stern, majestic profile that had long given it a distinctive character. Gradually stillness enveloped the once busy area. Some mills were abandoned, while historic structures like the Anchor, Cataract, Palisade, and Pillsbury B on the west side and the Phoenix on the east side, were razed. In 1965 operations ceased in the Washburn A—the weathered gray structure which still bore the plaque commemorating the deaths of men killed in the 1878 explosion—and the industry vanished from the west side. Only the Pillsbury A mill remained in operation across the river, enlarged but still retaining the classic outlines LeRoy S. Buffington had designed in 1880.[29]

As the mills closed, the conversion of the falls to hydroelectricity was completed. Some of the water released by the flour mills was used at the Hennepin Island hydro plant, which increased its capacity from 12,000 in 1908 to 17,000 horsepower by 1957. Most of the rest was employed to generate electricity at seven locations on the west bank. The output from these units was conveyed to a common station, called the Consolidated Hydro Plant, which in 1957 had a capacity of 6,068 horsepower. The conversion of the falls was at last completed in 1960, when General Mills, Incorporated, abandoned its water wheels and conveyed its millpowers. Now the falling water no longer furnished direct power, but was used to generate electricity.[30]

In the 1950s the output of the Lower Dam and Hennepin Island plants was absorbed into the Northern States system as the Twin City Rapid Transit Company converted from streetcars to buses. The firm gave up its lease on the Lower Dam in 1950 and on the Hennepin Island station in 1954. Northern States then rebuilt the plants and purchased the transit company's adjacent steam facilities. These additions, with the water released by the flour mills, placed almost the entire developed capacity of the cataract — 53,775 horsepower at that time — under the direct control of Northern States.[31]

The only notable exception was the water used at the St. Anthony Falls Hydraulic Laboratory. This experiment station of the University of Minnesota was established on Hennepin Island in 1936–39 through the co-operation of three agencies: the Works Progress Administration, which supplied construction funds; Northern States, which granted easements over the adjoining property; and the city of Minneapolis, which conveyed the site and five millpowers formerly used to operate its pumping stations. In a sense, the completion of the laboratory signified the maturing of the water-power development at the cataract. Local engineers in the past had relied upon the testing laboratory at Holyoke, Massachusetts, for help in solving complex problems. With the building of the St. Anthony laboratory, such services were performed by experts at the very brink of the falls.[32]

The city of Minneapolis helped write still another chapter in the twentieth-century story of the Falls of St. Anthony. Throughout its history, Minneapolis had another obsession that matched its water-power mania in intensity — the extension of navigation into the heart of the city. Even during the early years when the community was largely dependent upon the cataract, spokesmen at times ranked navigation above water power as a vital element in the city's welfare. "Some think," one observer wrote in the *Daily Minnesotian* of September 22, 1854, "that the Falls might be removed with some expense, so that boats could run uninterruptedly over them."

In the following century the water-power companies found that the navigation issue often affected their most vital interests. In its name they had requested federal funds to preserve the falls and construct the reservoirs. Conversely, to protect their monopoly they had opposed the Meeker and Lowry-Villard projects, which would have produced power as well as aided navigation. It seemed that the companies at the falls had the best of it in every contest, but twentieth-century Minneapolis pursued its old dream as tenaciously as it had in the nineteenth century.

Deprived of the navigation facilities they coveted, persuasive Minneapolitans continued to urge the federal government to act. United States army engineers responded in 1894 by announcing plans for two locks and dams—one to be located near Meeker Island, a short distance below the companies' projected Lower Dam installation, and the other in the vicinity of Fort Snelling. In 1909, after the Meeker Island structure had been completed and the one near Fort Snelling begun, the engineers decided that a single high dam at the latter location would create a deeper channel and make possible a hydroelectric development. Abandoning the Meeker Island installation, which had cost almost a million dollars, the engineers carried out their plan for elevating the Fort Snelling structure. The "High Dam," as it was called, was completed in 1917. It created a channel deep enough to extend navigation as far north as the Washington Avenue Bridge in Minneapolis, less than two river miles below the falls, and it made available 15,200 horsepower for conversion into electricity by a licensee whom the government would select.[33]

Although spokesmen for the water-power companies had earlier criticized suggestions for hydroelectric facilities at government dams below the cataract, they did not oppose the High Dam. Moreover, when it came time for the government to grant the license, they left the struggle to others. The chief contestants were Minneapolis and St. Paul, which, after briefly entertaining a plan to use the power jointly in a municipal plant, backed rival applicants. Minneapolis favored the Northern States Power Company (which had not yet acquired the water-power firms) while St. Paul's candidate was Henry Ford, whom its business leaders were encouraging to build an automobile assembly plant in the city. The issue was settled in 1923 when the government granted the license to Ford.

The High Dam, or "Ford Dam," as it is now known locally, was scarcely completed when Minneapolitans in the 1920s, 1930s, and 1940s bombarded Congress with requests to extend navigation above the falls. One advocate claimed that the harbor at the Washington Avenue Bridge was "comparable to having a road stop at the edge of town." Civic spokesmen urged Congress to provide appropriations for a lock and dam between the High Dam and the falls, for a lock and canal around the cataract on the west side of the river, and for a harbor with extensive facilities above the falls.

Arguments for the so-called "Upper Harbor" project echoed those advanced by boosters of river transportation early in the city's history. Navigation would work magic. It would help reduce freight rates, promote the welfare of railroads by increasing trade, bring to Minneapolis wheat from Canada and iron ore from northern Minnesota, and "give Minneapolis a firm foundation upon which to build a greater industrial city." One proponent wrote in 1925: "To state the exact truth about this Harbor is likely to expose us to the charge of exaggeration."[34]

Some Minneapolitans made such a charge. A local engineer, for example, declared in 1917 that the scheme was a "Pipe Dream," since the railroad had superseded the river as a vital factor in transportation. When the city in 1941 became committed to contributing funds for the project, other objections were expressed. "Minneapolis has about as much need for a second river harbor as a pig has for pockets," declared an opponent in 1948. As late as 1953 a citizen asked the city to cease its advocacy of the harbor and courageously face the fact that the benefits "which can be derived from it are inadequate to justify its greatly expanded cost."[35]

In spite of criticism and several false starts, the project got under way at last in 1950. Work on the first installation, near the Lower Dam, was completed in 1956. In 1959 construction of the lock and canal around the falls was started, and on September 21, 1963, the tugboat "Savage" pushed a barge laden with cast-iron pipe through the locks. On this proud day eminent Minnesotans gathered to salute the achievement. Senator Eugene J. McCarthy commented that Minneapolis was now tied to the "great cities of the United States that are part of the country's waterways system." Answering charges that the project was wasteful, Representative Walter H. Judd declared: "I don't know of any public works appropriation that I voted for that will bring as many benefits as this one in 50 or 100 years."[36]

The Upper Harbor project drastically altered the falls area. It destroyed the famed Minneapolis Mill canal which had nourished the city's milling industry, the generating stations of Consolidated Hydro, and other installations. When construction was completed in 1963, all that remained of the west-side district, once the pride of Minneapolis, were the gaping apertures of races leading to vanished or abandoned mills, and the Washburn A mill, which was to close two years later.

Destroyed, too, during the building of the Upper Harbor was Spirit Island, the legendary abode of Dark Day's ghost. Over the years the local press had photographed the island many times and retold the legend with unflagging enthusiasm.[37] Physically the island had become smaller and smaller as it was battered by waters from the falls and by the blasting for the apron which had been carried on periodically since the 1860s. In 1960 the last portions were cleared away.

Indirectly the Upper Harbor project also contributed to the dissolution of the Minneapolis Mill and St. Anthony companies as separate corporations. In 1946 the Federal Power Commission, whose authority had been increasing over the years, requested that the water-power firms apply for licenses to maintain and operate their dams and plants. The companies demurred on the grounds that the Mississippi at the falls was not navigable and that they were therefore exempt from federal jurisdiction. The Upper Harbor project changed the situation and made it clear that the river would soon be navigable. In addition the firms found that "whether it is palatable or not," the commission's growing powers had been consistently upheld by the courts. The companies made their first concession to the federal authority in 1950 when they applied for a license to use the new government dam resulting from the harbor project below the falls and to rebuild the Lower Dam hydroelectric plant. With the Lower Dam development thus subject to its regulations, the commission in 1952 informed the firms that it would be advisable for them to request a license for the other installations at the cataract. They did so the following year.[38]

Since the companies' charters no longer protected the water power from federal regulation, the firms were dissolved to become the St. Anthony Hydro Division of Northern States in 1957.[39] At that time they had been in existence for a hundred and one years. When the territorial legislature granted the firms' charters in 1856, Minneapolis had just been detached from the Fort Snelling military reservation, St. Anthony was at the zenith of its short history, the two communities had only a few thousand people, and both centers staked their futures on water power. When the corporate lives of the firms ended in 1957, St. Anthony was no more, and Minneapolis was a complex city of almost half a million people, with far-flung commercial interests as well as manufactures scattered from its heart to its suburban satellites.

Minneapolis has good reason to remember the Falls of St. Anthony, for much of its history is intertwined with them. From its birth until 1880, Minneapolis had been "Yoked unto the cataract's thunder/ As the 'wagon to a star.' "[40] The place and the time were right for the assumption of such a role by a waterfall. The place was mid-continent America, where a cataract on the Mississippi River could be easily tamed by the technology then available. The time was the mid-nineteenth century, when settlement was flowing into the Northwest, when water power was preferred to other sources of energy, and when it was particularly prized for manufacturing the type of raw materials which could be supplied by the tributary area.

Although the cataract's role was subordinated after 1880, it still mirrored facets of local, state, and national history. Here culminated the city's century-old desire for navigation, here the flour milling industry became pre-eminent in the United States, here the nation's first hydroelectric central station was established, and here—in step with other hydro developments in the country—a water power was brought to its most efficient utilization through electricity. Like similar organizations, the companies owning the falls operated in a steadily widening sphere of involvement. Their efforts to protect the water supply had brought them into conflicts with Minneapolis, St. Paul, and communities in northern Minnesota; the defense of their riparian rights had sent their representatives scurrying to the statehouse in St. Paul and to the nation's capital; and beginning in 1923 their policies were shaped by a large public utilities firm serving many communities in the Midwest.

Not the least interesting aspect of the cataract's history is the demonstration of the tenacity of an idea in community life. Long after water power had ceased to play a dominant role in the economy of Minneapolis, its citizens credited the falls with more importance than they had. Indicative of this feeling and of respect for the tradition was the retention of the cataract's image on the city's official seal. More concrete were the written comments from many segments of the community. A leading newspaper, the *Minneapolis Journal*, declared in 1908 that the "backbone of Minneapolis, next to her good character, is her great water power"; a team of local historians asserted in 1914 that to "the great cataract . . . the city owes its origins, its existence, and the principal elements which form its condition and character"; and in 1923 the executives of Pillsbury-Washburn and Northern States claimed that the falls "have been the most powerful instrument in the up-building of this city to its present position of primacy in the industrial world." [41]

As the historical consciousness of Minneapolitans matured, they advanced a plan to recognize St. Anthony's role. A report sponsored by the Minneapolis Downtown Council in 1961 asserted that the cataract could again be "a great landmark at the continent's heart" as it had been in the previous three centuries. Reviewing Hennepin's discovery of the falls, the tale of Dark Day, and the rise of a great city on the shores of the Mississippi, the report recommended the restoration of the area as an outdoor museum. Refurbish the district, it asked, build displays illustrating the industries once based on the power, and erect an observation tower. Honor the Falls of St. Anthony by completing the cycle and restoring it to its original natural beauty.[42]

Although nothing has as yet come of the council's suggestion, many tourists—attracted by the locks as well as by the sheathed cataract—now visit the area. Those with a little imagination can reconstruct its physical history. Looking downstream from the Third Avenue Bridge, they can see the dam across the river first built in 1856–57, the apron muffling the falls, and the Stone Arch Bridge. To the left are the St. Anthony millpond, the Main Street Station, the Pillsbury A mill, the Hennepin Island and the Lower Dam hydro plants, and Lucy Wilder Morris Park which commemorates the probable spot from which Hennepin saw the falls in 1680. To the right are the locks and the ragged outline of what was once the city's milling district. Nicollet Island near the eastern end of the Third Avenue Bridge is obscured by a shabby cover of houses, stores, secondhand shops, and missions, and some effort is required to recall that this was the beautiful spot to which Minneapolitans rushed in a frenzied effort to save the falls. Beyond the area to the west is the shimmering skyline of the new Minneapolis, no longer a water-power city but still a Queen City of the Northwest.

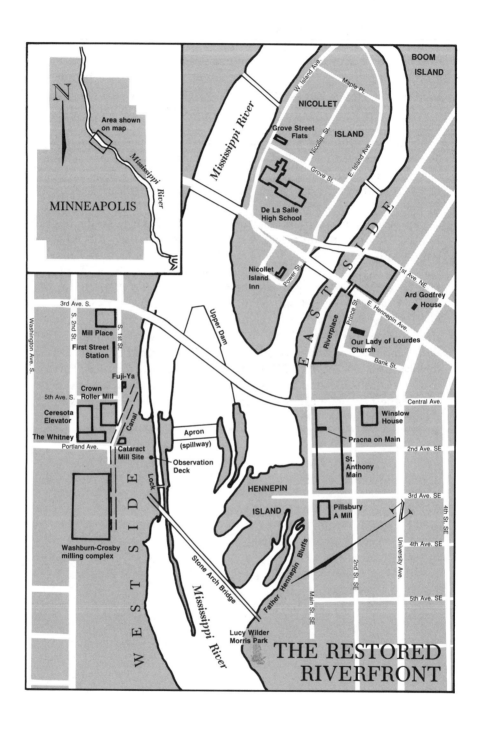

N

Area shown on map

Mississippi River

MINNEAPOLIS

Mississippi River

BOOM
ISLAND

W Island Ave.

Maple Pl.

NICOLLET

Grove Street
Flats

Nicollet St.

ISLAND

E. Island Ave.

Grove St.

Mississippi River

De La Salle
High School

1st Ave. NE

E A S T

Ard Godfrey
House

Nicollet
Island
Inn

Power St.

Prince St.

Riverplace

E. Hennepin Ave.

Our Lady of Lourdes
Church

Bank St.

3rd Ave. S.

Washington Ave. S.

S. 2nd St.

Mill Place

S. 1st St.

First Street
Station

Upper Dam

S I D E

Fuji-Ya

5th Ave. S.

Crown
Roller Mill

Central Ave.

Winslow
House

Ceresota
Elevator

Canal

Apron

(spillway)

Pracna on Main

2nd Ave. SE

The Whitney

Portland Ave.

Cataract
Mill Site

Observation
Deck

St.
Anthony
Main

Lock

HENNEPIN

3rd Ave. SE

4th St. SE

ISLAND

Pillsbury
A Mill

Washburn-Crosby
milling complex

N

4th Ave. SE

W E S T

Stone Arch Bridge

Father Hennepin Bluffs

2nd St. SE

University Ave.

5th Ave. SE

I S I D E

Mississippi River

Lucy Wilder
Morris Park

Main St. SE

THE RESTORED
RIVERFRONT

Epilogue, 1986:
A Riverfront Reborn

THE STORY OF THE FALLS OF ST. ANTHONY from the 1960s to 1986 is, like the earlier history, a complicated one involving public and private interests. Aspirations of public agencies, developers, and citizens' groups for refurbishing the falls area were expressed in many proposals after the Minneapolis Downtown Council sponsored its plan in 1961. Although the proposals differed widely, several emphasized common themes. Planners agreed that the riverfront should once again become a vital part of the city where people lived and worked and that the river should become more accessible to the public for recreation. They recognized, too, that the falls area was a special place on the river, significant as the spot where the city began and as the source of its early prosperity.[1]

Rejuvenation of the area evolved after World War II, during the age of urban renewal. Across the nation, many cities that had long outgrown the centers of their early development began renewal programs to eradicate blight and help stem the flight of businesses and people to the suburbs. During the first flush of enthusiasm for revitalization, urban planners in Minneapolis, like those in other cities, advocated sweeping away the old and building anew. Running counter to their proposals were the arguments of preservationists. The preservation movement, feeble in its early years, gained support as citizens saw notable structures that had been part of the city's historical fabric disappear from the urban landscape.

The falls area — both blighted and historically important — became an arena for the interplay of renewal concepts. Renascent interest in the Mississippi River at, above, and below the falls brought the site special attention. Reflecting on the phenomenon in 1980, Naomi Loper, then president of the Minneapolis Park and Recreation Board and a neighborhood and environmental activist, commented that af-

181

ter "years of neglect and general back-turning by society, the River has been discovered in a Big Way."

Loper noted particularly the strong interest in Nicollet Island: "Members of Southeast [Minneapolis] neighborhood associations saw so many designs for Nicollet Island over the years our eyes began to glaze over each time a new batch of drawings would come in from an architecture class."[2] Although the number of those designs was unprecedented, the idea of nonindustrial use had solid historical precedent. The island's location near the falls, its beauty, and its size — forty-eight acres — earned it the title "gem of the Mississippi." People wanted to live there, particularly after William W. Eastman and John L. Merriam acquired it in 1865 and began to build housing and sell lots on the upper portion.[3]

Some admirers of the island also recommended it as a fine setting for public buildings. In 1857, when boosters of St. Peter attempted to remove the state capital from St. Paul, legislative strategists bent on defeating them slipped "Nicollet Island" into the removal bill as a substitute location. And during an attempt in 1866 to merge Minneapolis and St. Anthony, acquisition of part of the island for public buildings and a park was made a condition for uniting the neighbors. As houses, industries, and commercial buildings spread over the island, regrets lingered. The *Minneapolis Tribune* in 1877 called the failure to acquire it for public use "a blunder of stupendous proportions, the lamentable results of which can never cease to be felt."[4]

In 1883 Horace W. S. Cleveland, a landscape architect influential in shaping the Twin Cities' park systems, reminded Minneapolitans of the blunder when he urged them to make the river an important part of their planning. Remember, he lectured, "that the Mississippi river is not only the grand natural feature which gives character to your city and constitutes the main spring of its prosperity, but it is the object of vital interest and the center of attraction to intelligent visitors from every quarter of the globe. . . . It is due, therefore, to the sentiments of the civilized world, and equally in recognition of your own sense of the blessings it confers upon you, that it should be placed in a setting worthy of so priceless a jewel."[5]

Cleveland's language was grandiloquent, but his recommendations were precise. Focusing attention on the deep and beautiful gorge the falls had cut during their centuries-long retreat from the mouth of the Minnesota River, he urged the Twin Cities to acquire riverside property for parkways and parks before it was too late. The cities, making Cleveland's vision their own, began building the boulevards in the late nineteenth century. On the east side the Minneapolis portion of the system met that of St. Paul; on the west side it connected with Minnehaha Park, abutting the river six miles below the falls, where a parkway in turn linked the river with the lake district.[6]

While the Twin Cities were building the parkways, visionaries created two designs for the falls area as part of comprehensive plans to reshape Minneapolis into "the city beautiful." The designs, proposed in 1906 and 1917, addressed far more difficult questions in the falls area than did those for the gorge section farther downriver. Industries still important to the city crowded the riverfront near the cataract, and renewal advocates, no matter how visionary they might be, were not bold enough to suggest their removal.

John N. Jager, who headed the group of Minneapolis architects producing a long-range city plan in 1906, felt that private interests on the west side should not be permitted "to mar what belongs to everybody, 'the beauty of the city.' " Nevertheless, he excluded the concentrated milling district below Fifth Avenue South from censure. The riverbank above this point, he commented, was "hideous where it should be beautiful, hiding the majestic and renowned St. Anthony falls, the most prominent feature in the history and topography of Minneapolis, instead of allowing their beauty to be admired from an advantageous point of view."[7]

The "reclamation and beautification" Jager suggested included an elevated boulevard accessible from the Hennepin Avenue Bridge and a new bridge at Fifth Avenue South. Except for unspecified improvements, the east bank appeared intact on the imaginative sketch of the new city. Not so Nicollet Island. Predictably, Jager and his associates envisioned the island as a park, with public baths, improved beaches, and structures housing industrial exhibits.

In presenting the Jager group's design as a plan worthy of consideration, the *Minneapolis Journal* conceded that it might seem "at first blush utopian and impractical."[8] It was, however, modest when compared with the *Plan of Minneapolis*, produced in 1917 by Edward H. Bennett, a Chicago architect, for the Civic Commission of Minneapolis. The riverfront figured prominently in Bennett's dazzling design. His plan recommended high- and low-level drives with "park embankments" on both sides of the river, linking the parks and parkways below the falls with new greenways above them. Finding an acceptable route through the west-side milling district posed critical questions. Bennett suggested a route that left the manufacturing system in place, but noted that the problem required "careful study." Not surprisingly, Nicollet Island — houses and businesses removed — was to fulfill its "manifest destiny" by becoming a park, with an encircling drive, gardens, sports facilities, and a stadium expansive enough to serve as an airfield.

The 1917 design, a significant prelude to intensive planning for the waterfront that began in the 1960s, came too early to receive serious consideration. Sporadic developments, however, enhanced the falls area. The beautiful Third Avenue Bridge, opened to traffic in 1918, satisfied the plan's design standards and provided an observation point for viewing the falls. Another window on the river opened in the 1920s when the Minnesota Society of the Daughters of American Colonists developed Lucy Wilder Morris Park on the east-side bluff below the falls. Although heavy overgrowth would later obscure the view and a steep stairway leading down the bluff to the riverbank was said to be more hospitable to Rocky Mountain goats than to people, the tiny park conformed with past and future ideas for open space on the waterfront.[9]

Other early initiatives in the falls area were rare. In 1905 the Hennepin County Territorial Pioneers' Association rescued the house of Ard Godfrey, Franklin Steele's early associate at the falls, and four years later presented it to the Minneapolis Park Board. Built in 1848 on the east side near the river, the house, which was relocated on nearby Richard Chute Square at University and Central Avenues Southeast, has recently been restored by the Woman's Club of Minneapolis. The *Minneapolis Journal* saved the John H. Stevens house, built on the west bank by the falls in 1849 and moved twice before 1896, when it was hauled by ten thousand Minneapolis school children to Minnehaha Park and presented to the park board; it was restored by the Junior League of Minneapolis in the 1980s. Both houses, as well as the notable Pillsbury A Mill on the east side, were included in the WPA's Historic American Buildings Survey in 1934.[10]

But businessmen, responding to changing economic conditions, technology, energy requirements, and space needs, had a greater role in determining the nature of the falls area's landscape than did pioneer preservationists. A major shift in that landscape came in the latter part of the nineteenth century, when sawmilling moved to its new center upriver, leaving no buildings behind to mark the sites of the city's first great industry. New structures built in 1866 and 1879 — one of them a flour mill — covered the site of the government mills, where use of water power began in the 1820s. During the heyday of flour production, when mills massed on the west side gave the district a distinctive character, steam stacks signalled the need for additional power and hydroelectric plants heralded yet another form of energy. After 1916, when flour production began to decline, many of the notable mills disappeared. Among them was the Cataract, the first private mill on the west side, built in 1859 and now commemorated by a millstone and engraved doorway lintels cemented into the remaining building foundations.[11]

Construction of the upper lock in 1959–1963 destroyed other important sites and structures. The site of the nation's first hydroelectric central station on Upton Island was destroyed; it is now commemorated by a hydraulic turbine and marker near the lock. The "great canal" that had carried water through the milling district was filled in and the gatehouse that controlled flowage from the river into the canal was razed. The Stone Arch Bridge, however, was adapted to accommodate the lock. Railroad traffic over the bridge ceased in 1981, and the structure, designated as a National Historic Engineering Landmark, now figures in designs for refurbishing the falls area.[12]

The new locks brought more than navigation to the city's core. The observation platform the United States Army Corps of Engineers built beside the lock, although not highly publicized, attracts thousands of visitors annually. From this excellent vantage point it is possible to watch river traffic pass through the lock, to view the falls, and, guided by an informative plaque, to locate important points in the area.[13]

As lock construction weakened the historical fabric at the falls in the late 1950s and early 1960s, preservationists faced another potential problem in the district. A massive renewal project called Gateway Center began in the nearby lower loop. Despite sporadic revival attempts, this area — the original site of Minneapolis — had been deteriorating for many years as the business district moved southward away from the river. But renewing a city by clearing an area for new construction, rather than integrating the new with the old, did not bode well for preservationists. After the Guaranty Loan Building (better known as the Metropolitan Building) in the Gateway Center area was demolished in 1961–1962, preservationists could cite a stunning example of an architectural gem destroyed in the whirlwind of renewal enthusiasm.[14]

Fortunately, the beginning of major revitalization at the falls was delayed until the 1970s, when the first surge of urban renewal had passed. This placed the efforts in a setting more hospitable to preservation. As Merlin H. Berg, a proponent of riverfront revival and rehabilitation, commented in 1982, "We are in the midst of a preservation fervor which has no parallel in American history. . . . Historic preservation has marched from an 'embattled cause' and now is part of the 'establishment.' " By the 1970s the Minneapolis Housing and Redevelopment Authority, the agency that spearheaded renewal, included rehabilitation of existing buildings as a desirable program element. Advocates for blending the old with the new found responsive audiences as the preservation movement grew from "the passion of a few" to "the interest of many."[15]

Legislation enacted from the 1960s helped protect historic resources and provide incentives for their development. The National Historic Preservation Act of 1966, a landmark in preservation legislation, fostered programs in the states by providing a process for reviewing the impact of federal projects on properties with historical significance. It also provided matching funds for state preservation offices and instituted a program of matching grants to further the preservation efforts of owners of properties on the National Register of Historic Places. And federal tax laws passed in 1976 and later encouraged rehabilitation of historic buildings and areas.[16]

No laggard in fostering a state program, the Minnesota legislature recognized historic sites as natural resources and opened the way for state funding in the Minnesota Omnibus Natural Resources and Recreation Act of 1963. In 1971 the state legislature, authorized by the National Historic Preservation Act, created several historic districts, including one incorporating the Falls of St. Anthony — which in turn was entered on the National Register of Historic Places. And in the same year the legislature adopted the Municipal Heritage Preservation Act, under which communities could form commissions to protect historically significant buildings or sites. In 1972 Minneapolis became the first Minnesota community to create such a commission.

Although many public interests had converged at the falls in the area's long history, never before had the interests been so numerous and so complex. The multilayered agencies tried to synchronize their efforts. The director of the Minnesota Historical Society, serving as the state historic preservation officer, was the liaison between the federal and state agencies in implementing the National Historic Preservation Act; he executed the program through the State Historic Preservation Office within the Society. The Minneapolis Heritage Preservation Commission, an advisory body to the city council which included a representative of the Hennepin County Historical Society, co-operated with the Minnesota Historical Society, extended local protection to city sites, and worked with other municipal agencies.

When the council adopted Central Riverfront Urban Design Guidelines in 1981, it included many that the commission had already formulated.[17]

The over-all development structure within Minneapolis city government, so complex that it was compared to Henry VIII's family tree, made co-ordination of riverfront revitalization challenging. A survey published in 1969 named twelve municipal units concerned with the river, including the Minneapolis Park Board (later Park and Recreation Board), the Minneapolis Planning Commission, the Office of the City Coordinator, the Minneapolis Industrial Development Commission (MIDC), and the Minneapolis Housing and Redevelopment Authority (MHRA). The structure was not static. An important change came in 1981 when the newly created Minneapolis Community Development Agency (MCDA), combining functions of a development division within the city co-ordinator's office, MIDC, and MHRA, assumed responsibilities for administering riverfront redevelopment projects. A component of the agency's program that was particularly significant to preservationists was the recognition and promotion of historical values in the falls area.[18]

Making strong efforts to co-ordinate riverfront plans and projects that emanated from municipal government, city officials encouraged voluntary consultations and at various times created interagency groups; in 1986 the Riverfront Technical Advisory Committee brought city experts together. Broad representation was also achieved in the Minneapolis Riverfront Alliance, a non-profit corporation that included representatives of MCDA, the Park and Recreation Board, the Minneapolis Heritage Preservation Commission, the Minnesota Historical Society, and private developers. Such efforts have been important in helping to integrate planning and to reconcile conflicting objectives revealed as agencies disagreed with one another, agencies disagreed with private developers, and neighborhood groups disagreed with agencies and private developers.[19]

The rejuvenation shaped by these forces of renewal, preservation, conflict, and conciliation began in 1962 when Reiko Weston, a Japanese immigrant, saw the Falls of St. Anthony while searching for a place to build a restaurant overlooking the river. "I saw this spot," she commented, "and I was so sure, this is the place." The location she chose was on the west bank on the river side of First Street South, between Fourth and Fifth avenues, where the Columbia flour mill had once stood. There, six years later, she opened the Fuji-Ya (which means "second to none"), a restaurant built over the remnants of the mill; its broad expanse of windows gave diners a river view. With the exception of the upper-lock facilities, the Fuji-Ya was the first new structure to appear for many years among the desolate west side's parking lots, gravel piles, and aged buildings used for storage.[20]

Across the street, a short distance from the Fuji-Ya, the First Street Station restaurant opened in 1975 in the former engine house of the Minneapolis Eastern Railway. The long, low, brick structure, built in 1914, had been abandoned in 1972. James Howe, who first saw the building when dining at the Fuji-Ya, remodeled it and soon after the restaurant opened enlarged it by adding three railroad box cars and a porte-cochère. The project was a sensitive adaptation of an existing structure and the first instance of adaptive re-use on the west side.[21]

The promising beginnings on the west side did not escalate into a boom. Although announcements of new projects occasionally appeared, several years passed before anything happened. Meanwhile, developments begun on the east side blossomed. In a historical perspective, the east-side boom was ironic. In the early years east-side aspirations were blunted by failures to develop the full potential of the water power and design a district capable of fostering major industrial growth. Now, while the west side lagged behind, the restaurants, shops, and housing units that blended the old with the new made the east side the pre-eminent place at the falls.

The rejuvenation began on Southeast Main, a cobblestone street that had once been a busy riverfront thoroughfare in the young city of St. Anthony. Between the Pillsbury A Mill and the Third Avenue Bridge, a two-block-long series of buildings — two of them dating from the 1850s — "had fallen derelict" as the industries, offices, and stores they had once housed moved out. The Pillsbury A Mill was the only structure still dedicated to its original use; the Main Street hydroelectric station, which had burned down and been rebuilt in 1911, closed in 1968.[22]

Peter Nelson Hall, a young architect with a strong interest in preservation and the falls, started the movement in 1969 when he purchased the Pracna building. Erected in 1890 as a saloon and home by Frank Pracna, the three-story structure with a red brick façade was a lively rendezvous for workmen from nearby industries until the onset of prohibition in 1919. By the time Hall acquired the Pracna, it had been used as a machine shop and warehouse. Hall began renovation immediately, and — like Pracna before him — used the upper floors as family living quarters for a time. Renovation continued after he

IN 1936 *Southeast Main Street was a little-used thoroughfare. This view shows the north side of the street from the Pracna building at left to the Salisbury-Satterlee building at right.*

BY 1987 *the same street was full of retail shops and restaurants. The Pracna building is to the right of the movie theater. Photograph by Alan Ominsky.*

THE TOWERS of Riverplace rose between the divided Hennepin Avenue Bridge, which spanned the east channel of the Mississippi, and the Third Avenue Bridge. The Nicollet Island Inn is the three-story buiding at lower right. Photograph by Regene Radniecki, 1984, courtesy Minneapolis Star and Tribune.

A Queen Anne-style house *built by Franklin C. Griswold in 1890 at 107–109 West Island Avenue on Nicollet Island. Photograph by Jack Renshaw, 1971.*

Significant progress *had been made in restoring the exterior of the Grove Street Flats on Nicollet Island when this photograph was taken in 1981. Photography by Michael Carroll, courtesy Minneapolis Star and Tribune.*

THE WHITNEY HOTEL *at Portland Avenue and First Street South was ready for its grand opening 1987. The Ceresota Elevator is to the left; to the right, across the river, is the Winslow House. Photograph by Alan Ominsky.*

THE FUJI-YA *on First Street South, between Fourth and Fifth avenues, in 1987.*
The Third Avenue Bridge and a tower of Riverplace can be glimpsed in the
background. Photograph by Alan Ominsky.

A NEW GATEHOUSE *was constructed in 1885 at South First Street between Fifth and Sixth avenues. It controlled flowage from the river into the "great canal." Courtesy Hennepin County Historical Society.*

AS ORIGINALLY PLANNED, *the Great River Road was to run directly over the remains of the gatehouse. When planners learned that the structure was too significant to destroy, the road was moved to the south. In 1986 Minnesota Historical Society archaeologists uncovered the gatehouse and remains of other buildings in the area, in order to mitigate the effects of road building and to determine the interpretive potential of the gatehouse. Photograph by Scott Anfinson.*

leased space to a corporation running a number of restaurants; in 1973 it opened Pracna on Main.[23]

Although observers acknowledged Hall's role in sparking activity on Southeast Main and advocating revitalization that was sensitive to the area's history, another developer captured the limelight. Louis Zelle, president of Jefferson Lines, Inc., whose company had acquired property on Southeast Main early in the twentieth century and later expanded its holdings, announced a plan for adaptive re-use of old buildings and new construction soon after the Pracna opened. Like the developers who would initiate later projects, he was encouraged to make a substantial private investment by a favorable tax structure and supportive public funding. St. Anthony Main — his restaurant, retail, entertainment, office, and residential development — grew in phases between 1976 and 1985, heartening riverfront proponents who had become more accustomed to proposals than to achievements.[24]

The St. Anthony Main complex began at the lower end of Main Street near Pillsbury A in brick buildings once used by the Salisbury and Satterlee mattress firm. As it expanded up the street, it absorbed buildings built in the 1850s — the brick Upton and the limestone Martin-Morrison, which were connected — and the brick Union Iron Works building (constructed in 1890) behind the Upton. A new structure intended to be compatible with the architecture of the old buildings bridged the gap between the Martin-Morrison and the Pracna. And the Pracna in turn connected with a new multiscreen movie theater extending under the Third Avenue Bridge. On Second Street, running parallel to Main, back from the river, Zelle also built the twelve-story Winslow House, a condominium tower named for the hotel near the river that had been a landmark in old St. Anthony.[25]

Internal and external walkways encouraged shoppers and diners to move through the St. Anthony Main complex. Adding to its ambience was the renovated cobblestone street, new street lighting, and landscaping provided by the city. The nearby Father Hennepin Bluffs, a regional park engulfing Lucy Wilder Morris Park, offered open space with trails, bridges, stairways to the river (designed for people), a pavilion, and picnic facilities.[26]

While St. Anthony Main was evolving, Riverplace, another eastside project, captured the attention of Minneapolitans. Announced in 1978 and opened in 1984, the development was built by Minneapolitan Robert Boisclair of the Boisclair Corporation and his Japanese partners joined as the East Bank Riverfront Partners. It was located opposite Nicollet Island facing Main Street on both sides of East Hennepin Avenue, in an area the city had earlier targeted for urban renewal. Like St. Anthony Main, Riverplace was a complex of shops, offices, and housing; it capitalized on the view and contributed to rejuvenation of the riverfront.[27]

The differences, however, were more striking than the similarities. While adaptive re-use of old buildings characterized St. Anthony Main, new construction dominated Riverplace. The low structures in St. Anthony Main blended into the landscape; the two towers featured in the Riverplace design — although compatible with the downtown skyline and high grain elevators in the milling district on the west side — were a departure for the east side near the falls. In addition, Zelle had consulted neighborhood groups in planning his project. Boisclair, who had attended De La Salle High School on Nicollet Island in the 1950s, seemed less attuned to the temper of southeast residents, despite his familiarity with the area and his experience as a developer.[28]

Boisclair's supporters — including influential De La Salle alumni Albert Hofstede, Minneapolis mayor in 1978–1979, and Louis DeMars, city council president at the same time — hailed Riverplace as a high-density project that would help stabilize the city's sagging population count and rejuvenate the east side. But opponents swiftly voiced their protests. Among them were State Representative Phyllis Kahn (who represented an East Side legislative district), members of the 57th District DFL Central Committee, and members of several Southeast neighborhood organizations who formed the Historic Riverfront Development Coalition and from this base drew support from other neighborhood organizations in the city.[29]

The coalition and others who joined the protest criticized the height of the towers, their proximity to the river and to historic Our Lady of Lourdes Roman Catholic Church, and the execution of so mammoth a project before the Heritage Preservation Commission had framed regulations for new construction in the historic district. They also protested benefits that the Boisclair project reaped from tax increment financing, a state-wide system by which a locality funded land acquisition, amenities, and facilities for development sites within specified districts; the locality was eventually to be repaid by increased taxes levied on the property after development. They charged that development at the Riverplace location would have occurred without such supports and that it was inappropriate to subsidize a project that did not provide for low-cost housing.

Heated comments (one labeling the project "a grotesque abuse of the riverfront") subsided as Boisclair made design compromises to meet some of the objections. He reduced the two towers' projected height from thirty-eight and thirty-four stories to twenty-seven, spaced them more widely to open views of Our Lady of Lourdes and the river, and placed them a little farther back from the river. He abandoned a plan to build one of the towers over the old Kronick warehouse, which its former owners had planned to renovate. He restored the almost century-old Brown-Ryan livery stable for adaptive re-use after it was moved to the Riverplace plaza from 20 Northeast Second Street. And, bowing to the historic character of the falls area, he dedicated a bust of William de la Barre, the great hydraulic engineer, in 1981 — the year Riverplace construction began. Although resentments still lingered when Riverplace opened in 1984, proponents and opponents could agree that the east side near the falls could no longer be called a neglected area.[30]

Compromises on the construction of Riverplace may have seemed slow in coming and tortuous to those witnessing the struggle. Compared with conflicts over Nicollet Island, however, the time span was short and the resolutions were definitive. By the 1960s the time had come to polish and place the "gem of the Mississippi" in its setting at the soon-to-be-refurbished riverfront. Since the early twentieth century, the island had been declining into a blighted area. From the residential enclave on the upper island, with houses dating from the 1870s, to the industrialized lower portion, fire, deterioration, demolition, and modifications made without comprehensive planning had taken their toll. After 1969, when the city adopted an urban renewal plan for the island, proposals involved historic preservationists, the MHRA/MCDA, the Park and Recreation Board, and the island's residents, who struggled "to retain their balance in the buffeting winds of city government."[31]

The MHRA, which in an early phase of renewal acquired property and razed buildings despite protests from the islanders, soon became sensitive to historic preservation. The creation of the St. Anthony Falls Historic District and the influence of the Heritage Preservation Commission encouraged selectivity in renewal. And surveys of island structures from historical and architectural perspectives — one of them commissioned by MHRA in 1973 — provided information helpful to everyone responsible for making decisions.[32]

The predominant controversies then focused on conflicting objectives of the MHRA/MCDA and the Park and Recreation Board, with the island's residents and developers working to protect their own interests. "When we look at the island," a park planning official commented in 1981, "we see all park. When MCDA thinks Nicollet Island, they see housing."[33]

From the mid-1970s to the mid-1980s, both agencies experienced frustrations. Commenting on the upper-island houses, where much of the controversy centered, an editorial writer observed that "city officials could be forgiven for wishing the things would just slide into the river and float away." While MHRA/MCDA was stabilizing some of the historic houses, the Park and Recreation Board pushed to acquire land for a riverfront regional park of some 150 acres with state funds available through the Metropolitan Council of the Twin Cities Area. The Board had compelling reasons to covet the island, for it could become the outstanding feature in the park. Hard-won agreements reached by 1986 included provisions for retaining houses on the upper island as a historic village, rehabilitating them, permitting a limited number of houses from other parts of the city to be moved to the village, and transferring land from the MCDA to the Board.[34] The adjustments between the agencies were as challenging as any of the real estate and water rights struggles that had highlighted the history of the falls area. The compromises, over-simplified here, are so sensitive that changes may be afoot while these words are being written.

Amid the interagency furor a development group adapted for use as a restaurant and inn a limestone structure erected in 1893 by a sash, door, and blind manufacturer on lower Nicollet Island. The MHRA had encouraged adaptive re-use of the three-story building — occupied for many years by the Salvation Army — after acquiring the property in 1972 as part of its renewal project. When opened in 1982 by the Nicollet Island Partners, Ltd., the Nicollet Island Inn was considered one of the city's "classiest restaurants and hotels." Its many attractions, however, were not strong enough to draw the patronage needed for survival, and the financially troubled inn closed in early 1986. The Park and Recreation Board, which in 1985 acquired the land and first rights to buy the building from the MCDA, leased the inn to a new operator, despite its earlier belief that a commercial enterprise did not fit in with its plans for the lower island.[35]

Through the Nicollet Island compromises and the purchase of nearby Boom Island, the Board acquired critical pieces of riverfront land needed for the regional park. Advocates of island housing and preservation also had cause for satisfaction when John Kerwin, an engineer and developer experienced in historic restoration, renovated the Grove Street flats on upper Nicollet. The limestone flats — a remnant of the luxury row houses Eastman had built in 1877–1878 — had deteriorated so badly that in 1971 the city declared them unfit for human habitation. Kerwin purchased the crumbling structure from a private owner in 1980, and, using the original floor plans, converted it into eighteen condominiums. Near the elegant restoration, completed in 1982, he then built a row of townhouses with a design intended to be compatible with the historic structure.[36]

Observing progress on the waterfront in the year the Grove Street condominiums opened, Mayor Donald M. Fraser wrote, "I believe the 1980s will be the decade of the River." Renewed activity in the west-side milling district, where revitalization had been stalled for several years, gave promise that the area would share in the progress. The Industry Square Development Company and the Center Companies, operating as the Mill River Limited Partnership, led the way by completing conversion of the St. Anthony Warehouse at First Street South and Third Avenue into an office building in 1985. The Hall and Dann Barrel Company had erected the four-story brick structure as two linked buildings between 1880 and 1906. After furnishing the millers with barrels and bags for many years, the factory became the St. Anthony Warehouse in 1920. The renovation overlooking the river, now called Mill Place, won an award in 1986 from the Minnesota Society of Professional Engineers for preservation of its original character.[37]

Down First Street South — past Mill Place, the First Street Station, and the Fuji-Ya into the heart of the milling district — the Hayber Development Group in 1985 began converting the 106-year-old Standard Mill at Portland Avenue into a luxury hotel called the Whitney. A worker at the site when the project began had problems visualizing the grimy old building as a hotel until he gazed across the Mississippi. "I didn't think there would be condominiums and hotels on the river," he said, "but that wound up looking pretty good." The Whitney Hotel, too, was looking pretty good as it neared completion in 1986. Its cream-brick exterior restored and its interior rebuilt into hotel rooms, penthouse suites, a dining room, and a bar, the six-story structure stood like a beacon in the delapidated district. Hayber's plans for further projects included two buildings clustered with the Standard — the Crown Roller Mill, a shell since it burned in 1983, and the Ceresota Elevator.[38]

The developments on the waterfront materialized because of the Falls of St. Anthony setting. A proposal made by the U.S. Army Corps of Engineers in 1983 threatened to damage that setting by diverting additional water from the falls, which were already dry for about 60 percent of the year. The Corps planned to increase hydropower production in response to the federal government's directive to increase the nation's use of water power. The plan provoked reactions touching on the historical role of the falls and current developments. Russell W. Fridley, director of the Minnesota Historical Society and State Historic Preservation Officer, pointed out that "the historical context of the Falls of St. Anthony is that of a natural resource developed for use rather than for beauty." Others contended that beauty, which required water flowing over the falls, was a key consideration in the redevelopment of the area. "It's not just river water that the hydroelectric-generating proposal would send down a tube," the *Minneapolis Star and Tribune* commented, "but potentially the city's hopes and ambitions for its riverfront as well."[39]

The Corps, which more than a century earlier had helped prevent the young industrial district from going "down a tube" by preserving the falls, quickly responded to the critics' concerns. In 1984 it proposed that flowage over the falls be reduced but magnified visually by adding ridges to the spillway (apron) surface. The Northern States Power Company, rather than the Corps, decided to plan for the additional power production. As of 1986, it had adopted in principle the feature the engineers had suggested and announced plans for building a facility on Hennepin Island near the plant opened in 1908, creating a three-acre park on the upper island, and connecting the park with St. Anthony Main. Aesthetic and other considerations, however, are under discussion and the debate may continue for some time.[40]

During the early phases of rejuvenation on the waterfront, an MHRA employee was asked when the riverfront would be completed. "Asking when the riverfront will be finished," he replied, "is like asking when the city will be finished. It never is."[41] Some projects now scheduled for the area near the falls, however, may materialize within the next few years. A span of the ornamented Broadway Avenue Bridge, built in 1887 and recently removed to make way for a new structure, has been relocated downriver to serve as a pedestrian walkway between Nicollet Island and the east riverbank. After considerable discussion about the need for replacement and the compatibility of proposed designs with the historic district, a new Hennepin Avenue suspension bridge is scheduled to replace the structure built in 1888, which in turn had replaced the second suspension bridge. The Park and Recreation Board, too, is developing lands and adding parcels needed for an integrated riverfront park. The Bergerud-Whitney

Corporation, whose principals are also members of the Hayber group, bought the First Street Station restaurant and the nearby Milwaukee Depot site fronting on Third Avenue South for a multipurpose development and have leased the Nicollet Island Inn from the Park Board. The developers of Mill Place announced proposals for converting buildings in the Washburn Crosby milling complex below the Whitney into offices and a milling museum, and for a new apartment tower near the buildings. And several agencies began working together to further an interpretive plan for the area.[42]

Construction of a portion of the Great River Road on the west bank in downtown Minneapolis has also begun. Proposed as a national project in 1938, the scenic highway along the Mississippi from Lake Itasca to the Gulf of Mexico has witnessed sporadic development. The program, which includes historic preservation and interpretation, parks, and scenic overlooks, has been an important factor in plans for the city's riverfront. When the first phase of the Minneapolis section (West River Parkway) has been built from Plymouth Avenue North downstream to Portland Avenue in the old milling district, realization of a continuous parkway along the river, envisioned so long ago, may be near. Preceding construction of the road, Minnesota Historical Society staff archaeologists, under a contract with the Park and Recreation Board, are excavating along the west bank to locate and explore sites important for preservation and interpretation.[43]

And what of the more distant future? When Hall and his family moved into the Pracna on the east bank, they felt "very much alone in the urban wilderness." Today city planners cite the riverfront as a prime downtown residential area where the population, they believe, may grow to ten thousand by the year 2000. However, problems experienced by Riverplace and some of the other restaurants and specialty shops have prompted questions about the future. Will the riverfront neighborhood grow fast enough and attract enough visitors to support developments already in place and sustain the momentum gained in the "decade of the river"? And will the tax structure and other conditions that favored the developments now in place continue to foster rehabilitation in the area near the cataract? Although the future is obscure, there are certainties revealed in the recent past: The riverfront is no longer the back door of the city, and the city has paid its respects to the falls area where its life began.[44]

Reference Notes

The following abbreviations are used throughout these notes:

MHS — Minnesota Historical Society
MMC — Minneapolis Mill Company
NA — National Archives
NSP — Northern States Power Company
SAC — St. Anthony Falls Water Power Company

CHAPTER 1 — A LANDMARK IN THE WILDERNESS

[1] William W. Folwell, *A History of Minnesota*, 1:13–29 (St. Paul, 1956).

[2] Hennepin, *A New Discovery of a Vast Country in America*, 184 (London, 1699).

[3] On the Indian names, see Elliott Coues, ed., *The Expeditions of Zebulon Montgomery Pike*, 1:91n. (New York, 1895), hereafter cited as Pike, *Expeditions*; Mentor L. Williams, ed., *Narrative Journal of Travels . . . 1820, Henry R. Schoolcraft*, 192 (East Lansing, Mich., 1953). For the quotation, see John Francis McDermott, ed., "Minnesota 100 Years Ago Described and Pictured by Adolph Hoeffler," in *Minnesota History*, 33:124 (Autumn, 1952).

[4] Hennepin, *New Discovery*, 184. See also Newton H. Winchell, "Hennepin at the Falls of St. Anthony," in Minnesota Academy of Science, *Bulletins*, 4:382 (Minneapolis, 1910).

[5] There are many versions of this legend. That given here follows Mary H. Eastman, *Chicóra and Other Regions of the Conquerors and the Conquered*, 32 (Philadelphia, 1854). For the verses below by Samuel W. Pond, see Harriet E. Bishop, *Floral Home; or, First Years of Minnesota*, 198 (New York, 1857).

[6] Folwell, *Minnesota*, 1:30; A. J. Hill, trans., "Relation of M. Penicaut," in *Minnesota Historical Collections*, 3:6 (St. Paul, 1880). The first edition of Hennepin's book, published in Paris, was entitled *Description de la Louisiane, Nouvelle Decouverte au Sud'Ouest de la Nouvelle France*. For the Carver quotation below, see his *Travels through the Interior Parts of North-America*, 66, 69, 70 (London, 1778).

[7] Mary W. Berthel, *Minnesota Under Four Flags*, n.p. (St. Paul, 1946).

[8] Folwell, *Minnesota*, 1:90; *American State Papers: Miscellaneous*, 1:942.

[9] Pike, *Expeditions*, 1:83, 227.

[10] Pike, *Expeditions*, 1:227, 231. For the quotation below, see page 311.

[11] *American State Papers: Indian Affairs*, 1:755; Pike, *Expeditions*, 1:238n.

[12] Francis Paul Prucha, *Broadax and Bayonet: The Role of the United States Army in the Development of the Northwest, 1815–1860*, 4, 9, 17–20 (Madison, 1953); Folwell, *Minnesota*, 1:71, 72, 131–134; Theodore C. Blegen, *Minnesota: A History of the State*, 81 (Minneapolis, 1963).

[13] Long, "Voyage in a Six-Oared Skiff to the Falls of Saint Anthony in 1817," in *Minnesota Historical Collections*, 2:34 (St. Paul, 1889). See also Folwell, *Minnesota*, 1:134.

[14] Folwell, *Minnesota*, 1:144, 438, 446; Forsyth, "Fort Snelling: Col. Leavenworth's Expedition to Establish It In 1819," in *Minnesota Historical Collections*, 3:140, 165 (St. Paul, 1880). On Mrs. Gooding and the quotation below, see page 155.

[15] John M. Callender, *New Light on Old Fort Snelling*, 9–15 (St. Paul, 1959).

[16] Theodore C. Blegen, "The 'Fashionable Tour' on the Upper Mississippi," in *Minnesota History*, 20:378–386 (December, 1939). Jarvis to William Jarvis, August 2, 1835, Jarvis Papers in the New York Academy of Medicine, New York City. The Minnesota Historical Society (hereafter abbreviated as MHS) has photo copies.

[17] Beltrami, *A Pilgrimage in Europe and America*, 2:205 (London, 1828); Latrobe, *The Rambler in North America*, 2:218 (New York, 1835); Bertha L. Heilbron, ed., "A 'Craven Lad' in Frontier Minnesota," in *Minnesota History*, 27:287 (December, 1946); Bremer, *The Homes of the New World*, 2:286 (London, 1853).

[18] Williams, ed., *Schoolcraft Narrative Journal*, 191.

[19] Catlin, *Letters and Notes on the Manners, Customs, and Condition of the North American Indians*, 2:131, plate 230 (London, 1841); *Northampton Courier* (Massachusetts), May 27, 1856. The MHS has a typed copy.

[20] For a concise review of these illustrators, see Newton H. Winchell and Warren Upham, *The Geology of Minnesota*, 2:318–329 (St. Paul, 1888).

[21] Leavenworth to Daniel Parker, November 10, 1819, Letters Received, Office of the Adjutant General, Record Group 94, National Archives. The MHS has a photo copy. Hereafter records in the National Archives are indicated by the symbol NA, followed by the record group (RG) number. It should be noted that the Mississippi River at the falls flows in a southeastward direction so that references to the east and west banks are approximations.

[22] Snelling to Thomas Jesup, August 16, 1824, Fort Snelling Consolidated Correspondence File, Office of the Quartermaster General, NARG 92. The MHS has a microfilm copy.

[23] Colhoun Diary, July 3, 1823, microfilm copy in MHS, original in private hands; George Henry Gunn, "Peter Garrioch at St. Peter's," in *Minnesota History*, 20:126 (June, 1939).

[24] Snelling to Jesup, August 16, 1824, Fort Snelling Consolidated Correspondence File, NARG 92; Folwell, *Minnesota*, 1:139.

[25] Folwell, *Minnesota*, 1:216, 438; June Drenning Holmquist and Jean A. Brookins, *Minnesota's Major Historic Sites: A Guide*, 9–11, 15 (St. Paul, 1963).

CHAPTER 2 — THE RISE OF ST. ANTHONY, 1837–1855

[1] Benjamin H. Hibbard, *A History of the Public Land Policies*, 144, 152–154 (New York, 1924); Victor J. Michaelson, *Some Legal Aspects of Public and Private Waters in Minnesota*, 7 (Minnesota Department of Conservation, Division of Waters, *Bulletins*, no. 4 — St. Paul, 1951); Rome G. Brown, *Limitations of Federal Control of Water Powers: An Argument Before the National Waterways Commission*, 2 (New York, [1911]).

[2] Folwell, *Minnesota*, 1:92, 216–220.

[3] Folwell, *Minnesota*, 1:217; *Sale of Fort Snelling Reservation*, 16 (40 Congress, 3 session, *House Executive Documents*, no. 9 — serial 1372).

[4] See *Sale of Fort Snelling Reservation*, 17; *Fort Snelling Investigation*, 48 (35 Congress, 1 session, *House Reports*, no. 351 — serial 965); Folwell, *Minnesota*, 1:218–226, 244.

⁵ Folwell, *Minnesota*, 1:159, 422. For a map of the reservation, see page 17.

⁶ J. D. Doty to John Bell, August 12, 1841, a handwritten copy in the Henry H. Sibley Papers, MHS; Rodney C. Loehr, "Franklin Steele, Frontier Businessman," in *Minnesota History*, 27:310 (December, 1946); Henry T. Welles, *Autobiography and Reminiscences*, 2:12 (Minneapolis, 1899); "Biography of Franklin Steele," a nine-page manuscript eulogy prepared at the time of Steele's death in 1880, MHS. The latter includes a statement that it was President Andrew Jackson who advised Steele to go West.

⁷ Lawrence Taliaferro Journal, July 15, 1838, Taliaferro Papers, MHS; *St. Paul Daily Pioneer*, June 21, 1874; Folwell, *Minnesota*, 1:452–454.

⁸ Return I. Holcombe and William H. Bingham, eds., *Compendium of History and Biography of Minneapolis and Hennepin County*, 61–63 (Chicago, 1914); Warren Upham and Rose B. Dunlap, comps., *Minnesota Biographies, 1655–1912*, 66, 222, 655, 662 *(Minnesota Historical Collections*, vol. 14 — St. Paul, 1912).

⁹ Holcombe and Bingham, eds., *Compendium*, 61.

¹⁰ James L. Greenleaf, "Report on the Water-Power of the Mississippi River and Some of Its Tributaries," in Department of the Interior, Tenth Census, *Reports on the Water-Power of the United States*, part 2, p. 128, 169 (Washington, D.C., 1887). Greenleaf and others give the total drop of the river in the falls area as 70 to 75 feet. A table appearing in part 1, p. xxx–xxxii, of George F. Swain's "General Introduction" to the above reports gives fall data for the nation's largest developed water powers. On Minnesota's forests, see Agnes M. Larson, *History of the White Pine Industry in Minnesota*, 5–7 (Minneapolis, 1949); James E. Defebaugh, *History of the Lumber Industry of America*, 1:275 (Chicago, 1906). A detailed description of the forests bordering the Mississippi appears in the *St. Paul and Minneapolis Daily Pioneer Press*, December 24, 1880. The quotation is from the *St. Anthony Express*, February 7, 1852.

¹¹ Larson, *White Pine Industry*, 14–25; Daniel Stanchfield, "History of Pioneer Lumbering on the Upper Mississippi and Its Tributaries," in *Minnesota Historical Collections*, 9:342 (St. Paul, 1901).

¹² Robert S. Rantoul, *Personal Recollections*, 26 (Cambridge, Mass., 1916); *Stimpson's Boston Directory*, 137 (Boston, 1846); *Prairie du Chien Patriot* (Wisconsin), October 13, 1846; B. H. Cheever to Caleb Cushing, July 10, 1846, Cushing Papers, Library of Congress. The MHS has microfilm copies of all items cited from this collection. For the Cushing-Rantoul venture in the St. Croix Valley, see James Taylor Dunn, *The St. Croix: Midwest Border River*, 82, 85 (New York, 1965).

¹³ Stanchfield, in *Minnesota Historical Collections*, 9:328; Cheever to Alexander Ramsey, October 13, 1849, Ramsey Papers, MHS.

¹⁴ Stanchfield, in *Minnesota Historical Collections*, 9:328–331, 333, 339; Cheever to Ramsey, October 13, 1849, Ramsey Papers; *Express*, October 27, 1855. Cheever and the *Express* give $12,000 as the amount the easterners paid Steele, but Stanchfield states that the sum was $10,000.

¹⁵ Stanchfield, in *Minnesota Historical Collections*, 9:333–335; Rodney C. Loehr, "Caleb D. Dorr and the Early Minnesota Lumber Industry," in *Minnesota History*, 24:128–130 (June, 1943).

¹⁶ The dam is described, with some variations, in the testimony of William R. Marshall, Sumner W. Farnham, E. S. Brown, and Ard Godfrey in Ashley C. Morrill, James A. Lovejoy, *et al. v.* the St. Anthony Falls Water Power Company, File No. 6098, in the office of the clerk of district court, Hennepin County Courthouse, Minneapolis. References to this firm are abbreviated hereafter as SAC. On the sawmill, see *Wisconsin Herald* (Lancaster), June 24, 1848; Larson, *White Pine Industry*, 34; Grace Lee Nute, ed., "A Western Jaunt in 1850," in *Minnesota History*, 12:163 (June, 1931). Both the mill and dam are described in Isaac At-

water, ed., *History of the City of Minneapolis*, 527, 537 (New York, 1893); and in E. S. Seymour, *Sketches of Minnesota*, 123 (New York, 1850). The latter states that the mill used the water at an eight-foot head.

[17] Stanchfield, in *Minnesota Historical Collections*, 9:335–339.

[18] Larson, *White Pine Industry*, 34; Steele to Sibley, December 18, 1848, Sibley Papers.

[19] The *Express* of October 27, 1855, states that Steele purchased Boom Island from Peter Quinn in 1846, but a quit-claim deed in the Sibley Papers, dated January 22, 1848, shows that Steele acquired it from Pierre Bottineau.

[20] Stanchfield, in *Minnesota Historical Collections*, 9:329; Proclamation (copy) in Incoming Correspondence, and Letter Book, August 31, September 11, 1848, both in St. Croix Falls Land Office Records in the Minnesota State Archives, St. Paul. Steele's purchase is recorded in Abstract of Sales, St. Croix Falls Land Office, July 24–September 8, 1848, General Land Office Records, NARG 49. William Cheever purchased the land where the University of Minnesota now stands. In 1849 he platted it as "St. Anthony City," a village later absorbed by Steele's St. Anthony. See Deed Book A-1, p. 20, office of the register of deeds, Hennepin County Courthouse, Minneapolis, and Marion D. Shutter, *History of Minneapolis*, 1:658 (Minneapolis, 1923).

[21] Shutter, *Minneapolis*, 1:86, 435; William R. Marshall, manuscript plat of St. Anthony Falls, MHS.

[22] *Express*, October 27, 1855; W. A. Cheever to B. H. Cheever, March 7, 1848, Cushing Papers. Drafts for "improvements at the Falls" drawn on Rantoul and payable in Boston are listed in Steele Account Book, July 10, 1847–November 3, 1848, Steele Papers, MHS.

[23] Steele to Sibley, November 27, 1848, Sibley Papers.

[24] Steele to Godfrey, October 11, 1848, Steele Papers; Stanchfield, in *Minnesota Historical Collections*, 9:334. Godfrey's purchase is recorded in two deeds dated October 10, 1849, in Ramsey County Deed Book A, 363–366, in the Minnesota State Archives.

[25] Ramsey County Deed Book A, 166.

[26] See Ramsey County Deed Book A, 368; *Express*, October 27, 1855; *Minneapolis Daily Chronicle*, February 24, 1867. The townsmen's attitude toward Steele is exemplified by an article about him in the *Express*, April 15, 1853. For a rare story praising Taylor, see the *Minnesota Pioneer* (St. Paul), October 17, 1850.

[27] John W. North to George S. Loomis, October 13, 1850, North Papers. The papers are owned by and quoted with the permission of the Henry E. Huntington Library and Art Gallery, San Marino, Calif. The MHS has microfilm copies of all items cited from this collection. On the mills, see *Minnesota Pioneer*, November 14, 1850; *Minnesota Democrat* (St. Paul), December 24, 1851. On the suits, see Taylor *v.* Steele and Taylor *v.* St. Anthony Mill Company, File Nos. 158 and 170 in the office of the clerk of district court, Ramsey County Courthouse, St. Paul. A summons in File No. 158 names Ira Kingsley and Anson Northup as the two contesting pre-emptors. Steele settled his dispute with these rival claimants and secured his hold on Hennepin Island in 1854. For details of the settlement, see Ira Kingsley to Edmund Rice (power of attorney) May 12, 1854, and an indenture between Kingsley and Steele, June 28, 1854, in Northern States Power Company Deed and Lease File, in the offices of the company, Minneapolis. References to this firm are hereafter abbreviated as NSP.

[28] A copy of the contract is in Steele *v.* Taylor, File No. 278, Ramsey County District Court.

[29] Material here and in the following two paragraphs is drawn from Steele *v.* Taylor, File No. 278, Ramsey County District Court. Taylor claimed that Steele's agent could not get certificates from the specified banks, not because they did not issue them, but because Steele wanted to borrow the money and then deposit it.

[80] Secombe v. Taylor, File No. 397, Ramsey County District Court.

[81] Steele v. Taylor, File No. 278, Ramsey County District Court.

[82] North to Loomis, May 15, 1853, January 1, 1854, North Papers.

[83] Steele v. Taylor, 1 Minnesota 274 (Gil. 210); Secombe v. Steele, 61 United States Reports 94. The Minnesota Supreme Court's ruling in Steele v. Secombe is recorded in Territorial Docket A, 1852–58, File No. 82, in the office of the clerk of the Supreme Court, Minnesota State Capitol, St. Paul.

[84] North to Loomis, September 3, October 13, 1850; May 1, 15, 1853, North Papers.

[85] Loehr, in Minnesota History, 27:311, 318; Minnesota Pioneer, May 29, 1851; Express, October 27, 1855. On the boom companies, see note 43, below. Steele's name appears among the incorporators of several railroads in the 1850s. For an example, see Minnesota Territory, Laws, 1853, p. 27–32.

[36] Steele to Sibley, January 21, February 18, 1851, Sibley Papers.

[37] Stevens to Sibley, March 2, 7, 1851, Sibley Papers.

[38] Vincent C. Hopkins, Dred Scott's Case, 4, 156 (New York, 1951); on the purchase by Sanford, Gebhard, and Davis discussed here and below, see Hennepin County Register of Deeds, Book 2, p. 53–56, Book 3, p. 364–368. On Davis and Gebhard, see Henry Wilson, comp., The Directory of the City of New-York, 1852–53, 160, 235 (New York, 1852); Wilson, comp., Trow's New York City Directory, 1855–56, 316 (New York, 1855).

[39] Sanford to Sibley, May 9, 1853, Gebhard to Sibley, May 9, 1853, Sibley Papers. On the purchase of Godfrey's interest (May 23, 1853), see Hennepin County Register of Deeds, Book 2, p. 50.

[40] Power of Attorney to Chute, November 4, 1854, in Hennepin County Register of Deeds, Book 3, p. 154. On Chute, see "Some Reminiscences Dictated by Charles R. Chute, June 20–21, 1921," a typewritten manuscript in the Richard Chute Papers, MHS, hereafter cited as Chute, "Reminiscences"; Atwater, ed., History of Minneapolis, 532; Welles, Autobiography, 2:61, 186; Chute's testimony in Morrill, Lovejoy, et al. v. SAC, File No. 6098, Hennepin County District Court; and Ferdinand Suydam, et al. v. William Ewing, Richard Chute, et al., Supreme Court for the City and County of New York, NARG 21. On Steele's transfer of a one-eighth interest to Chute and Prince for $20,500 (May 1, 1855), see Hennepin County Register of Deeds, Book D, 411–417. See also Prince to Chute, October 25, 1854, Chute Papers; Upham and Dunlap, Minnesota Biographies, 616.

[41] Express, August 13, December 17, 1853, July 21, October 27, 1855.

[42] On the sawmills and their production, see Express, May 31, 1851, July 30, 1852, October 27, 1855; Larson, White Pine Industry, 34; Daily Minnesotian (St. Paul), February 7, 1856. Production figures for lumber in this period are unreliable. On leases and mill operators, see Welles, Autobiography, 2:13; Memorandum of Agreement between Steele and C. D. and A. H. Dorr, July 23, 1852, Steele Papers; Steele v. S. W. Farnham, File No. 526, Ramsey County District Court; Atwater, ed., History of Minneapolis, 537; Articles of Agreement between A. W. Taylor and Farnham and Stimson, October 21, 1851, File No. 278, Ramsey County District Court.

[43] Stanchfield, in Minnesota Historical Collections, 9:343. On the incorporation of the Mississippi, St. Anthony, and Rum River Boom companies, respectively, see Minnesota Territory, Laws, 1851, p. 18–22, 33–36; 1852, p. 23–25.

[44] On log rafting below the falls, see Minnesota Pioneer, April 15, 1852; Welles, Autobiography, 2:22. The quotations are from the Express, June 9, 1855; Horace R. Bigelow Diary, November 21, 1853, MHS.

Other wood-using industries also prospered. In 1855 A. King and Loring and James A. Lovejoy built two shingle mills on Cataract Island; Stearns and Mansur, who were manufacturing furniture in St. Anthony as early as 1851, constructed a new factory at the falls in 1853; and the same year O. H. Rogers and Company erected a four-story building on the east bank to house planing and turning machines, a cabinet and chair factory, and a sash, door, and blind establishment. See *Express*, June 7, 1851, August 6, 1853, October 27, 1855; Shutter, *Minneapolis*, 1:335.

⁴⁵ Steele Ledger, 1851–53, p. 208, Steele Papers; Atwater, ed., *History of Minneapolis*, 576; *Northwestern Miller*, 8:121; *Minneapolis Tribune*, May 15, 1881 (quote), hereafter cited as *Tribune*. All citations in this book are to the daily *Tribune*. On the community's enthusiasm for the mill, see *Express*, October 8, 1852, November 26, 1853.

⁴⁶ Leasing arrangements are in Samuel Chute *v.* John W. Eastman, *et al.*, File No. 2417, Hennepin County District Court. On the mill, see Atwater, ed., *History of Minneapolis*, 577; *Express*, July 1, 1854, October 27, 1855; *Northwestern Miller*, vol. 30, Holiday issue, 31 (1890); *Daily Minnesotian*, October 25 (quote), November 27, 1854; Shutter, *Minneapolis*, 1:350.

⁴⁷ Shutter, *Minneapolis*, 1:85; Minnesota Manuscript Census Schedules, St. Anthony, 1850, MHS; *Express*, January 28, 1854, January 13, October 27, 1855.

⁴⁸ *Express*, June 7, July 12, 1851, April 29, May 6, 1853; *New-York Daily Tribune*, July 12, 1850; Horace B. Hudson, ed., *A Half Century of Minneapolis*, 36 (Minneapolis, 1908); *Weekly Minnesotian*, November 20, 1852; Ann North to Loomis, November 6, December 9, 1849, North Papers; Lucile M. Kane, "Governing a Frontier City: Old St. Anthony, 1855–72," in *Minnesota History*, 35:122 (September, 1956); Minnesota Territory, *Laws*, 1855, p. 10–18; St. Anthony, "Council Proceedings," June 18, 1855, a manuscript volume in the office of the city clerk, Minneapolis.

CHAPTER 3 — THE BIRTH OF MINNEAPOLIS, 1836–1855

¹ Stambaugh's partner in this effort was William L. D. Ewing of Illinois. See Lawrence Taliaferro, "Auto-Biography," in *Minnesota Historical Collections*, 6:221 (St. Paul, 1894). For Stambaugh's efforts, see Stambaugh to Jesup, February 17, 1836; Jesup to Stambaugh (copy), May 19, 1836; Stambaugh to Cross, September 7, 1836, and Cross's endorsement; Stambaugh to [Andrew Jackson], October 9, 1836; Cross to C. A. Harris (copy), October 19, 1836; William Davenport to Roger Jones, May 27, 1837. For pressures on the war department, see Richard M. Young and J. M. Robinson to Jesup, December 18, 1838, enclosed with Stambaugh's letter to Jackson; Stambaugh to J. D. Doty, March 26, 1841, and Jesup's endorsement; Stambaugh to Jesup, April 20, 1841. All correspondence cited above is in Fort Snelling Consolidated Correspondence File, NARG 92; photo copies in MHS.

² Harris to Luther Reily, April 1, 1838, and endorsements, Fort Snelling Consolidated Correspondence File, NARG 92 (photo copy MHS); A. D. Stuart to [Sibley], November 28, 1838, and Sibley to Lucius Lyon, February 10, 1839, Sibley Papers. The MHS has a photostatic copy of the latter; the original is in the University of Michigan Library, Ann Arbor. Sibley was technically right in stating that the falls in 1839 were in the possession of the government since Steele had not yet bought his claim on the east side.

³ Henry Stanton to Joel R. Poinsett, January 16, 1839 (manuscript copy), Sibley Papers.

⁴ W. T. Norton, "Forgotten Statesmen of Illinois: Hon. Robert Smith," in *Journal of the Illinois State Historical Society*, 8:437 (October, 1915); *Fort Snelling Investigation*, 142; Ramsey County Deed Book A, 248, 250–252; William L. Larned to Sibley, December 8, 1852, February 23, 1853, Sibley Papers.

⁵ *Sale of Fort Snelling Reservation*, 36. The house was built some time between 1824 and 1833.

⁶ *Sale of Fort Snelling Reservation,* 38, 39.

⁷ John H. Stevens, *Personal Recollections of Minnesota and Its People, and Early History of Minneapolis,* 24, 27–29 (Minneapolis, 1890); Atwater, ed., *History of Minneapolis,* 981; Holcombe and Bingham, eds., *Compendium,* 106. The quote is from the *Express,* January 13, 1855.

⁸ *Sale of Fort Snelling Reservation,* 39, 58; Sibley to Alexander Ramsey, April 23, 1850, Ramsey Papers; [George E. Warner], *History of Hennepin County and the City of Minneapolis,* 372 (Minneapolis, 1881). On Mitchell's association with Rice in another transaction, see Folwell, *Minnesota,* 1:370.

⁹ Smith to Sibley, February 1, 1853, Sibley Papers. Rice's sale is shown in Hennepin County Register of Deeds, Book A, 34. The deed is dated October 19, 1853, and conveys a three-sixteenths interest. For Northup's and Russell's claims, see Declaratory Statements Nos. 220 and 897, in Pre-emption Proofs, Patent Records, Stillwater Land Office, NARG 49.

Fridley, a lawyer, was a citizen of Kane County, Illinois, living there from 1835 until his death in 1898, according to his obituary in the *Twice-A-Week Republican* (Geneva, Illinois) June 4, 1898. Huy, a lumberman, settled in Minneapolis in 1852. See Upham and Dunlap, *Minnesota Biographies,* 359. Brown resided at various times in the 1850s in St. Anthony. See Hennepin County Register of Deeds, Book K, 413; *Edward Martin v. B. F. Brown, et al.,* File No. 223, Hennepin County District Court.

¹⁰ Conclusions concerning the occupations of the claimants were reached by comparing the list of persons who bought reservation land (1855) in *Fort Snelling Investigation,* 424–430; the list of incorporators of the townsite of Minneapolis appended to the plat in Hennepin County Register of Deeds, Plat Book A-1, p. 23; Upham and Dunlap, *Minnesota Biographies;* and the United States Manuscript Census Schedules, 1857, for Hennepin and Ramsey counties, the originals of which are in the National Archives. The MHS has photostatic copies. For an example of the influences brought to bear in the applications for claims, see A. S. Molony to John Stevens, September 29, 1851, Stevens Papers, MHS.

¹¹ North to G. S. Loomis, January 12, 1851, North Papers.

¹² For an example, see Francis Lee to Sibley, November 4, 1852, Sibley Papers.

¹³ *Minnesota Pioneer,* January 22, 1852 (quote); Alexander Faribault to [Sibley], March [n.d.], 1850, Steele to Sibley, March 12, 1850, Sibley Papers; *Express,* June 17, December 9, 1854.

¹⁴ The quotation, written by an unidentified author, appears in Atwater, ed., *History of Minneapolis,* 80. See also *Express,* March 24, 1855.

¹⁵ On the extension of the survey lines, see *Express,* July 16, 1853; for an example of an arrangement made by settlers for protecting claims, see Articles of Agreement, Franklin Steele and Joseph R. Brown with thirty-four settlers [listed], May 20, 1850, Martin McLeod Papers, MHS. See also Charles J. Ritchey, "Claim Associations and Pioneer Democracy in Early Minnesota," in *Minnesota History,* 9:86–91 (June, 1928); Shutter, *Minneapolis,* 1:97; *Express,* July 23, 1852, April 8, 1853, July 22, 1854; and Resolutions of the Military Claim Association, signed by Henry M. Rice, April 2, 1853, Stevens Papers.

¹⁶ Atwater, ed., *History of Minneapolis,* 33; *Express,* February 21, 1852.

¹⁷ Minnesota Territory, *Laws,* 1849, p. 161.

¹⁸ Sibley to Alexander Ramsey, May 7, 22, 1850, Ramsey Papers; *Congressional Globe,* 31 Congress, 2 session, 432–434; *Fort Snelling Investigation,* 48; United States, *Statutes at Large,* 10:36.

¹⁹ *Express,* December 24, 1853, December 9, 1854; Steele to Stevens, August 20, 1854, Rice to Stevens, February 4, 1855, Stevens Papers. Smith was in the vanguard of those urging government surveys, which were completed in 1853. Two other mill-claim owners — Roswell P. Russell and Marquis L. Olds — occupied strategic

positions in the Minneapolis land office when it opened in 1854. See Atwater, ed.,
History of Minneapolis, 41; Smith to John Wilson, October 16, 1852, and J. J.
Abert to Jefferson Davis, October 25, 1853, in Fort Snelling Abandoned Military
Reservation File, NARG 49.

[20] Smith to John Wilson, September 21, 1854, Minneapolis and Lower Minneapolis Townsite File, NARG 49.

[21] Minnesota Territory, *Laws,* 1854, p. 162; Folwell, *Minnesota,* 1:431. For examples of the pressures exerted by Minnesotans, see A. E. Ames to Stevens, January 7, 14, February 7, 23, 1855, and Henry M. Rice to Stevens, February 4, 1855,
Stevens Papers.

[22] *Congressional Globe,* 33 Congress, 2 session, 487–489. See also Folwell, *Minnesota,* 1:431; Rice to Stevens, February 4, 1855, Stevens Papers.

[23] *North-Western Democrat* (Minneapolis), March 31, 1855; *Fort Snelling Investigation,* 424–430. Possible explanations of the small number of purchasers are
that only original claimants of large blocks of land, since subdivided, would
show among the buyers, and that only heads of families would be listed.

[24] Hennepin County Register of Deeds, Book A, 12, 34, 48, Book D, 361, 422–
428, 431–438, 440–450; Minneapolis Mill Company, Property Record Book, in NSP
files. References to Minneapolis Mill are hereafter abbreviated as MMC. The four
owners not mentioned in the text were: Joseph Day, Jacob S. Elliott, Isaac Newton, and George K. Swift.

[25] Washburn to Smith, December 7, 1852, Washburn to "Dear Brother," April
24, 1853, both in Cyrus Woodman Papers, State Historical Society of Wisconsin,
Madison; Clare L. Marquette, "The Business Activities of C. C. Washburn," 133,
175, 211 (University of Wisconsin, Ph.D. thesis, 1940), microfilm copy, MHS. On
Morrison, see Upham and Dunlap, *Minnesota Biographies,* 526; Atwater, ed.,
History of Minneapolis, 615; *Daily Minnesotian,* February 20, 1855.

[26] *Minnesota Pioneer,* August 28, 1851; *Express,* February 18, 1854; Atwater, ed.,
History of Minneapolis, 536; Edward A. Bromley, "The Old Government Mills at
the Falls of St. Anthony," in *Minnesota Historical Collections,* vol. 10, part 2,
p. 643 (St. Paul, 1905).

[27] *Minnesota Pioneer,* February 13, 20, June 13, 1850, August 28, 1851; Atwater,
ed., *History of Minneapolis,* 536; Bromley, in *Minnesota Historical Collections,*
vol. 10, part 2, p. 641.

[28] *Express,* August 6, 1853, June 17, 1854, October 27, 1855; *Daily Minnesotian,*
November 12, 1856; Shutter, *Minneapolis,* 1:307–309, 394, 437, 571–575, 606, 609.

[29] *Express,* December 24, 1853; *Tribune,* August 1, 1880.

[30] *Express,* November 5, 12, 1852.

[31] Minnesota Territory, *Laws,* 1852, p. 51, 1854, p. 86; Hennepin County Register
of Deeds, Plat Book A-1, p. 23; Jessie Marcley, *The Minneapolis City Charter,*
3–5 (Minneapolis, 1925).

[32] *Express,* May 14, 1852, April 15, 1854; *Minnesota Republican* (St. Anthony and
Minneapolis), December 1, 1857. The ambivalent attitude toward the East which
characterized the communities continued to be sharply defined throughout the
nineteenth century and evidences of it still remained in 1965.

[33] *Express,* June 10, 1854. Examples of criticism of the East and faith in the
West appear in the *Express,* February 14, March 6, June 18, December 31, 1852;
Tribune, June 20, 1867.

[34] Bertha L. Heilbron, ed., "Bridging the Mississippi," in *Minnesota History,*
29:32 (March, 1948); *Express,* September 20, 1854, January 20, 27 (quote), 1855.

[35] Figures on St. Paul's population in 1855 vary widely. See J. Fletcher Williams,
A History of the City of Saint Paul, 359 (Minnesota Historical Collections, vol. 4 —
St. Paul, 1876); "Census of the Twin Cities," in *Northwest Magazine,* September,
1885, p. 17; *Daily Pioneer and Democrat* (St. Paul), December 27, 1855; *Weekly*

Pioneer and Democrat, October 30, 1856. See also *Express,* cited in *Daily Minnesotian,* July 21, 1854.

[36] Lucile M. Kane, "Rivalry for a River," in *Minnesota History,* 37:309–311 (December, 1961); John North to G. S. Loomis, February 20, 1853, North Papers. A review of the commercial and manufacturing benefits St. Anthony and Minneapolis hoped to gain from navigation appears in the *Falls Evening News* (St. Anthony and Minneapolis), December 18, 1858.

CHAPTER 4 — EAST SIDE — WEST SIDE, 1856–1869

[1] For the charters discussed here and below, see Minnesota Territory, *Laws,* 1856, p. 215, 236–239.

[2] On the dam described here and below, see Greenleaf, in *Reports on the Water-Power of the United States,* part 2, map following 162, and 171–177; Minneapolis and St. Anthony Union Board of Trade, *Reports,* 1868, p. 3; Herbert W. Meyer, *Builders of Northern States Power Company,* 89 [Minneapolis, 1957]; Shutter, *Minneapolis,* 1:331; *Daily Minnesotian,* December 22, 1858; *St. Paul Daily Press,* January 26, 1867; William de la Barre to Robert F. Pack, p. 12, a report of 60 pages, dated November, 1924, in NSP Correspondence Files, hereafter cited as De la Barre to Pack, November, 1924; testimony of E. S. Brown in Morrill, Lovejoy, *et al. v.* SAC, File No. 6098, Hennepin County District Court. Figures for the total length of the dam and related installations vary from 3,574.5 to 3,670 feet. Most sources state that the bolts fastening the dam to the river bed were oak, but a few claim that they were made of iron. See, for example, *Falls Evening News,* November 28, 1857.

[3] SAC, Minutes, April 26, May 9, 10, 1856, in NSP files. Steele held 1,800 shares of stock; Davis, 1,200; Sanford, 600; Gebhard, 600; Chute, 300; and Prince, 300. The capital stock was increased at the meeting from $160,000 to $640,000.

[4] Richard Chute to Beach and Beman, September 25, 1868, Chute Papers.

[5] Chute to Davis and Gebhard, February 6, 1861, Steele Papers.

[6] On the Sibley land purchase, see *Express,* August 30, 1856; on the sale of the mortgage and the lawsuits, see W. H. Gebhard *v.* SAC, File No. 755; F. C. Gebhard and T. E. Davis *v.* SAC, File No. 1739; W. H. Gebhard *v.* SAC, *et al.,* File No. 1753, all in the Hennepin County District Court. For an account of the westerners' strenuous efforts to meet payments on the debt to W. H. Gebhard, see Chute to Steele, November 15, 1860, Steele Papers.

[7] Chute to Beach and Beman, September 25, 1868, and C. R. Chute, "Reminiscences," 13, Chute Papers; Butterfield to Steele, July 18, 1865, and Chute to Steele, September 27, October 4, 1865, Steele Papers. The total sums were arrived at by adding the amounts of the individual notes mentioned in these sources.

[8] Henry Reynolds to Steele, March 31, 1860, Steele Papers.

[9] Chute to Steele, January 26, 1859 (quote), February 4, April 13, 23, August 28, 1860, and Chute and Prince to Steele, November 5, 1859, Steele Papers; Chute to Beach and Beman, September 25, 1868, Chute Papers. In 1859 the stockholders considered issuing bonds worth $150,000 but never did so. See *Statement of St. Anthony Falls Water-Power Company First Mortgage Bonds,* 3 (New York, 1859), a leaflet in the MHS.

[10] Chute to Steele, March 2, 1859, Steele Papers.

[11] Chute's efforts are described in his letters to Steele of March 10, 29, April 13, 26, September 28, 1859, and April 13, 1860, Steele Papers. The quotations are from the last two letters.

[12] Chute to Steele, February 6, 1861, Steele Papers.

[13] Frederick Gebhard to Steele, October 16, 1860, September 3, 1861; Chute to Steele, February 6, 1861; all in the Steele Papers.

[14] Chute to Steele, April 23, 1860, January 15, 1864, Steele Papers.

[15] Chute to Steele, September 27, 1865, April 12, 1866 (quote), Steele Papers; *Minneapolis Daily Chronicle,* May 24, 1867.

[16] M. Brayman to Steele, January 5, 1866, Steele Papers; Chute to Beach and Beman, September 25, 1868, Chute Papers; SAC, Minutes, September 29, 1868; *Tribune,* September 10, 1868. In addition to those named in the text, the purchasers were: A. B. Barton, Thomas F. Andrews, J. K. Sidle, H. G. Sidle, H. F. Brown, J. R. Gilfillan, John Dudley, and A. C. Morrill.

[17] *Tribune,* September 10, 11, 1868. The complaint may be found in John Martin *et al. v.* Richard Chute *et al.,* File No. 3080, Hennepin County District Court.

[18] SAC, Minutes, September 29, 30, October 3, 1868; Martin *v.* Chute, File No. 3080, Hennepin County District Court.

[19] MMC, Minutes, May 15, 1856, October 7, 1857, November 15, 1865. On November 15, 1865, Robert Smith's stock was actually held by his brother William.

[20] Norton, in *Illinois State Historical Society Journal,* 8:428; *Biographical Directory of the American Congress, 1774–1961,* p. 1622, 1779, 1780 (Washington, D.C., 1961); Marquette, "The Business Activities of C. C. Washburn," 212; Charles E. Flandrau, *Encyclopedia of Biography of Minnesota,* 1:142 (Chicago, 1900); Israel G. Hunt, *Elihu and Cadwallader Washburn: A Chapter in American Biography,* 14 (New York, 1925); Atwater, ed., *History of Minneapolis,* 546, 550.

[21] William C. Edgar, *The Medal of Gold,* 61 (Minneapolis, 1925).

[22] Ignatius Donnelly made the remark. After he was reprimanded for it, he observed that he spoke "necessarily under some heat." See *Congressional Globe,* 40 Congress, 2 session, 235.

[23] C. C. Washburn to Cyrus Woodman, September 17, 1865, Woodman Papers; MMC, Minutes, November 15, 1865, October 9, 1869. Since no meetings were held between November, 1868, and October, 1869, there is no record that the stock passed directly from William Smith to C. C. Washburn. It is known, however, that Washburn held it on the latter date. Washburn's name first appears as company president in the minutes of November 15, 1865.

[24] Washburn to Woodman, January 1, 1858, Woodman Papers; Smith to Washburne, September 20, 30, 1858, Elihu B. Washburne Papers, Library of Congress. Elihu, unlike his brothers, used a terminal "e" on his name.

[25] MMC, Minutes, May 15, 17, 1856. For examples of personal loans to the company, see Smith to E. B. Washburne, September 30, 1858, Washburne Papers; Welles, *Autobiography,* 2:84.

[26] MMC, Minutes, May 15, 17, 1856; June 4, 1857; March 22, July 22, 1858; June 20, July 30, August 2, 1859; May 7, August 6, October 5, November 21, 1866; June 10, 1867. On the charter amendment, see *Special Laws,* 1858, p. 286.

[27] Welles, *Autobiography,* 2:83–85; MMC, Minutes, September 21, October 7, 1857. The property in question was owned jointly by Steele and Ralph W. Kirkham.

[28] Hilary B. Hancock, "Subsisting Leases From the Minneapolis Mill Company," May 25, 1867, John S. Pillsbury Papers, MHS; MMC, Minutes, June 10, 1867. The amount of free water granted was eight millpowers and eight hundred additional horsepower. Since the financial records for the company are fragmentary, the exact financial situation cannot be analyzed.

[29] Greenleaf, in *Reports on the Water-Power of the United States,* part 2, p. 172.

[30] The quotation is from an unidentified clipping in Francis P. Sweet Scrapbook, vol. 3, n.p., MHS. See also *Minneapolis Daily Chronicle,* November 22, 1866; *Northwestern Miller,* 8:137.

[31] On Bigelow's engagement and the canal plans discussed below, see *Proposals*

of the Minneapolis Mill Company, for the Sale of Their Land and Water Power, 1857, a leaflet in the MHS. See also map on the inside covers of this volume.

[32] *St. Paul Daily Press,* January 26, 1867; *Northwestern Miller,* 8:153. The quotation is from Joseph P. Frizell, "The Water-Power of the Falls of St. Anthony," in American Society of Civil Engineers, *Transactions,* 12:416 (October, 1883). On the later extension of the canal, see Chapter 8, note 19, below.

[33] George E. Loughland, "History of the Development of St. Anthony Falls," 1934, in NSP Correspondence Files. The "head," strictly speaking, can be defined as the height at which water enters the wheels. The "fall" is the total drop from the point of entry to the point of exit.

[34] The agreement, dated July 23, 1856, is in NSP Deed and Lease File.

[35] SAC *v.* Lovejoy and Brockway, File No. 2038, Hennepin County District Court; Richard Chute Memorandum, October 28, 1858, and Chute to Steele, March 29, 1861, Steele Papers. An example of an advertisement offering to rent the mills as a unit or separately is in the *Falls Evening News,* November 23, 1857.

[36] The regulations discussed here and below are embodied in *Proposals of the Minneapolis Mill Company,* 1857. The "Proposals of the Hadley Falls Company" are in the archives of the Holyoke Water Power Company, Holyoke, Massachusetts.

[37] *Proposals of the Minneapolis Mill Company,* 1857; Frizell, in American Society of Civil Engineers, *Transactions,* 12:419; William de la Barre to the Minnesota Tax Commission, August 16, 1915, NSP Correspondence Files. In a 1964 interview with the author, Herbert W. Meyer, formerly of NSP, said that when the early leases were signed it was assumed that the head was only 22 feet minus a one-foot drop in the canal, or 21 feet. Although a 22-foot head and 30 cubic feet of water per second would produce 75 theoretical horsepower, a 21-foot head would produce only 71.59. The difference between the theoretical and the actual horsepower delivered at the turbine shaft depended upon such factors as the wheel setting, the size of intake and discharge tubes, and the turbine design.

[38] All changes in millpower rates are recorded in the minutes of the firm.

[39] See Hancock, "Subsisting Leases," 1867, Pillsbury Papers.

[40] United States Manuscript Census Schedules, 1857, St. Anthony, enumerate 4,689 persons. See also *United States Census,* 1870, *Population,* 178.

[41] Manuscript Census Schedules, 1857, Hennepin County; *United States Census,* 1870, *Population,* 178; Bigelow to Smith, August 29, 1857, a printed circular letter bound with *Proposals of the Minneapolis Mill Company,* 1857. Total flour ground on the east side (including Hennepin Island) in 1869 was 45,700 barrels, while the west side produced 210,400. Lumber produced on the east side amounted to 22,813,792 board feet; on the west side to 67,920,803 board feet. The latter figure includes the production of five steam sawmills. See Union Board of Trade, *Reports,* 1869, p. 12, 13.

[42] On the formation of the Board of Trade, see *Express,* July 12, 1856. For the Lowell quotation, see *North-Western Democrat,* July 12, 1856. Figures on the value of products are from *United States Census,* 1860, *Manufactures,* 279; 1870, p. 535.

[43] This paragraph is based on material appearing in *Express,* November 11, 1854; *Tribune,* April 11, May 15, 1868, November 17, 1872, and February 27, 1877.

[44] Larson, *White Pine Industry,* 36; Union Board of Trade, *Reports,* 1869, p. 12, which list the thirteen water-power mills as well as five steam mills. On the Hennepin Island mill, which was owned by S. W. Farnham and James A. Lovejoy, see their testimony in Morrill, Lovejoy, *et al. v.* SAC, File No. 6098, Hennepin County District Court. Renters on the east side were compiled by the author from NSP Deed and Lease File.

In addition to those named in the text, the following built mills on the west-side row: William E. Jones; Ankeny, Robinson and Clement; Townsend and

Company; and Crocker Brothers and Lamoreaux. See Hancock, "Subsisting Leases," 1867, Pillsbury Papers; *St. Paul Daily Press,* December 3, 1865; *Tribune,* September 5, 1868, July 16, 1869, December 1, 1870, November 21, 1875; Atwater, ed., *History of Minneapolis,* 555.

[45] On wheat yields, see Minnesota Commissioner of Statistics, *Reports,* 1872, p. 12; on flour production in 1860, see Minneapolis Board of Trade, *Reports,* 1881, p. 57; Union Board of Trade, *Reports,* 1869, p. 13.

The west-side mills were the City (formerly the government gristmill), Cataract, Dakota, Washburn, Union, Arctic, Minneapolis, and Taylor. See Atwater, ed., *History of Minneapolis,* 536; *Northwestern Miller,* vol. 30, Holiday issue, 32 (1890); *St. Paul Daily Press,* April 10, 1867; and Union Board of Trade, *Reports,* 1869, p. 13.

The east-side mills were the St. Anthony, the Minnesota or Island, the River or Farmers, and the Summit. The last three were on Hennepin Island. The gristmill built by Rogers and Steele burned in 1857 and was not rebuilt. See Shutter, *Minneapolis,* 1:350; *Northwestern Miller,* vol. 30, Holiday issue, 31 (1890).

[46] Atwater, ed., *History of Minneapolis,* 634–640, 643, 644, 646; *Minneapolis Daily Chronicle,* November 22, 1866; *Tribune,* January 7, 1868, May 27, 1869; *St. Paul Daily Press,* January 26, 1867. Important among the metal-working shops were the Minnesota Iron Works, the Minneapolis Iron Works, the St. Anthony Iron Works, the North Star Iron Works, and Scott and Morgan.

[47] *Proposals of the Minneapolis Mill Company,* 1857; E. D. Scott, *The "Home" Record,* 8 [Minneapolis, 1872]; Minnesota Commissioner of Statistics, *Reports,* 1861, p. 77; *Minnesota State News* (St. Anthony), August 24, 1861. On his effort to get woolen mills, see Chute to Davis and Gebhard, February 6, 1861, Steele Papers.

[48] The two mills were the North Star Woolen Mill, which Eastman, Gibson and Company began to operate in 1864, and the Minneapolis Woolen Mill, which began production in 1868. The carding mill on the east side was established in 1861 by David Lewis; that on the west side by Miner Hilliard about 1865. Eastman, Gibson, and Company, Articles of Co-partnership, April 7, 1864, George A. Brackett Papers, MHS; *Tribune,* January 7, September 4, 1868; Union Board of Trade, *Reports,* 1868, p. 11.

[49] The Hennepin Island Paper Mill, as it was called, was established by Charles C. Secombe, and the Minneapolis Paper Mill by Lyman W. Montgomery. On the former, see *Minnesota State News,* July 8, November 19, 1859, December 22, 1860; *St. Paul Daily Press,* July 12, 1865; *St. Paul Daily Pioneer,* November 16, 1865, February 17, 1866; *Minneapolis Daily Chronicle,* November 22, 1866; *Tribune,* May 21, 1868, July 8, 1869. The firm's lease is mentioned in SAC, Minutes, July 13, 1869. On the Minneapolis Paper Mill, see Shutter, *Minneapolis,* 1:385; *Minneapolis Daily Chronicle,* November 22, 1866; *Tribune,* January 7, September 5, 1868; Hancock, "Subsisting Leases," 1867, Pillsbury Papers.

[50] Minnesota, *Special Laws,* 1866, p. 88–132, 1867, p. 43–85, 1872, p. 56–91; *Falls Evening News,* April 10, 1858; *Minnesota State News,* January 28, 1860; *St. Paul Daily Press,* January 9, 31, 1866; *St. Paul Daily Pioneer,* March 20, 1866.

[51] *United States Census,* 1950, *Population,* vol. 2, part 23, p. 11.

[52] Bigelow to Smith, August 29, 1857, in *Proposals of the Minneapolis Mill Company,* 1857; *North-Western Democrat,* July 12, 1856 (quote).

CHAPTER 5 — THE FALLS ARE GOING OUT!

[1] For other assertions of faith in the falls, see *Tribune,* January 7, 1868, March 20, 1869. St. Paul newspapers frequently published stories about the possibility

that the falls might disappear. See, for example, *Daily Press*, February 18, 1868; *Daily Dispatch*, April 26, 1869.

[2] The limestone layer is known as the Lower Trenton, the sandstone as the St. Peter. On the geology discussed here and below, see Newton H. Winchell, "The Recession of the Falls of St. Anthony," in *Quarterly Journal of the Geological Society of London*, 34:889–900 (November, 1878); Frederick W. Sardeson, "Beginning and Recession of Saint Anthony Falls," in Geological Society of America, *Bulletins*, 19:29–35 (March, 1908). The implications of the recession for the water-power companies are discussed by Franklin Cook in United States Engineers, *Annual Reports*, 1870, p. 339 (41 Congress, 3 session, *House Executive Documents*, no. 1, part 2—serial 1447).

[3] *Express*, June 3, 1854. For examples of the occasional recognition that erosion might reduce the falls to rapids, see *Express*, June 17, 1853; *Minnesota State News*, June 10, 1859.

[4] Comments on the destructive effects are in the following *Annual Reports* of the United States Engineers, in *House Executive Documents*, 41 Congress, 3 session, no. 1, part 2, p. 279; 42 Congress, 3 session, no. 1, part 2, p. 302 (serial 1559); 47 Congress, 2 session, no. 1, part 2, p. 236 (serial 2092). A board of army engineers reporting in 1874 stated: "It is strange that the interests dependent upon the preservation of the Falls of St. Anthony should continue to employ means tending so strongly to its entire destruction." See 43 Congress, 2 session, *House Executive Documents*, no. 1, part 2, p. 286 (serial 1636).

[5] MMC, Minutes, November 17, 1865, June 4, 1866; *St. Paul Daily Press*, August 8, 1866.

[6] *Daily Press*, May 26, June 8, July 21, 1867; *Tribune*, June 9, July 21, 1867. For the amount spent, see John S. Pillsbury and Curtis H. Pettit to Ignatius Donnelly, March 21, 1868, Ignatius Donnelly Papers, MHS. On the request for co-operation, see MMC, Minutes, November 11, 1867.

[7] Warren, in 41 Congress, 2 session, *House Executive Documents*, no. 1, part 2, p. 210 (serial 1413).

[8] Pillsbury and Pettit to Donnelly, March 21, 1868, Donnelly Papers; *Congressional Globe*, 40 Congress, 2 session, p. 3710–3712.

[9] *Congressional Globe*, 40 Congress, 2 session, p. 3888.

[10] *Congressional Globe*, 40 Congress, 2 session, p. 3889 (quote), 4255–4258, 4300.

[11] Petition, December 4, 1868, from the Board of Trade to the Minneapolis Council, in Petitions File, and Minneapolis, "Council Proceedings," December 4, 1868, both in the Minneapolis City Clerk's Office; SAC, Minutes, December 7, 1868.

[12] *Special Laws*, 1868, p. 364–367.

[13] For the vote, see Minneapolis, "Council Proceedings," February 21, 1868; St. Anthony, "Council Proceedings," March 3, 1868; *Tribune*, February 19, 21, 1868.

[14] *Special Laws*, 1869, p. 182–187. While the bill was pending, the Minneapolis Council attempted unsuccessfully to have it amended to permit the city to become part owner of the Minneapolis Mill Company. See "Council Proceedings," February 26, 1869; Petitions File, March 5, 1869.

[15] Minneapolis, "Council Proceedings," March 19, 1869, record the vote in the election of March 16 as 1,109 for the bonds and 164 against. St. Anthony, "Council Proceedings," April 10, 1869, record the vote on April 6 as 381 in favor and 192 against. For the firms' promises, see their statements of June 15, 16, 1869, to the Minneapolis and St. Anthony councils, and Minneapolis Council, "Report," of June 18, 1869 (quote), all in Petitions File. See also Minneapolis, "Council Proceedings," July 24, 1869.

[16] Board of Construction, Report to Minneapolis Council, June 17, 1869, and to St. Anthony Council, December 30, 1869, Petitions File.

[17] *Tribune*, July 27, August 4, 12, 1869; Board of Construction, Report to St. Anthony Council, December 30, 1869, Petitions File.

[18] See also *Tribune*, August 4, 1869.

[19] *St. Paul Daily Press*, September 15, 1869.

[20] The situation is reviewed in Richard Chute to Franklin Steele, September 27, 1865, Steele Papers. For an example of the conveyance of Nicollet Island water rights, without the island itself, see Steele to Davis, Sanford, and Gebhard, April 8, 1852; Hennepin County Register of Deeds, Book 2, p. 53.

[21] The mortgage, dated August 4, 1851, is in Hennepin County Register of Deeds, Mortgage Record Book 1, p. 3. A review of the foreclosure is in a memorandum entitled "Statement of Matters Between Steele and Dousman," January 21, 1868, Steele Papers. A letter from Henry M. Rice to Dousman, January 21, 1865, in the Dousman Papers (State Historical Society of Wisconsin) demonstrates that the separation of land and water rights was recognized by at least one outsider; and a letter from Henry T. Welles to Steele, April 4, 1866, in the Steele Papers, alleges that Dousman had never been concerned about acquiring the water rights attached to the island.

[22] W. W. Eastman and John L. Merriam *v.* SAC and Samuel H. Chute, File No. 2427, Hennepin County District Court. On Merriam, see Edward D. Neill, *History of Ramsey County and the City of St. Paul*, 348, 441, 569 (Minneapolis, 1881).

[23] The agreements are in the *Tribune*, September 29, 1870.

[24] Upham and Dunlap, *Minnesota Biographies*, 389, 856.

[25] SAC, Minutes, May 18, 1869; a supplement to the *St. Anthony Falls Democrat*, April 15, 1870, filed in the John S. Pillsbury Papers, containing an extensive statement by Eastman. The exchange between the tunnel proprietors and members of the St. Anthony firm is also discussed in detail in a letter to the editor, signed by the directors of the water-power company, in the *Tribune*, September 29, 1870. In the latter source there is no mention of a bulkhead. The authors state that the tunnel proprietors "put into the tunnel a wooden gate at the head of Hennepin Island, and during the summer prosecuted their work without taking any other precautions to protect the tunnel."

[26] *St. Paul Daily Press*, October 6, 1869.

[27] The quotation is from an unidentified clipping, October 15, 1905, in NSP Scrapbook No. 1, p. 96, NSP files. See also *St. Paul Daily Press*, October 6, 1869.

[28] The material here and below is from the *St. Paul Daily Press*, October 6, 1869. See also *Tribune*, October 5, 6, 7, 8, 9, 1869; *St. Anthony Falls Democrat*, October 15, 1869.

[29] *Daily Press*, October 7, 1869.

[30] The theme of "injury to the whole state" continued in the *Daily Press* for a number of days. See, for example, October 21, 1869. It is interesting to note, however, that the St. Paul newspapers did not refrain from publishing stories showing their habitual enmity toward Minneapolis. See the *Press* of October 22, 1869.

[31] The quotation is from Welles, *Autobiography*, 2:159. For accounts of the work, see *Tribune*, October 16, 20, 21, 22, 29, 31, 1869. The issue of October 29 indicates an awareness that the major task remained to be done.

[32] On the Union Committee, see "Minutes of a Meeting of St. Paul, St. Anthony and Minneapolis Citizens," October 6, 1869, in Petitions File, and SAC, Minutes, November 3, 1869. On the financial arrangements, see *Tribune*, October 8, 1869, September 29, 1870.

[33] See also SAC, Minutes, October 13, November 15, 1869; *Tribune*, September 29, 1870.

[34] Eastman and Merriam *v.* SAC, File No. 2427; SAC *v.* Eastman and Merriam, File No. 3593; John Eastman *et al.* (owners of the Island mill) *v.* W. W. Eastman and Merriam, File No. 3596, all in Hennepin County District Court. For the supreme court opinions, see 17 *Minnesota* 48–51 (Gil. 31–33); 20 *Minnesota* 277–313 (Gil. 249–271).

[35] On Francis, see *Tribune,* July 21, 1870. For the committee's decision, see 43 Congress, 2 session, *House Executive Documents,* no. 1, part 2, p. 280.

[36] See also *Tribune,* July 20, August 11, 25, November 6, 1870.

[37] On the appeal to Minneapolis Mill, see SAC, Minutes, December 10, 15, 1869. For information on the work and the floods, see *Tribune,* January 21, March 6, April 5, 15, 16, September 29, 1870.

[38] For Cook's appointment and his report, see 41 Congress, 3 session, *House Executive Documents,* no. 1, part 2, p. 279, 282. The concern of the United States Corps of Engineers is also demonstrated in 41 Congress, 2 session, *House Executive Documents,* no. 1, part 2, p. 210.

[39] On the campaign and the engineers' work, see *Tribune,* November 6, 9, 1869, September 6, 1870, July 7, 1871; Welles, *Autobiography,* 2:175. For full engineering data on the project, see 42 Congress, 2 session, *House Executive Documents,* no. 1, part 2, p. 294–298 (serial 1504), and 42 Congress, 3 session, *House Executive Documents,* no. 1, part 2, p. 296–306. For the appropriation, see 49 Congress, 1 session, *House Executive Documents,* no. 1, part 2, p. 1721 (serial 2372).

[40] 42 Congress, 3 session, *House Executive Documents,* no. 1, part 2, p. 299.

[41] 42 Congress, 3 session, *House Executive Documents,* no. 1, part 2, p. 301–303.

[42] The action of the St. Anthony Council was in the form of a resolution, which was published in the *Tribune,* July 23, 1871. See also Minneapolis, "Council Proceedings," July 24, August 30, 1871.

[43] The citizens' complaints are found in *Tribune,* July 29, 30, August 1, 2, 3, 4, 5, 6, 24, 27, 1871. More than one story appears in some issues.

[44] *Tribune,* July 22 (quote), August 27, 29, 1871. On the millpond work, see 42 Congress, 3 session, *House Executive Documents,* no. 1, part 2, p. 299. On the bonds, see *Special Laws,* 1872, p. 395, 403; Minneapolis, "Council Proceedings," February 24, 1872; St. Anthony, "Council Proceedings," April 4, 1872. For the union of St. Anthony and Minneapolis, see Kane, in *Minnesota History,* 35:129; *Special Laws,* 1872, p. 91.

[45] *Minneapolis City Directory,* 1873, p. 1; Minneapolis, "Council Proceedings," April 15, 20, 1872. For Bassett's report, see *Tribune,* April 16, 1872.

[46] On May 3 the *Tribune* repeated the suggestion that the city take over the water power and added that if the city was not prepared to do so, the purchase might be made by wealthy Minneapolitans, whose property values were "entirely dependent upon our water power."

[47] *Special Laws,* 1873, p. 406–408; *Tribune,* February 25, 26, 27, August 6 (quote), 1873. The ratio of the vote rejecting the bond issue was 4 to 1. The *Tribune* of August 6, 1873, contains an appeal for private subscriptions, and on February 12, 1874, the newspaper reported that $14,000 had been contributed. For the total amount spent, see 49 Congress, 1 session, *House Executive Documents,* no. 1, part 2, p. 1722. The crisis was long remembered by Minneapolis citizens. For later examples summarizing the fear and anxiety of the time, see *Minneapolis Journal,* June 5, 1897; William D. Washburn's statement of 1905 in NSP Scrapbook No. 1, p. 96; and Welles, *Autobiography,* 2:160.

[48] The report of the board of engineers is in 43 Congress, 2 session, *House Executive Documents,* no. 1, part 2, p. 279–286. The appropriations ($100,000 on March 3, 1875, and $125,000 requested for 1876–77) as well as a progress report on construction are in 44 Congress, 1 session, *House Executive Documents,* no. 1, part

2, p. 62 (serial 1675). For the measurements of the dike and a map showing the government installations built to preserve the falls, see *Tribune*, November 20, 1876. For a recapitulation of the roles played by the government, the citizens, and the water-power companies between 1866 and 1879, as well as data on a Congressional appropriation of $120,000 made on August 14, 1876, see 46 Congress, 2 session, *House Executive Documents*, no. 1, part 2, p. 1160, 1162–1165 (serial 1905).

[40] See 49 Congress, 1 session, *House Executive Documents*, no. 1, part 2, p. 1722–1725, and Chapter 7, note 29, below.

CHAPTER 6 — THE TROUBLED DECADE OF THE 1870s

[1] The impact of the panic of 1873 on Minnesota was much less severe than that of 1857. See Mildred L. Hartsough, *The Twin Cities as a Metropolitan Market*. 162 (Minneapolis, 1925).

[2] See also *Tribune*, October 21, 1870; *Daily Press*, October 22, 1870.

[3] The *Tribune* of October 21, 1870, gives $75,000 as the value of the mills, while the *Daily Press* of the same date estimates the total property loss at $150,000. See also *Daily Press*, October 22, 1870; *Tribune*, December 14, 1870. On the sale of the sawmill sites, see five deeds all dated May 22, 1871, in NSP Deed and Lease File. Purchasers of the sites were: (1) Levi Butler, O. C. Merriman, James L. Lane, and L. M. Lane; (2) Frederick Butterfield; (3) John Martin and John B. Gilfillan; (4) George H. Andrews, John S. Pillsbury, and Woodbury Fisk; (5) John Dudley, Eunice Farnham, and James A. Lovejoy.

[4] Chute to Franklin Steele, February 24, 1871, Steele Papers.

[5] Chute to Steele, February 24, 1871, Steele Papers; *Tribune*, March 4, April 1, 1871.

[6] Receipt, Steele to Butterfield, June 8, 1871, Steele Papers; Chute, "Reminiscences," 15, Chute Papers; *Tribune*, November 30, 1875. In 1874 several local stockholders who had bought out the Sanford-Gebhard-Davis interest sold their shares to John S. Pillsbury and John Dudley, leaving the company at that time in the possession of these two men, the Chutes, and Butterfield. See *Daily Dispatch*, July 8, 1874.

[7] See 17 *Minnesota* 48–51 (Gil. 31–33); 20 *Minnesota* 277–313 (Gil. 249–271); 24 *Minnesota* 437–443. On the St. Anthony firm's grant to Eastman, see a deed dated November 23, 1878, in NSP Deed and Lease File.

[8] Island Power Company, Articles of Incorporation, Book D, 430, in the Secretary of State's Office, Minnesota State Capitol, St. Paul; and a deed from the partners dated February 10, 1879, in NSP Deed and Lease File. See also *Tribune*, December 6, 1879; Atwater, ed., *History of Minneapolis*, 663. On Barton, see United States Manuscript Census Schedules, Minneapolis, 1870, MHS.

[9] *Tribune*, January 5, 1876, March 13, 1878 (quote). On the houses, see also *Tribune*, June 16, October 27, 1877, July 27, 1878.

[10] SAC v. the City of Minneapolis, File No. 32451, Hennepin County District Court, details the ownership transfers. According to this source, the property passed from Kingsley to Farnham through a series of foreclosures between 1856 and 1858. Lovejoy was operating the mill with Farnham in 1858; he became a part owner with Farnham and Ashley C. Morrill around 1860. Anson Northup had a pre-emption claim on the island, but in 1853 he withdrew in favor of Kingsley. See letters from John Wilson to Register and Receiver, Stillwater Land Office, and others, September 24, 1853, in Series G, Pre-emption Bureau, vol. 28, p. 47, NARG 49.

[11] Morrill, Lovejoy, *et al. v.* SAC, File No. 6098, Hennepin County District Court.

¹² See 26 *Minnesota* 224.

¹³ 26 *Minnesota* 228. The suit did not settle the matter. On November 26, 1879, the St. Anthony company sued Morrill *et al.* requesting that the Farnham and Lovejoy dam angling into the west channel be removed on the grounds that it prevented the free flow of water past the water-power firm's riparian land. The case was dismissed in 1882 when the St. Anthony company bought the property. See File No. 10252, Hennepin County District Court.

¹⁴ Chute to Steele, December 1, 1870, Steele Papers; *Tribune*, January 1, 1875.

¹⁵ On the company's persistence in keeping its request before the council, see *Tribune*, January 1, 1875, January 19, 1876. On the objections, see W. C. Patterson to Steele, December 17, 1875, Steele Papers; Chute to Butterfield (draft), January 27, 1875, Chute Papers.

¹⁶ SAC to Merle Potter, June 8, 1931, NSP Correspondence Files; *Tribune*, August 10, 1875; *Northwestern Miller*, 8:137. The waters are advertised on a billhead dated July 7, 1877, in the Curtis H. Pettit Papers, MHS.

¹⁷ *St. Paul Daily Globe*, March 20, 1880; Minneapolis Board of Trade, *Reports*, 1879, p. 62. Butterfield died in Vichy, France, in 1883. See Richard Chute Diary, June 24, 1883, Chute Papers.

¹⁸ Joseph G. Pyle, *The Life of James J. Hill*, 1:24, 32, 151–166, 286–289 (New York, 1917).

¹⁹ The quotations are from an unidentified newspaper clipping datelined March 20, 1880, Chute Papers; and *Tribune*, May 20, 1880.

²⁰ Marquette, "The Business Activities of C. C. Washburn," 264; C. C. Washburn to Cyrus Woodman, November 4, 1874, Woodman Papers; Algernon S. Washburn to C. C. Washburn, September 9, 1874, C. C. Washburn Papers, State Historical Society of Wisconsin.

²¹ The information on rates was compiled by the author from data in NSP Deed and Lease File and in MMC, Minutes. On the gross receipts, see William D. Hale to A. W. Stratton, May 31, 1877, letterpress book, Hale Papers, MHS. On the free millpowers granted, see MMC, Minutes, January 2, 1880.

²² H. B. Hancock to Bassett, January 12, 1871, NSP Correspondence Files; MMC, Minutes, May 7, 1873.

²³ On Frizell, see MMC, Minutes, October 23, 1875. The lessees were notified in a printed circular dated October 23, 1875, a copy of which is in the Hale Papers.

²⁴ H. H. Douglass to Cahill, Fletcher, and Company, October 3, 1880, MMC letterpress book, NSP files.

²⁵ MMC, Minutes, November 21, 1866, October 23, 1875.

²⁶ On Douglass, see MMC, Minutes, October 5, 1877; *Northwestern Miller*, 15:29.

²⁷ See Washburn's letter to the editor in the *Tribune*, July 16, 1878, in which he says that he spent $15,000 to get the spur built to his mills.

²⁸ Minneapolis Eastern, Articles of Incorporation, Book D, 361, in the Minnesota Secretary of State's Office; *Tribune*, July 15, 16, October 23, November 1, 2, 1878. The latter contains two stories, one giving Bassett's version of the affair and one presenting C. C. Washburn's arguments. For a review of the condemnation and the award, see "Agreement" between Minneapolis Eastern and Minneapolis Mill, November 15, 1878, Hennepin County Register of Deeds, Miscellaneous Deed Book 8, p. 334–349.

²⁹ Material here and below is from the *Tribune*, November 2, 1878.

³⁰ On the agreement, see note 28, above. See also *Tribune*, November 2, 18, 1878, February 1, 1879; *St. Paul Daily Globe*, November 21, 1878; MMC, Minutes, October 3, 1883.

³¹ Meeker Island, which no longer exists, was located between the present Franklin Avenue and Milwaukee Railway bridges in Minneapolis. For a fuller treatment of the navigation story and the Meeker Dam episode discussed below, see Kane,

in *Minnesota History*, 37:309–323. Steamboats occasionally reached points below the falls within the cities' limits. See *Minneapolis Daily Chronicle*, April 16, 1867; *Tribune*, June 6, 1867, May 22, 1874.

[32] Minnesota Territory, *Laws*, 1857, p. 230–234. On Meeker, see Upham and Dunlap, *Minnesota Biographies*, 501.

[33] The memorial has not been found. It is referred to in Meeker to Ignatius Donnelly, January [n.d.], 1866, Donnelly Papers. On the petition, see 39 Congress, 2 session, *House Executive Documents*, no. 58, p. 45–50 (serial 1292). The quotation is on page 45.

[34] Meeker to Donnelly, January 11, February 14 (quote), 1866, Donnelly Papers.

[35] Meeker to Donnelly, February 14, March 15 (quote), 28, April 3, 21, 1866, Donnelly Papers; Donnelly to Curtis H. Pettit, February 15, 1866, Pettit Papers.

[36] *Congressional Globe*, 39 Congress, 1 session, 579, 2292; United States, *Statutes at Large*, 14:74; Meeker to Donnelly, April 16, 1866 (quote), Donnelly Papers. Cook's conclusions are reported in the *St. Paul Daily Press*, February 19, 1867.

[37] *Statutes at Large*, 15:169. The act empowered the state legislature to dispose of the lands to get the lock and dam constructed but did not name a specific recipient for the grant.

[38] On the sale, see Meeker to Donnelly, March 27, April 21, 1866, March 1, 1867, S[tephen] Miller to Donnelly, April 6, 1866; and H[ezekiah] Fletcher to Donnelly, March 28, 1866, Donnelly Papers. For the deed, dated February 7, 1867, by which Meeker conveyed the property to the new group, see Hennepin County Register of Deeds, Book 14, p. 184.

[39] Articles of Incorporation, Book B, 166, Minnesota Secretary of State's Office. The organizational meeting is described in the *Tribune*, February 12, 1869. Dorilus Morrison was elected president; W. P. Westfall, vice-president; Edward Murphy, secretary; and Rufus J. Baldwin, treasurer. A committee was appointed to "look after" the land grant. For the award of the grant, see *Special Laws*, 1869, p. 350–352.

[40] *Congressional Globe*, 41 Congress, 3 session, 52, 65, 792, 838, 847, 1884, 2004; 42 Congress, 2 session, 395, 452; 42 Congress, 3 session, 82, 123, 702. See also *Tribune*, December 29, 1872, January 8, 1873.

[41] *Tribune*, December 29, 1872. St. Paul newspapers for this period seem to have ignored the stock transfer.

[42] For accounts of Board of Trade meetings, interviews with Minneapolis citizens, editorial comments, and letters to the editor, see *Tribune*, December 17, 24, 25, 28, 29, 31, 1872, January 1, 7, 8, 1873. For examples of opposition, see telegrams, Richard Chute, James A. Lovejoy, and others to Alexander Ramsey, April 24, December 7, 1872, Ramsey Papers. Among the specious arguments used in Chute's telegram and by other opponents was that the amendment was a "private scheme for absorption of all pine lands in the state." For examples of support, see letters to Ramsey from Eugene M. Wilson, April 25, 1872, Edward Murphy, May 1, 1872, and A. B. Barton [January, 1873], Ramsey Papers.

[43] *Congressional Globe*, 42 Congress, 3 session, 82, 123, 702; *Tribune*, April 21, 1874. In the absence of company records and with only sporadic press comment available, it is impossible to determine why the firm did not build the dam and develop the water power. Among the possibilities, surely, is the fact that after the failure of the amendment the land grant was considerably less valuable than it would have been had the measure passed. It is possible, too, that the Washburns and Chute succeeded in sabotaging the development efforts, that the failure to proceed was due to a lack of resolution and energy, or that the panic of 1873 blighted the enterprise.

[44] *Tribune*, January 28, 1879.

[45] W. D. Washburn to A. S. Washburn, November 16, 1868, A. S. Washburn Papers, MHS.

CHAPTER 7 — THE QUEEN CITY OF THE NORTHWEST

[1] The developed capacity of the falls at the end of the 1870s cannot be determined exactly. It is known from a study of the NSP Deed and Lease File that by the close of the decade 92.5 millpowers, theoretically yielding 6,947.5 horsepower, had been granted by Minneapolis Mill. Since the water granted by the St. Anthony company was variously defined by cubic feet, horsepower, and millpower, and since some grants (such as those owned by Farnham and Lovejoy and the Hennepin Island paper mill) were not defined at all, no total can be calculated.

[2] United States Census, 1870, Industry and Wealth, 535, 683; 1880, Manufactures, 412. The relative importance of manufacturing at the falls was greater than the percentage figures indicate, for among the "manufactures" listed in the census as being away from the cataract were such activities as blacksmithing, carpentering, stone and marble work, photography, and watch and clock repairing. On the other hand, some allowance must be made for the fact that a few steam-powered sawmills were operating away from the falls at this time and that there is no reliable way to isolate them from the figures on water-powered mills.

[3] United States Census, 1870, Industry and Wealth, 683; 1880, Manufactures, 412. On flour production, see Minneapolis Board of Trade, Reports, 1880, p. 58.

[4] American Miller, cited in Tribune, December 6, 1878. The announcement that Minneapolis was the nation's largest flour producer appeared in Minneapolis Board of Trade, Reports, 1880, p. 54.

[5] For examples of the falls communities' early interest in railroads and their conflict with St. Paul, see Express, December 10, 1852, December 31, 1853; Minnesota State News, January 28, September 17, 1859, August 4, 1860; Minneapolis Daily Chronicle, January 11, 1867; Tribune, January 7, December 3, 1868, March 19, October 2, 4, 1870, September 9, 1874. For the city's progress in securing railroads in the 1870s, see Robert Watson to Richard Chute, December 10, 1879, Chute Papers; Frank P. Donovan, Jr., Mileposts on the Prairie: The Story of the Minneapolis & St. Louis Railway, 28, 37, 45–52 (New York, 1950); Tribune, March 14, 21, 1879.

[6] Hartsough, The Twin Cities as a Metropolitan Market, 48, 81, 83–85, 87; Folwell, Minnesota, 3:48, 49, 460–462; Donovan, Mileposts on the Prairie, 9, 12, 15, 22–26, 28, 39–42, 54; Lester B. Shippee, "An Early Northern Railroad," in Mississippi Valley Historical Review, 5:141, 142 (September, 1918). On the Minneapolis and Duluth, see also Tribune, July 23, 1871.

[7] United States Census, 1950, Population, vol. 2, part 23, p. 9; part 26, p. 6; part 34, p. 6; part 41, p. 8. On wheat production, see Commissioner of Statistics, Reports, 1872, p. 12; 1881, p. 16. See also Mildred L. Hartsough, "Transportation as a Factor in the Development of the Twin Cities," in Minnesota History, 7:225 (September, 1926); Charles B. Kuhlmann, The Development of the Flour-Milling Industry in the United States with Special Reference to the Industry in Minneapolis, 149–153, 289–293 (Boston and New York, 1929).

[8] Commissioner of Statistics, Reports, 1877, p. 164, 172; Minneapolis Board of Trade, Reports, 1877, p. 78; 1880, p. 66–68; Henrietta Larson, The Wheat Market and the Minnesota Farmer, 133 (New York, 1926); Kuhlmann, Development of Flour-Milling, 142, 144. On livestock and meat packing, see Tribune, June 3, 1875. The millers' organization dissolved a few years after the formation of the Minneapolis Chamber of Commerce in 1881. The millers then bought wheat through the chamber and participated in its management.

[9] Folwell, Minnesota, 3:388–400.

[10] Kuhlmann, Development of Flour-Milling, 112, 126, lists the following mills built in the 1870s: Zenith, Holly, Empire, Palisade, Washburn A, Galaxy,

Anchor, Hennepin, Humboldt, Pettit, and Peoples, a steam-powered mill. For descriptions of them, see *Tribune*, February 14, 1874, November 14, 1875; undated memorandum, Hale Papers.

[11] Washburn to Cyrus Woodman, October 16, 1873 (quote), April 24, September 13, 1874 (quote), Woodman Papers; Minneapolis Board of Trade, *Reports*, 1876, p. 41.

[12] *Tribune*, November 7, 1875.

[13] Quotations here and in the following paragraph are from the *Tribune*, May 3, 1878. See also Edgar, *Medal of Gold*, 77–80; Nannie Riheldaffer Diary, May 2, 1872, in John G. Riheldaffer Papers, MHS.

[14] Other examples of national coverage are: *New York Tribune*, May 3, 4, 6, 1878; *St. Louis Republican*, cited in the *Minneapolis Tribune*, July 29, 1878; *Harper's Weekly*, May 25, 1878. The quotation is from a reminiscent letter by William de la Barre to H. E. Howes, May 3, 1918, in MMC letterpress book.

[15] For material here and in the following paragraph, see *Tribune*, May 3, 1878 (quote); Kuhlmann, *Development of Flour-Milling*, 124.

[16] On the mills, see Minneapolis Board of Trade, *Reports*, 1878, p. 51; 1880, p. 54; Kuhlmann, *Development of Flour-Milling*, 126. The figures do not include two small steam mills on the fringe of the district — the Eagle (located at Ninth Avenue South, between Washington and Third) and the Trades (located at 108 South Second Street) — which had a combined capacity of 175 barrels. *Minneapolis City Directory*, 1880, p. 442.

[17] *Northwestern Miller*, vol. 30, Holiday issue, 31 (1890).

[18] *Northwestern Miller*, 11:147; *Tribune*, May 15, 1881. An unidentified clipping in NSP Scrapbook No. 2, p. 190, gives the subsequent history of the Phoenix, which was razed in 1956.

[19] *Northwestern Miller*, 11:147, 217, 126:647, 664; Kuhlmann, *Development of Flour-Milling*, 132. It is difficult to determine the exact date when the Pillsbury A became the largest mill in the world. The *Tribune* of August 29, 1885, made this boast, and an advertisement of May 1, 1896, reprinted in *Pillsbury People*, house organ of the Pillsbury Flour Mills Company, June, 1944, p. 14, challenged any mill in the world to come within 15,000 barrels of its production of 61,827 barrels on a six-day run. The mill is still operated by the Pillsbury Company. Although greatly remodeled, it is one of the city's historic landmarks.

[20] Kuhlmann, *Development of Flour-Milling*, 86, 113; Dorilus Morrison to W. F. Davidson, September 21, 1871, William F. Davidson Papers, MHS.

[21] Kuhlmann, *Development of Flour-Milling*, 113–120. The quotation is on page 119. The leading winter-wheat manufacturing centers were St. Louis, New York City, and Richmond, Virginia. See Marquette, "The Business Activities of C. C. Washburn," 250.

[22] Kuhlmann, *Development of Flour-Milling*, 120–123.

[23] The statements on consolidation are based on lists of mills and their owners and operators in Union Board of Trade, *Reports*, 1869, p. 13; Minneapolis Board of Trade, *Reports*, 1880, p. 54. The 1880 count does not include the Eagle and the Trades. For details on the firms involved and the reasons for the trend, see Kuhlmann, *Development of Flour-Milling*, 131–133; James Gray, *Business Without Boundary: The Story of General Mills*, 38 (Minneapolis, 1954).

[24] Union Board of Trade, *Reports*, 1869, p. 12; Minneapolis Board of Trade, *Reports*, 1876, p. 47.

[25] *United States Census*, 1870, *Industry and Wealth*, 683; 1880, *Manufactures*, 412; Union Board of Trade, *Reports*, 1869, p. 12; Minneapolis Board of Trade, *Reports*, 1880, p. 61. The production of William D. Washburn's mill at Anoka, reported in the 1880 figures, has been subtracted by the author.

[26] Minneapolis Board of Trade, *Reports*, 1880, p. 62. The author calculated

east-side production statistics through a knowledge of the operators' names. On the new east-side row, see deeds from SAC to the five purchasers, May 22, 1871, in NSP Deed and Lease File.

[27] *Tribune,* November 14, 1875.

[28] Minneapolis Board of Trade, *Reports,* 1876, p. 47. An approximate production figure was arrived at by adding the output of west-side mills known to be water powered in 1876. They were: Morrison Brothers, Pettit and Robinson, J. B. Bassett, the Minneapolis Mill Company (two mills), and Eastman and Bovey.

[29] On the purchase and removal of the sawmills, see *Tribune,* May 2, 9, 1876, March 14, 1887; *Daily Pioneer Press,* January 14, 1880; MMC, Minutes, January 5, 1887. The position of the United States Engineers is stated in 44 Congress, 2 session, *House Executive Documents,* no. 1, part 2, p. 699 (serial 1743); see also Chapter 5, note 49, above. Markets and operating arrangements discussed below were compiled by the author from MMC letterpress books, 1879–83. Production statistics were calculated from Minneapolis Board of Trade, *Reports,* 1880, p. 62. The figure includes Bassett's mill as well as the six row mills then in operation.

[30] On the steam mills of the 1850s and 1860s, see [Warner], *History of Hennepin County and . . . Minneapolis,* 377; *Daily Minnesotian,* June 6, 1855, June 24, 1857; *St. Paul Daily Press,* December 3, 1865; *Minneapolis Daily Chronicle,* November 22, 1866; *Tribune,* April 1, 1868; Union Board of Trade, *Reports,* 1869, p. 12. On the advantages of the north Minneapolis location, see *Mississippi Valley Lumberman,* April 11, 1879, p. 1; *Tribune,* April 7, 1879.

[31] For descriptions of the steam mills, see Atwater, ed., *History of Minneapolis,* 544, 557, 564, 566; *Mississippi Valley Lumberman,* January 5, 1877, p. 2; *Tribune,* February 10, 19, 1870, May 31, 1878, May 26, 1880. The production figure was obtained by totaling the output of individual mills in Minneapolis Board of Trade, *Reports,* 1880, p. 62.

[32] See *Mississippi Valley Lumberman,* June 22, 1877, p. 4; John B. Appleton, "The Declining Significance of the Mississippi as a Commercial Highway in the Middle of the Nineteenth Century," in Geographical Society of Philadelphia, *Bulletins,* 28:267–284 (January–October, 1930). Evidences of the continued attraction of southern trade as well as aspirations for transportation links with the area are in the *Weekly Minnesotian,* November 13, 1852; *Express,* November 5, 1852; *Tribune,* September 5, 1868, March 10, 1870, October 18, 1877, April 1, 1878; *Northwestern Miller,* 8:266.

[33] *Daily Press,* January 23, 1866; Articles of Incorporation, Book B, 312, Minnesota Secretary of State's Office; *Tribune,* June 16, 1869, February 5, March 25, 1870 (quote).

[34] On production and machinery, see John Storck and Walter D. Teague, *Flour for Man's Bread,* 270 (Minneapolis, 1952); *St. Anthony Falls Democrat,* November 3, 1870; *Tribune,* April 12, May 11, August 12, 1870, October 6, 1872, January 1, 1874. On the decline of the business, see *Tribune,* December 29, 1876, June 13, July 19, October 2, 1877, January 27, 1879; C. C. Washburn to Morrison, December 7, 1878, Morrison Papers, MHS.

[35] See "Council Proceedings," November 23, 1870; *Tribune,* November 26, 1870, June 1, 1871. For examples of agitation for cotton mills, see *Tribune,* June 6, 20, 1877; Minneapolis Board of Trade, *Reports,* 1878, p. 59.

[36] Victor S. Clark, *History of Manufactures in the United States, 1860–1914,* 2:105, 182, 395 (Washington, D.C., 1928); *Tribune,* June 1, 1871, June 6, 20, 1877.

[37] The carding mills are listed in the Minneapolis city directories for the period. On the woolen mills, see Atwater, ed., *History of Minneapolis,* 657; *Tribune,* December 11, 1876.

[38] *Tribune,* August 9, 1876, February 5, 1877; MMC, Minutes, January 2, 1880.

[39] On its products, customers, and sources of wool, see *Tribune,* June 28, 1872,

August 15, 1875; Sales Book, 1877–80, North Star Woolen Mill Company Papers, MHS. See also Minneapolis Board of Trade, *Reports*, 1876, p. 52; 1878, p. 59; William G. Northup to the author, November 23, 1960.

[40] On the North Star Iron Works, see *Tribune*, November 28, 1875; on Monitor, see *Tribune*, August 6, 1873, February 1, 1876; on Minnesota Iron, see *Tribune*, September 27, 1878, and Atwater, ed., *History of Minneapolis*, 664. The *Tribune*, May 10, 1872, has information on the removal of the furniture factory, at that time owned by Barnard and Clark. Among the plants remaining at the falls were the Northwestern Fence Works and the St. Anthony Iron Works. See *Mississippi Valley Lumberman*, March 30, 1877, p. 4; *Tribune*, November 10, 1872.

[41] On the Hennepin Island mill, see *Tribune*, February 11, 1870, March 6, 1878; Atwater, ed., *History of Minneapolis*, 657. On the Minneapolis mill, see *Tribune*, October 20, 1877, January 14, 1878; Minneapolis Board of Trade, *Annual Exhibit of the Manufacturing and Commercial Industry of the City of Minneapolis, 1872*, 17 (Minneapolis, 1873).

[42] Swain, in *Reports on the Water-Power of the United States*, part 1, p. xii.

[43] *United States Census*, 1870, *Population*, 178; 1880, *Manufactures*, xxvi; 1880, *Population*, 226, 536.

[44] *United States Census*, 1880, *Population*, 536.

CHAPTER 8 — STRETCHING THE POWER

[1] Shutter, *Minneapolis*, 1:135–137, 142, 146, 153, 229–237, 422, 464, 647; Harry P. Robinson, "Minneapolis: A Year's Growth of the City by the Falls," in *Northwest Magazine*, January, 1885, p. 1–14.

[2] *Tribune*, July 4, 1880.

[3] On the destruction of the sawmill rows, see *Tribune*, March 14, 1887; *Mississippi Valley Lumberman*, September 16, 1887, p. 6, May 4, 1888, p. 7. For a list of sawmills and production figures, see Minneapolis Chamber of Commerce, *Annual Reports*, 1889, p. 162. Of a total production of 275,855,648 board feet, steam mills accounted for 234,608,648 board feet, according to the author's calculation. For the subsequent history of sawmilling in Minneapolis, see Larson, *White Pine Industry*, 229–246. McMullen's mill did not burn in 1887.

Among the few nonflour milling firms remaining were: the North Star Woolen Mill, which continued in business on the west side until 1949, the Minneapolis Paper Mill, the Northwestern Fence Works (formerly the Herzog Manufacturing Company), the Union Iron Works, and miscellaneous industries housed in the Island Power Company building on lower Nicollet Island. See North Star Woolen Mill Company, Minutes, May 16, 1881 (microfilm, MHS), originals in the possession of the company; Atwater, ed., *History of Minneapolis*, 647, 657; Shutter, *Minneapolis*, 1:384. For businesses housed in the Island Power Company building, see *Minneapolis City Directory*, 1888, p. 1468, 1480, 1486, 1488, 1495, 1503, 1518, 1522, 1565, 1572, 1606.

[4] Minneapolis Chamber of Commerce, *Annual Reports*, 1889, p. 136; *United States Census*, 1890, *Manufactures*, part 2, p. 337, 345, 401, 513.

[5] On the mills, see Minneapolis Board of Trade, *Reports*, 1880, p. 54; Minneapolis Chamber of Commerce, *Annual Reports*, 1889, p. 135; H. P. Robinson, "The Minneapolis Mills," in *Northwest Magazine*, February, 1884, p. 6. By 1889 the three large milling firms were Washburn, Crosby and Company, Minneapolis Flour Manufacturing Company, and Pillsbury-Washburn Flour Mills Company, Ltd. See Kuhlmann, *Development of Flour-Milling*, 131–138. For conflicting evidence on the relative size of the Pillsbury A, see note 19 of Chapter 7, above.

[6] SAC, Minutes, September 6, 1880, August 19, 1882.

[7] SAC, Minutes, August 19, 1882. For examples of the management problems,

see Notice by W. H. Bailey to Squatters, January 30, 1882; L. S. Gilette to Hill, August 13, 1883, July 7, 1884; Gilette to Benton and Roberts, November 18, 1885; John T. Fanning to Hill, May 12, 1886; Fanning to William W. Eastman, November 30, 1887 — all in SAC letterpress book, NSP files.

[8] MMC, Minutes, 1883–88. On the asylum, see Shutter, *Minneapolis*, 1:194, 197; *Tribune*, October 25, 1964, Women's Section, part 1, p. 2.

[9] On Douglass, see *Northwestern Miller*, 15:29; on De la Barre, 34:15.

[10] Washburn to Hale, January 17, 1883, Hale Papers. De la Barre's rise in Minneapolis Mill and the firm's prosperity under his management are detailed in the company's minutes for the years cited below. Gross receipts rose from $57,734.54 in 1876 to $66,084.69 in 1888. Dividends were paid in 1883 (25 per cent), in 1884 (20 per cent and 33⅓ per cent), in 1886 (12 per cent), in 1887 (13 per cent), in 1888 (12½ per cent and 10 per cent), and in 1889 a distribution of $22,410.52.

[11] *St. Paul Daily Globe*, August 31, 1878 (quote).

[12] Undated statement, *ca.* 1915, prepared by MMC for the Minnesota Tax Commission, NSP Correspondence Files.

[13] H. H. Douglass to C. C. Washburn, January 22, 1879; Douglass to thirteen milling firms, February 6, 1879, both in MMC letterpress book; *Globe*, cited in *Tribune*, March 13, 1879.

[14] Undated statement, *ca.* 1915, prepared by MMC for the Minnesota Tax Commission, NSP Correspondence Files; De la Barre to A. M. Bailey, September 10, 1887, in MMC letterpress book; and MMC, Minutes, January 15, 1885. See also *Northwestern Miller*, 18:487.

[15] For an example, see De la Barre to W. D. Washburn, January 19, 1885, MMC letterpress book.

[16] De la Barre to Pack, November, 1924, p. 34, NSP Correspondence Files; *Northwestern Miller*, 18:102; 19:77, 101, 365; 20:518; 22:595; 26, Holiday issue, 2 (1888); 28:491, 522, and Holiday issue, 2 (1889).

[17] *Northwestern Miller*, 11:401 (quote); 20:244; 22:595 (quote). In 1888 De la Barre, who warned against the hazards of computing such cost differences, stated that the best average he could arrive at was 3 cents a barrel for water power and 6⅜ cents for steam. Neither figure took into account original plant cost, depreciation, or interest charges on investment. See De la Barre to William E. Worthern, February 4, 1888, MMC letterpress book.

[18] MMC, Minutes, January 2, 1884, January 15, May 30, 1885.

[19] C. E. Plank to A. R. Renquist, March 5, 1953, NSP Correspondence Files; George E. Loughland, "Minneapolis Mill Company," December 11, 1936, NSP Historic Data File. See also *Northwestern Miller*, 19:29; 23:5, 543; 24:381; 25:446; 26:164; 32:631, 720; 33:41. The canal had been extended in 1866–67 from 215 to 600 feet. At that time an additional 115 feet were contracted for but not built. See *St. Paul Daily Press*, January 26, 1867.

[20] In 1890, after most of the improvements Minneapolis Mill promised were completed, De la Barre sternly reminded transgressors of their bargain. See De la Barre to Minneapolis Millers Union, March 25, 1890; to W. D. Washburn, March 27, 1890; to Hennepin Paper Company, May 23, 1890; circular letter to lessees of MMC, December 1, 1890 — all in MMC letterpress book.

[21] See De la Barre to Cahill, Fletcher, and Company, January 24, 1884, MMC letterpress book; Galaxy Mill Company to MMC, January 2, 1887, NSP Correspondence Files; MMC, Minutes, January 15, 1885.

[22] For examples of complaints, see C. C. Washburn Flouring Mills Company to De la Barre, December 26, 1889, NSP Correspondence Files; MMC, Minutes, May 30, 1885; *Northwestern Miller*, 18:487, 23:29, 24:381, 28:679.

[23] De la Barre to Sidle, Fletcher, and Holmes Company, May 8, 1886, MMC letterpress book.

²⁴ De la Barre to A. M. Long, September 9, 1885, and to H. W. Holmes, April 7, 1888, MMC letterpress book. See also Minutes, June 25, 1885; De la Barre to C. A. Pillsbury and Company, August 18, 1885; De la Barre circular letter, undated, in MMC letterpress book, 1883–85.

²⁵ On the early use of a water pool, see H. H. Douglass to C. C. Washburn, February 19, 1879, MMC letterpress book. By 1883 Minneapolis Mill seemed to be taking the initiative in starting pools; see De la Barre circular letter, November 30, 1883, MMC letterpress book. For descriptions of other pools, see *Northwestern Miller*, 21:125; 23:29, 53.

²⁶ See *Northwestern Miller*, 22:643; 23:53; 24:353; 29:3.

²⁷ *Northwestern Miller*, 21:245. For other examples of violations of pool arrangements, see Washburn Mill Company to [William D. Hale], February [n.d.], 1885, Hale Papers; *Northwestern Miller*, 21:149, 23:5.

²⁸ On the Pillsbury A steam plant, see *Northwestern Miller*, 17:249. On the overdrawing of grants, see *Mississippi Valley Lumberman*, August 14, 1885, [p. 2]. The St. Anthony company leased ten millpowers to Pillsbury A on July 1, 1881, and an additional ten on November 22, 1883; see NSP Deed and Lease File.

²⁹ For the decision, see SAC *v.* Orlando C. Merriman, *et al.,* in 35 *Minnesota* 42–50. See also *Mississippi Valley Lumberman*, July 11, 1884, p. [3]; August 14, 1885, p. [4]; July 30, 1886, p. [4]; August 26, 1887, p. 6.

³⁰ *Mississippi Valley Lumberman*, August 14, 1885, [p. 4].

³¹ *Northwestern Miller*, 22:29; 24:695; 28:550. The work on the channel and the dam cost $150,000.

³² On the rumored contest, see *Northwestern Miller*, 21:29; 24:695; 25:369. Millpond levels are discussed by Ralph D. Thomas, "Water Power Development on the Mississippi River above St. Paul," in Affiliated Engineering Societies of Minnesota, *Bulletins*, 2:241–243 (September, 1917).

³³ See Chapters 4 and 6, above. Minneapolis City Council, *Proceedings*, 1880–81, p. 193–196; *Northwestern Miller*, 11:145, 20:389, 28:550.

³⁴ See *Mississippi Valley Lumberman*, September 23, 1887, p. 6.

³⁵ Deeds dated May 15, 1880, February 8, 1882, in Hennepin County Register of Deeds, Books 85 and 104, p. 566, 488.

³⁶ On the burning of the mill and the acquisition of the property by the city, see Atwater, ed., *History of Minneapolis*, 657; deed (copy), July 9, 1883, in NSP Deed and Lease File. On the earlier pumping station, see Minneapolis, "Council Proceedings," June 17, 1867, April 14, 1868, December 31, 1872; Minneapolis Board of Trade, *Reports*, 1877, p. 27. Information on the 1885 station is in *Tribune*, April 22, 1885; SAC *v.* the City of Minneapolis, File No. 32451, Hennepin County District Court. The population figure is reported by the Minnesota Secretary of State, *Census, Appendix A*, 26 ([St. Paul], 1885).

³⁷ SAC *v.* the City of Minneapolis, File No. 32451.

³⁸ *Tribune*, January 11, February 1, 1888.

³⁹ SAC *v.* the City of Minneapolis, File No. 32451; 41 *Minnesota* 270–278. In 1892 a referee appointed by the court set the amount of water to be furnished at three and a half millpowers.

⁴⁰ De la Barre to James J. Hill, August 14, 1884, and to Mississippi and Rum River Boom Company, October 10, 1887, in MMC letterpress book; *Northwestern Miller*, 22:349.

⁴¹ For examples of the efforts to control the passage of logs over the falls, see H. H. Douglass to F. Driscoll [St Paul Boom Company], June 3, 1882, and De la Barre to the Mississippi and Rum River Boom Company, April 16, 1888, both in MMC letterpress book. On the sluice, see 48 Congress, 1 session, *House Executive Documents*, no. 1, part 2, p. 1432 (serial 2184). For the end of log driving, see Larson, *White Pine Industry*, 225.

⁴² The first Suspension Bridge, built in 1854, had been replaced by a second

one on the same site in 1875. See Kane, "First Bridge over the Mississippi," in *Gopher Historian*, Spring, 1964, p. 16; De la Barre to Charles J. Allen, September 11, 1885; to Mayor George A. Pillsbury, September 12, 1885; and De la Barre, "Statement," November 12, 1885 (quote), all in MMC letterpress book. On the injunction, see *Northwestern Miller*, 21:29; 22:199. On the modified design, see "Hilgard's Design for a Steel Arch Bridge at Minneapolis," in *Scientific American*, 55:1 (October 23, 1886).

⁴³ *Proposals of the Minneapolis Mill Company*, 1857 (quote); Commissioner of Statistics, *Reports*, 1861, p. 77; 1871, p. 156. For examples of the repetition of these figures, see *St. Paul Daily Press*, June 4, 1861; *Tribune*, December 17, 1880, April 18, 1881. The figure given in the latter source is 105,000.

⁴⁴ Greenleaf, in *Reports on the Water-Power of the United States*, part 2, p. 169.

⁴⁵ On the heads, see De la Barre, Memorandum, *ca.* June, 1889, in MMC letterpress book. See also Daniel W. Mead, *Water Power Engineering*, 1–13, 237, 243–260 (New York, 1908); *Northwestern Miller*, 12:95; Frizell, in American Society of Civil Engineers, *Transactions*, 12:420. On the Meeker Dam controversy, see Chapter 6, above.

⁴⁶ "Water Flow Records," begun in 1875, in the offices of NSP. There is no evidence that earlier company managers made use of them.

⁴⁷ *Tribune*, October 28, 1913; W. A. Jones to De la Barre, June 2, 1899, NSP Correspondence Files; Greenleaf, in *Reports on the Water-Power of the United States*, part 2, p. 21–27, 138.

⁴⁸ De la Barre to Thomas Lowry, June 2, 1894, MMC letterpress book.

⁴⁹ See a published article by De la Barre, March 21, 1932, but otherwise unidentified in NSP Scrapbook No. 2, p. 71; De la Barre, "Memorandum," *ca.* June, 1889, and De la Barre to F. W. Cappelen, August 20, 1913, both in MMC letterpress book; "Water Flow Records." The all-time low was reported by H. W. Meyer in an interview with the author, 1964.

⁵⁰ Greenleaf, in *Reports on the Water-Power of the United States*, part 2, p. 142–148. The annual evaporation rate was reported by Meyer in an interview with the author, 1964.

⁵¹ Greenleaf, in *Reports on the Water-Power of the United States*, part 2, p. 147, 260.

⁵² For a review of early reservoir plans, see A. A. Humphreys and H. L. Abbot, *Report upon the Physics and Hydraulics of the Mississippi River*, 406 (United States Army Corps of Topographical Engineers, *Professional Papers*, no. 4 — Washington, D.C., 1876). Griffith's plan is detailed in David Heaton, *Summary Statement of the General Interests of Manufacture and Trade Connected with the Upper Mississippi*, 9 (Minneapolis, 1862). The quotation is from 41 Congress, 3 session, *House Executive Documents*, no. 1, part 2, p. 284.

⁵³ For a useful summary of the engineers' work, see 46 Congress, 2 session, *House Executive Documents*, no. 1, part 2, p. 1193–1198.

⁵⁴ 44 Congress, 1 session, *House Executive Documents*, no. 1, part 2, p. 436, 439 (serial 1676); 46 Congress, 2 session, *House Executive Documents*, no. 1, part 2, p. 1198.

⁵⁵ Warren's statement is in 39 Congress, 2 session, *House Executive Documents*, no. 58, p. 31; on Cook's expedition, see 41 Congress, 2 session, *House Executive Documents*, no. 285, p. 2–11 (serial 1426). On the lands at Pokegama, see W. D. Washburn to C. C. Washburn, May 14, 19, 1869, C. C. Washburn Papers; W. D. Washburn to W. D. Hale, January 25, 1883, Hale Papers.

⁵⁶ On Washburn's work, see *Tribune*, March 17, 1881, October 24, 1882, November 14, 1885; Resolution (copy) sent to Mrs. W. D. Washburn, October 12, 1912, in MMC letterpress book; Washburn to Alexander Mackenzie, July 23, 1905, item 26, File No. 49126, Office of the Chief of Engineers, NARG 77.

⁵⁷ *Tribune*, May 17, 1880.

[58] *Tribune*, October 17, 1879, April 26, 1880.

[59] *Mississippi Valley Lumberman*, February 9, 1877, p. 4; *Tribune*, January 27 (quote), April 26, 1880.

[60] *Mississippi Valley Lumberman*, August 30, 1878, p. 4; September 13, 1878, p. 4.

[61] *Tribune*, January 20, 26, 1881.

[62] Robert W. Buselmeier, "The Engineer Corps Manages Water," in *Conservation Volunteer*, July–August, 1957, p. 24–26; 50 Congress, 1 session, *House Executive Documents*, no. 1, part 2, p. 1681–1693 (serial 2535); Edward J. Dugan, "Mississippi River Reservoirs," in *Minnesota Surveyors' and Engineers' Society, Proceedings*, 1912, p. 72; J. G. Pyle, "The Reservoir System," in *Harper's New Monthly Magazine*, 69:622 (September, 1884).

[63] *Mississippi Valley Lumberman*, November 16, 1883, p. [4]; June 27, 1884, p. [4] (quote); August 12, 1887, p. 2; September 2, 1887, p. 2; September 9, 1887, p. 5; June 1, 1888, p. 2.

[64] De la Barre to W. D. Hale, November 10, 1886, Hale Papers; *Northwestern Miller*, 26:533, 28:118.

[65] See Charles J. Allen to W. D. Washburn, August 16, 1887, NSP Correspondence Files; De la Barre to Francis R. Shunk, February 5, 1908, MMC letterpress book.

[66] *Northwestern Miller*, 8:137, 28:550; De la Barre, "Memorandum," *ca.* June, 1889, MMC letterpress book; *Tribune*, June 6, 1875 (quote).

CHAPTER 9—PORTENT OF THINGS TO COME

[1] See Emil Mosonyi, *Water Power Development*, 95 (Budapest, Hungary, 1957).

[2] Harold C. Passer, *The Electrical Manufacturers, 1875–1900*, 11, 14–18, 75, 78–80 (Cambridge, Mass., 1953); Clark, *History of Manufactures in the United States*, 2:378; Forrest McDonald, *Let There Be Light*, 4 (Madison, Wis., 1957).

[3] Passer, *Electrical Manufacturers*, 19, 92, 219; McDonald, *Let There Be Light*, 9, 15.

[4] On the Lake Elmo plant, see the *St. Paul Daily Globe*, June 21, 1879, which claimed that this was the "first introduction of the electric light in the Northwest." See also *Mississippi Valley Lumberman*, August 12, 1881, p. [1]; *Tribune*, February 7, March 12, April 20, October 21, 1882 (quote).

[5] *Scientific American*, 25:145 (September 2, 1871).

[6] Minnesota Electric Light and Electric Motive Power Company, "Articles," in the firm's minute book, NSP files.

[7] Minnesota Electric, Minutes, November 28, 1881, March 18, July 15, 1882. See also McDonald, *Let There Be Light*, 8–10.

[8] Minnesota Electric, Minutes, May 4, June 1, 1882; Minnesota Brush Electric Company, Minutes, August 20, 1882, in NSP files. The amount of water attached to the cotton millsite was not defined; the amount leased from Minneapolis Mill in 1882 was two millpowers. On equipment and prices, see Meyer, *Builders of Northern States Power Company*, 2.

[9] The lights were tested on the evening of September 5 and were turned on to provide regular service on September 6. See the *St. Paul and Minneapolis Daily Pioneer Press*, September 6, 1882; *Tribune*, September 6, 1882; and "Report of the Secretary," January 12, 1884, in Minnesota Brush Minutes. On the Appleton plant, see McDonald, *Let There Be Light*, 16. Although there has been speculation that the Minneapolis plant was the first hydroelectric central station in the world, it is known that a plant in Godalming, Surrey, England, was in operation by February 18, 1882. See "Electric Lighting by Water Power," in *Scientific American*, 46:102 (February 18, 1882).

[10] On the Minneapolis Gas Light Company, which was organized in 1870, see Shutter, *Minneapolis*, 1:160; Minneapolis Gas Light Company *v.* the City of Minneapolis, File No. 14453, Hennepin County District Court. The latter contains the firm's articles of incorporation, which are not recorded. On its customers, see Mrs. Lester J. Eck, "Early History of Gas Street and Building Lighting," 1–9, MHS; "Conference Leader's Outline," 1963, in Minneapolis Gas Company files. On the firm's readiness to furnish electricity, see *Tribune*, November 2, 4, 1881.

[11] On the lights, see *Tribune*, September 16, 1882 (quote); "Report of the Secretary," January 12, 1884, in Minnesota Brush Minutes. On the lack of power, see Minnesota Electric, Minutes, July 15, 1882, and Minnesota Brush, Minutes, August 20, 1882, June 30, 1883; MMC, Minutes, June 27, 1883, January 2, 1884; and a letter from Minnesota Brush to MMC, February 27, 1884, NSP Correspondence Files. For King's statement, see *Tribune*, March 17, 1882.

[12] Minneapolis City Council, *Proceedings*, 1881–82, p. 252, 257 (quote).

[13] *Proceedings*, 1881–82, p. 257.

[14] *Tribune*, February 17, 1882.

[15] Minneapolis Council, *Proceedings*, 1882–83, p. 58; Minnesota Brush, Minutes, June 19, 1890, and reports of the company's secretary, in the firm's Minutes, January 10, 1887, January 17, 1891, January 25, 1892.

[16] Eck, "Early History of Gas Street and Building Lighting," 1–8; Minnesota Electric, Minutes, May 25, 1882.

[17] *Minnesota Tribune*, March 11, 1883.

[18] Council, *Proceedings*, 1883–84, p. 52.

[19] Council, *Proceedings*, 1883–84, p. 53, 90; "Report of the Secretary," January 12, 1884, in Minnesota Brush Minutes. Only a small part of the city's negotiations is discussed here. For further details, see the published council *Proceedings* for the years 1882–89.

[20] Minnesota Brush, "Report of the Secretary," January 12, 1885; *Minnesota Tribune*, January 17, 1884; *Proceedings*, 1883–84, p. 426; 1884–85, p. 124.

[21] Minnesota Brush, "Report of the Secretary," January 12, 1885.

[22] "Reports of the Secretary," January 21, 1886 (quote), January 10, 1887, and "General Manager's Report," January 11, 1888 — all in Minnesota Brush Minutes. See also Eck, "Early History of Gas Street and Building Lighting," 8.

[23] "Report of the Secretary," January 10, 1887; "General Manager's Report," January 11, 1888; and "Annual Report," January 20, 1890 (quote) — all in Minnesota Brush Minutes.

[24] On the United States Electric Lighting Company, see *Tribune*, February 17, April 20, 1882; *Mississippi Valley Lumberman*, July 25, 1884, p. [7]; and "Report of the Secretary," January 12, 1885, in Minnesota Brush Minutes. On the Safety company, see Articles of Incorporation, Book G, 73, Minnesota Secretary of State's Office; *Mississippi Valley Lumberman*, March 17, 1882, p. [4]; *Tribune*, May 31, 1882.

[25] See Articles of Incorporation, Book U, 514, Minnesota Secretary of State's Office; *Tribune*, March 19, 1887; Meyer, *Builders of Northern States Power Company*, 3. For comment on the competition, see "Report of the Secretary," January 20, 1890, and "Resolution," November 15, 1888 — both in Minnesota Brush Minutes. See also an unpaged manuscript by Herbert W. Meyer, entitled "The Minneapolis Division," in the possession of the author. For a review of early arc and incandescent lighting in Minneapolis, see Edward P. Burch, "Electrical Engineering in Minnesota, 1881 to 1899," in Minnesota Federation of Architectural and Engineering Societies, *Bulletins*, 19:5 (July, 1934).

[26] "Report of the Secretary," January 12, 1884 (quote), in Minnesota Brush Minutes; "The Brush-Swan Electric Light," in *Scientific American*, 47:423 (December 30, 1882).

[27] "Report of the Secretary," January 12, 1885. See also Meyer, "The Minneapolis Division."

[28] "Resolution," November 17, 1882 (quote), in Minnesota Brush Minutes, and Minutes, January 23, 1883.

[29] Minnesota Brush, Minutes, November 1, 1887, August 17, October 30, November 15, 1888, January 4, 8, 1889; "General Manager's Report," January 11, 1888 (quote).

[30] "Reports of the Secretary," January 12, 1884, January 12, 1885.

[31] Minnesota Brush, Minutes, June 30, 1883; "Report of the Secretary," January 12, 1885 (quote).

[32] Articles of Incorporation, Book J, 80, Minnesota Secretary of State's Office; Minnesota Brush, Minutes, September 25, 1884; "Report of the Secretary," January 12, 1885.

[33] MMC, Minutes, January 2, 1884, October 14, 1886.

CHAPTER 10 — HYDROELECTRICITY COMES OF AGE

[1] See, for example, Frizell, in American Society of Civil Engineers, *Transactions*, 12:422.

[2] Kuhlmann, *Development of Flour-Milling*, 134; Herman Steen, *Flour Milling in America*, 64 (Minneapolis, 1963); *Northwestern Miller*, 28:[547]-550; Minneapolis Chamber of Commerce, *Annual Reports*, 1890, p. 140.

[3] *Northwestern Miller*, 28:554.

[4] *United States Census*, 1950, *Population*, vol. 2, part 23, p. 11; Larson, *The Wheat Market and the Minnesota Farmer*, 137, 227-230; Edwin H. Lewis, *Wholesaling in the Twin Cities*, 6 (Minneapolis, 1952); Hartsough, *The Twin Cities as a Metropolitan Market*, 51-53, 58, 69, 70; Larson, *White Pine Industry*, 246. On linseed oil, see Marion E. Cross, *From Land, Sea, and Test Tube: The Story of Archer-Daniels-Midland Company*, 14 (Minneapolis, 1954).

[5] Hill to Washburn, May 28, 1881, NSP Correspondence Files. On the bridge and depot, see *Minnesota Tribune*, November 23, 1883; Pyle, *Life of James J. Hill*, 1:392.

[6] Donald E. Nelson, General Counsel, NSP, to the author, January 8, 1964; MMC and SAC, Minutes, 1889-1908; Charles J. Martin to De la Barre, October 16, 1899, De la Barre Papers, MHS.

[7] De la Barre to Union Carbide Company (quote), February 14, 1903, in MMC letterpress book; De la Barre address in Minnesota Federation of Architectural and Engineering Societies, *Bulletins*, May, 1932, p. 11. De la Barre, "Recollections of a Milling Engineer," in *Northwestern Miller*, 105:851, 871; *Tribune*, January 29, 1924.

[8] Frank Spencer to De la Barre, June 12, 1907, De la Barre Papers.

[9] See, for example, De la Barre to Albert S. Crane, October 24, 1903, SAC letterpress book; to the Atlanta Water and Electric Power Company, March 16, 1903, De la Barre Papers.

[10] De la Barre to Frank Spencer, March 2, 1898 (quote), SAC letterpress book. On the construction, see De la Barre to C. A. Pillsbury, April 17, 1897, SAC letterpress book; to John Wade, August 27, 1902, and to E. L. Corthell, August 8, 1904, MMC letterpress book; unsigned memoranda, 1904, and October 15, 1908, prepared by MMC for the Minnesota Tax Commission and the Minnesota Bureau of Corporations, respectively, both in NSP Correspondence Files.

[11] On log drives and improvements, see De la Barre to John Wade, August 27, 1902; for an example of difficulties with sawmill operators, see De la Barre to W. A. Jones, July 2, 1892, both in MMC letterpress book.

[12] De la Barre to E. W. Savage, November 27, 1894, to John Wade, August 27,

1902, in MMC letterpress book. See also De la Barre to C. A. Pillsbury, June (n.d.), 1893, NSP Correspondence Files. On De la Barre's insistence that manufacturers improve their installations, see his letters to Herzog Manufacturing Company, November 11, 1890, SAC letterpress book, and to A. C. Loring, December 5, 1903, MMC letterpress book.

[13] De la Barre to W. J. Hield, December 26, 1901, SAC letterpress book; to A. C. Loring, November 23, 1897, MMC letterpress book.

[14] See Chapter 4, above; De la Barre to C. A. Pillsbury, August 18, 1897, MMC letterpress book; Memorandum, September 28, 1909, NSP Correspondence Files.

[15] On the disappearance of industries and the city's two pumping plants in 1904, see *Northwestern Miller*, 43:273; McMullen and Company to John Andrus, January 20, 1899, NSP Deed and Lease File; De la Barre to Henry L. Little, October 20, 1899, MMC letterpress book; *Minneapolis City Directory*, 1901, p. 523; NSP Scrapbook No. 1, p. 12, 48.

[16] Minneapolis Chamber of Commerce, *Annual Reports*, 1889, p. 135; 1908, p. 112; Kuhlmann, *Development of Flour-Milling*, 165.

[17] On these developments, see *Northwestern Miller*, 55:346, 363; and *United States Census*, 1900, *Manufactures*, part I, p. cccxxi, cccxxiii; *Duluth News-Tribune*, August 30, 1908, p. 1.

[18] Minneapolis General Electric Company, Minutes, August 10, September 15, 1894, in NSP files; SAC to Minneapolis General Electric Company, September 1, 1894, NSP Deed and Lease File; undated memorandum, Hale Papers. On the Main Street Station, see De la Barre to W. A. Black, August 11, 1906, SAC letterpress book; Meyer, *Builders of Northern States Power Company*, 4; and Meyer, "The Minneapolis Division."

[19] Minneapolis General Electric, Minutes, July 15, 1899, March 13, 1900, June 30, 1909; indenture between the Island Power Company and Minneapolis General Electric, October 9, 1909, in Island Power Company, Minutes, NSP files.

[20] Meyer, *Builders of Northern States Power Company*, 3–5; Minnesota Brush, Minutes, April 29, 1892; Minneapolis General Electric, Minutes, November 1, 1892, March 4, 1899.

[21] Stone and Webster to Minneapolis General Electric, May 3, 1906, NSP Correspondence Files; Meyer, *Builders of Northern States Power Company*, 5.

[22] On plans for the Meeker development, see *Tribune*, October 29, 1882, in which the firm is inaccurately named; *Northwestern Miller*, 28:735; *Northwest Magazine*, March, 1888, p. 21.

[23] Shutter, *Minneapolis*, 1:167–171; *Tribune*, March 12, 1890; *Electric Railways of Minneapolis & St. Paul*, 5 (Interurbans, *Special No. 14*—Los Angeles, 1953).

[24] Unidentified clipping, Press Clipping Book, Box No. 148, and Villard to Lowry, [February, 1890], March 4, May 27, 1890, letterpress book, in Henry Villard Papers, Harvard University; McDonald, *Let There Be Light*, 19; *Tribune*, March 12, 1890 (quote).

[25] *St. Paul and Minneapolis Pioneer Press*, March 2, 1890 (quote); *Tribune*, March 28, 1890; *Northwest Magazine*, April, 1890, p. 10.

[26] *Tribune*, March 6, 1890 (quote); *Northwestern Miller*, 30:733; unidentified clipping, Press Clipping Book, Box No. 148, Villard Papers.

[27] On the dam here and below, see De la Barre to Pack, November, 1924, p. 19–21 (quote), NSP Correspondence Files; *Northwestern Miller*, 29:423; clipping, June 4, 1890, NSP Scrapbook No. 1, p. 9; Edward P. Burch, "The Utilization of Water Power for the Electric Railway System of Minneapolis and St. Paul," in North-West Railway Club, *Proceedings*, April, 1900, p. 12–29. The figure on the total cost of the project was furnished to the author by the NSP Plant Accounting Department.

[28] De la Barre, "Report" to C. A. Pillsbury, June, 1893, and Thomas Lowry to De la Barre, October 18, 1894, NSP Correspondence Files; SAC to Twin City Rapid

Transit Company, December 5, 1896, NSP Deed and Lease File; *Electric Railways of Minneapolis & St. Paul,* 5, 17.

[29] The quotations appear in *Tribune,* March 21, 1897; *Electrical Engineer,* 23:581 (June 2, 1897); undated clipping, NSP Scrapbook No. 1, p. 21.

[30] On Hedderly's warning, see De la Barre to "Col. Benton," June 15, 1891, SAC letterpress book. On De la Barre's position and Pillsbury's offer, see Minnesota Loan and Trust Company and William W. Eastman *v.* SAC, File No. 73976, Hennepin County District Court; E. T. Abbott to A. H. Hedderly, February 12, 1900 (copy), NSP Correspondence Files.

[31] *Tribune,* March 29, 1901, p. 2; File No. 73976, Hennepin County District Court; Rome G. Brown to De la Barre, September 20, 1895; and M. B. Koon to De la Barre, May 27, 1901, both in NSP Correspondence Files.

[32] File No. 73976, Hennepin County District Court; 82 *Minnesota* 506–516; undated clippings from *Tribune* in NSP Scrapbook No. 1, p. 32.

[33] De la Barre to Henry L. Little, April 2, 1901, MMC letterpress book.

[34] *Tribune,* December 24, 1905, p. 16; De la Barre to Henry L. Little, December 16, 1905, MMC letterpress book; to S. Morgan Smith Company, June 22, 1908, SAC letterpress book. The cost figure was furnished to the author by the NSP Plant Accounting Department. Thomas, in Affiliated Engineering Societies of Minnesota, *Bulletins,* 2:244.

[35] Thomas, in Affiliated Engineering Societies, *Bulletins,* 2:244, 245.

[36] J. W. Rickey to De la Barre, January 18, 1906; De la Barre to C. G. Goodrich, March 14, 1906; to A. W. Leonard, April 19, 1906—all in SAC letterpress book; to W. D. Washburn, April 24, 1906, MMC letterpress book; and to Goodrich, October 25, 1906, NSP Correspondence Files. The lease, dated October 1, 1907, is in NSP Deed and Lease File.

[37] *United States Census,* 1900, *Population,* vol. 1, part 1, p. 219; 1910, vol. 2, p. 971; *Minneapolis City Directory,* 1908, p. 23; unidentified clipping (quotes), NSP Scrapbook No. 1, p. 54.

[38] De la Barre statement in "Report of Public Hearing Before Board of Engineers, September 12–14, 1905," item 36, p. 341, in File No. 49126, NARG 77, microfilm copy MHS. De la Barre gives the total horsepower in 1905 as 43,068; to this the author has added the 12,000 horsepower of the Hennepin Island plant to get the figure given in the text.

[39] MMC *v.* St. Paul Board of Water Commissioners, File No. 55120, Hennepin County District Court.

[40] File No. 55120, and SAC *v.* the Board, File No. 55121, both in Hennepin County District Court; 56 *Minnesota* 485–491. The quotation is on page 487.

[41] [Rome G. Brown?], Memorandum, [1893?] (quotes), NSP Correspondence Files; 168 *United States Reports* 349.

[42] De la Barre to Washburn, August 6, 1894, NSP Correspondence Files; Buselmeier, in *Conservation Volunteer,* July–August, 1957, p. 26. On the benefits resulting from the reservoirs, see United States Engineers, *Annual Reports,* 1906, p. 1464–1469. On mileage, see Greenleaf, in *Reports on the Water-Power of the United States,* part 2, p. 138.

[43] De la Barre to Frank Spencer, July 17, 1908, NSP special letterpress book; to Charles L. Potter, April 8, 1913; and MMC to John Wade, May 30, 1907, both in MMC letterpress book.

[44] See *Mississippi Valley Lumberman,* September 2, 9, 1887, p. 2, 5; *Duluth News-Tribune,* July 17, 1905, p. 4; R. L. Hoxie to G. L. Gillespie, November 14, 1903, item 1, File No. 49126, NARG 77, microfilm copy MHS. The statement by Jones is in the *Tribune,* January 21, 1896.

[45] *United States Census,* 1950, *Population,* vol. 2, part 23, p. 11.

[46] 59 Congress, 1 session, *House Executive Documents,* no. 2, p. 1675 (serial 4947).

[47] The quotation is from a statement by J. E. Murphy of McGregor in an unidentified clipping, NSP Scrapbook No. 1, p. 42. On the controversy, see George McC. Derby, F. P. McQuillan, and Matt Kemp to Senator Knute Nelson, June 20, 30, July 20, 1905, Nelson Papers, MHS; *Little Falls Transcript*, September 8, 1905, [p. 3].

[48] *United States Census, 1950, Population,* vol. 2, part 23, p. 11. On the emergence of Duluth, see *Tribune*, October 25, 1885; Larson, *White Pine Industry,* 247–261; Kuhlmann, *Development of Flour-Milling,* 161–165.

[49] See, for example, *Duluth News-Tribune*, June 22, p. 4, July 10, p. 4, September 4, 1905, p. 4; De la Barre to W. D. Washburn, July 31, 1905, MMC letterpress book.

[50] De la Barre to Derby, MMC letterpress book, and Derby's reply, NSP Correspondence Files.

[51] De la Barre to Washburn, July 25, 1905, MMC letterpress book.

[52] De la Barre to Washburn, July 19, 1905, MMC letterpress book.

[53] For the quotations, see De la Barre to W. D. Washburn, July 31, 1905, MMC letterpress book; De la Barre to the editor, in *Tribune*, July 25, 1905, p. 4. On the rallying of support, see a circular letter, September 1, 1905, addressed to water-power companies in Little Falls, St. Cloud, Sauk Rapids, and Watab, SAC letterpress book.

[54] See De la Barre to W. D. Washburn, July 19, 1905, MMC letterpress book; "Report of Public Hearing," item 36, File No. 49126, NARG 77.

[55] For the quoted statements, see "Report of Public Hearing," item 36, p. 83, 314, NARG 77. See also pages 96, 134, 137, and 139 for comments on discrimination and abandonment.

[56] "Report of Public Hearing," item 36, p. 224–226, NARG 77. His name is improperly given as Robert V. Eva in the testimony.

[57] De la Barre to the Upper Mississippi Improvement Association, September 29, 1905, MMC letterpress book. On Gole and Brown, see "Report of Public Hearing," item 36, p. 220, 264, NARG 77; for an example of a conciliatory statement by a spokesman for St. Paul, see page 190.

[58] United States Engineers, *Annual Reports,* 1906, p. 1449–1474. The quotation is on page 1470.

[59] On subsequent conflicts over the reservoirs, see Minnesota Legislative Research Committee, *Report of the Upper Mississippi Reservoir and Minnesota River Valley Development Interim Commission,* 9–19 ([St. Paul?], 1961); *Grand Rapids Herald-Review,* March 27, 1935, p. 1; *St. Paul Pioneer Press,* September 9, 1960, p. 9.

[60] Statement, January 6, 1886, SAC letterpress book; MMC, Minutes, October 10, 1888, August 31, 1909; SAC, Minutes, August 31, 1909, p. 9.

CHAPTER 11 — THE END OF AN ERA

[1] Frank Spencer to De la Barre, May 7, 1907, July 27, August 13, 1908 (quote), De la Barre Papers; William H. Dunwoody to James McDaniel, August 19, 1908, Dunwoody Papers, MHS; unidentified clipping, September 10, 1909, NSP Scrapbook No. 1, p. 127.

[2] On the receivership arrangements, see *Minneapolis Journal,* August 8, 1908, p. 1; "Statement by the Creditors' Committee of the Pillsbury-Washburn Flour Mills Co., Ltd.," August 29, 1908, NSP Correspondence Files; De la Barre to Louis Boisot of First Trust, January 16, 1913, NSP special letterpress book. On the financial details, see Paine and Company to "Dear Sir," March 31, 1911 (copy), NSP Correspondence Files; *London News,* undated clipping, and unidentified clipping of September 10, 1909, NSP Scrapbook No. 1, p. 104, 127.

[3] De la Barre to H. K. Davis, December 1, 1913, NSP Correspondence Files.

[4] The figures were computed by the author from annual financial statements in the minute books of the two companies from 1909 to 1923. Pillsbury-Washburn emerged from receivership in 1909, but the financial arrangements involving the water-power companies devised under the plan of reorganization continued until 1923. Full data on the plan of reorganization is found in Second National Bank of St. Paul *et al. v.* Pillsbury Washburn Flour Mills Co., Ltd., Case No. 834 Equitable, Circuit Court, Fourth Division, Agency Container No. 298, Record Group 29, Federal Records Center, Kansas City, Missouri.

[5] De la Barre to water-power companies' board of directors, October 27, 1911; to Charles Lock, September 20, December 5, 1916; to H. K. Davis, September 8, 1922 (quote), all in NSP Correspondence Files. On the apron, see also MMC, Minutes, October 25, 1912, October 22, 1913.

[6] On the reservoir, see United States Engineers, *Annual Reports*, 1912, part 1, p. 818; on the bridge, see De la Barre to Andrew Rinker, February 28, 1912, SAC letterpress book, and *Tribune*, October 28, 1913; on sawmilling and log drives, see Larson, *White Pine Industry*, 225, 399–401.

[7] Unidentified clipping, November 20, 1909, NSP Scrapbook No. 1, p. 119; De la Barre to Pack, November, 1924, p. 33 (quote), and De la Barre to Alfred Shephard, July 23, 1920 (quote), both in NSP Correspondence Files; MMC, Minutes, December 8, 1920.

[8] On water-power sites above the falls, see Thomas, in Affiliated Engineering Societies of Minnesota, *Bulletins*, 2:238; Gene H. Hollenstein, *Power Development in Minnesota*, 23–25 (Minnesota Department of Conservation, Division of Waters, *Bulletins*, no. 20—St. Paul, 1962); De la Barre to Rome G. Brown, May 11, 1914, and to Alfred Shephard, July 23, 1920, NSP Correspondence Files; MMC, Minutes, December 8, 1920 (quote).

[9] For a summary of federal and state authority, see Michaelson, *Some Legal Aspects of Public and Private Waters in Minnesota*, 1–4.

[10] For examples of arguments over federal controls, see Gifford Pinchot's testimony in *Hearings on the Development and Control of Water Power Before the National Waterways Commission, November 21–24, 1911*, 147–152 (62 Congress, 2 session, *Senate Executive Documents*, no. 274—serial 6174); Rome G. Brown, "The Conservation of Water-Powers," in *Harvard Law Review*, 26:602, 615–622 (May, 1913).

[11] The legislation is reviewed in Brown, *Limitations of Federal Control of Water Powers*, 53–98; Robert D. Baum, *The Federal Power Commission and State Utility Regulation*, 1–3 (Washington, D.C., 1942).

[12] On the companies' attitudes, see De la Barre to Charles Lock, August 5, 1914, NSP Correspondence Files; Brown, *Limitations of Federal Control of Water Powers*, 6 (quote).

[13] Minnesota Drainage Commission, *Report of the Water Resources Investigation of Minnesota, 1909–10*, 11, 21, 51–54, 60 (St. Paul, 1910).

[14] For the text of the bill, see Minnesota Legislature, Thirty-seventh session, 1911, House File 76. On the companies' objections and the conference, see *Minneapolis Journal*, March 19, 1911, p. 13; Ralph D. Thomas to Charles Oberey, March 4, 1911, De la Barre to F. W. Stearns, February 17, 28, March 7, 1911, all in MMC letterpress book.

[15] *St. Paul Pioneer Press*, March 21, 1911, p. 1; *Minneapolis Journal*, March 21, 1911, p. 4; Brown to John A. Fairlie, January 12, 1911, NSP Correspondence Files.

[16] See Brown to De la Barre, May 24, 1912, NSP Correspondence Files; *Minneapolis Journal*, March 19, 1911, p. 13 (quote).

[17] On the House and Senate, see *Minneapolis Journal*, March 25, 1911, p. 12; *Tribune*, April 13, 1911, p. 5; De la Barre to H. K. Davis, April 13, 1911, NSP spe-

cial letterpress book. The opinion appears in *Minneapolis Journal*, April 13, 1911, p. 6.

[18] On threatened legislation, see Brown to De la Barre, July 12, 1912, NSP Correspondence Files; M. H. Gerry to Watab Paper Company, January 19, 1923, MMC letterpress book; De la Barre to the Northwest Paper Company, February 15, 1923, SAC letterpress book. See also *Session Laws*, 1937, p. 794–800.

[19] De la Barre to H. K. Davis, October 18, 1923, NSP Correspondence Files; *Northwestern Miller*, 135:40, 51; 136:242.

[20] Meyer, *Builders of Northern States Power Company*, 6, 149; Meyer, "The Minneapolis Division."

[21] *Byllesby Monthly News*, house organ of H. M. Byllesby and Company, January, 1923, p. 6; November, 1925, p. 6; NSP, *Annual Reports*, 1923, p. 16.

[22] H. W. Meyer, "Twin City Regional Power," in Minnesota Federation of Architectural and Engineering Societies, *Bulletin*, August, 1928, p. 9–12; on the Thomson plant, see 70 Congress, 1 session, *Senate Executive Documents*, no. 92, part 26, p. 343, 468 (serial 8858); on the Keokuk plant and Pacific slope developments, see Department of Commerce, Bureau of the Census, *Central Electric Light and Power Stations and Street and Electric Railways, 1912*, 123, 129–132 (Washington, D.C., 1915); Edward D. Adams, *Niagara Power*, 1:vii, ix (Niagara Falls, N.Y., 1927).

[23] Donald Nelson, General Counsel, NSP, to the author, January 8, 1964; Meyer, *Builders of Northern States Power Company*, 93.

[24] SAC, Minutes, December 31, 1923.

[25] G. E. Loughland, "William de la Barre — 1849–1936 — and the Falls of St. Anthony," in *Byllesby Management*, house organ of Public Utility Engineering and Service Corporation, Chicago, May, 1936, p. 7–10.

[26] See Chapter 10, p. 157; *Byllesby Monthly News*, January, 1923, p. 6.

[27] For the Dingley tariff and milling-in-bond, see United States, *Statutes at Large*, 30:207; Gray, *Business Without Boundary*, 65; Victor G. Pickett and Roland S. Vaile, *The Decline of Northwestern Flour Milling*, 8, 16, 59 (Minneapolis, 1933). The other factors are discussed in the latter source, pages 6–10, 54.

[28] Minneapolis Chamber of Commerce, *Annual Reports*, 1908, p. 112; 1940, p. 63; *Northwestern Miller*, 162:893; Pickett and Vaile, *Decline of Northwestern Flour Milling*, 70. The Minneapolis figures are for the calendar year, while that for Buffalo is for the milling year of 1930–31. The 1960 figure was furnished to the author by the research department of the *Northwestern Miller*.

[29] On the mills, see the *Minneapolis Journal*, April 3, 1924, p. 1 (Palisade); November 15, 1928, p. 19 (Cataract); December 1, 1931, p. 1 (Pillsbury B); unidentified clipping, December 25, 1937, NSP Scrapbook No. 2, p. 97 (Anchor); *Northwestern Miller*, 255:12 (Phoenix).

[30] For information on these plants, see "United Land and Power Company," 1951, and "Initial Statement of Northern States Power Company (Minnesota) to the Federal Power Commission," 1957, staff reports in NSP Plant Accounting Division; C. E. Plank to the author, June 12, 1958; Kane, "Foundations of a City," in *Minnesota History News*, December, 1960, p. 1. In 1907 a few mills began using electricity as auxiliary power. For a typical arrangement, see "Agreement" between Minneapolis General Electric and the Washburn, Crosby Company, April 28, 1916, NSP Deed and Lease File.

[31] Meyer, *Builders of Northern States Power Company*, 92, 94; Plank to the author, June 12, 1958; L. F. Wadsworth of NSP to the author, March 4, 1965.

[32] *Research and Facilities St. Anthony Falls Hydraulic Laboratory*, 1 (University of Minnesota, Hydraulic Laboratory, *Circulars*, no. 5 — Minneapolis, 1950); De la Barre to Pack, November, 1924, p. 28, NSP Correspondence Files; *Holyoke* (Massachusetts) *Transcript-Telegram*, September 14, 1960, p. 4A.

[33] Information here and below is covered in detail by Kane, in *Minnesota History*, 37:309–323. See also 53 Congress, 3 session, *House Executive Documents*, no. 1, part 2, p. 1682 (serial 3298). For the horsepower figure, see United States Engineers, *Annual Reports*, 1924, part 1, p. 1124.

[34] *Tribune*, June 26, 1925, p. 1; untitled leaflet, September 18, 1925, addressed to Minneapolis citizens by Mayor George E. Leach, in NSP Scrapbook No. 1, p. 219.

[35] E. T. Abbott to Howard Strong, March 13, 1917, NSP Correspondence Files; *Minneapolis Star*, August 2, 1948, p. 14, March 12, 1953, p. 8; Minneapolis City Council, *Proceedings*, 1941, p. 272.

[36] Kane, "Feuds, Fusses and Colorful Old Days When Minneapolis Tamed the River," in *Greater Minneapolis*, November, 1961, p. 28; *Minneapolis Star*, September 21, 1963, p. 10A; *Tribune*, September 22, 1963, p. 1, Upper Midwest Section (quotes).

[37] See, for example, *Minneapolis Journal*, December 24, 1905, p. 10; May 25, 1919, p. 1, City Life Section.

[38] Federal Power Commission to the water-power companies, November 22, 1946, and the companies' reply, February 26, 1947 (copies); Cyrus Erickson, "Memorandum," November 10, 1952 (quote), all in NSP Legal Department; "Initial Statement of Northern States Power Company to the Federal Power Commission," 1957, NSP Plant Accounting Division.

[39] Nelson to Kane, January 8, 1964.

[40] Joel Benton, "St. Anthony's Falls," in *Northwest Magazine*, April, 1887, p. 5.

[41] *Minneapolis Journal*, March 31, 1908, p. 17; Holcombe and Bingham, eds., *Compendium*, 1; SAC, Minutes, December 31, 1923.

[42] Barton-Aschman Associates, Inc., *St. Anthony Falls—Nicollet Island: Landmarks at the Continent's Heart*, 6–21 (Minneapolis, 1961).

EPILOGUE, 1986: A RIVERFRONT REBORN

[1] On the 1961 plan, see page 178. Several of the subsequent reports are cited below.

[2] *Southeast* (Minneapolis), October, 1980, p. 7.

[3] The quotation is in *St. Paul Daily Press*, April 19, 1866. See also pages 69 and 84.

[4] H. P. Hall, *H. P. Hall's Observations, Being More or Less a History of Political Contests in Minnesota from 1849 to 1904*, 38–44 (St. Paul, 1904); Minnesota Legislature, *Special Laws*, 1866, p. 123; *Minneapolis Tribune*, January 8, 1877. See also page 60.

[5] William H. Tishler and Virginia S. Luckhardt, "H. W. S. Cleveland: Pioneer Landscape Architect to the Upper Midwest," in *Minnesota History*, 49:281, 282 (Fall, 1985); Cleveland, "Suggestions for a System of Parks and Parkways for the City of Minneapolis," in Minneapolis Board of Park Commissioners, *Annual Report*, 1884, p. 5–9 (quotation on p. 6).

[6] On formation of the gorge, see page 62. On the parkways, see Cleveland, *The Aesthetic Development of the United Cities of St. Paul and Minneapolis*, 13–16 (Minneapolis, 1888); Theodore Wirth, *Minneapolis Park System, 1883–1944*, 157–161 (Minneapolis, 1945); Donald Empson, "The History of the Mississippi River Boulevard in St. Paul," 17–25, 29 (manuscript in possession of the author). On latter-day planning, see [City of Minneapolis], *Mississippi/Minneapolis: A Plan and Program for Riverfront Development*, 18, 78, 79, 81, 82 ([Minneapolis], 1972).

[7] Here and below, see *Minneapolis Journal*, December 2, 1906, where the Jager report is published. Jager's proposals are placed in a modern context in City Planning Commission, *Official City Plan of the City of Minneapolis, Minnesota*, I-II-4 (Minneapolis, 1953).

[8] *Minneapolis Journal*, December 2, 1906. On Bennett's proposal, here and below, see Andrew Wright Crawford, *Plan of Minneapolis*, 125, 126, 149, 150, 160–162 (Minneapolis, 1917). The plate following page 150 shows the boulevard system but gives no details on the routes at the falls; for quotations, see pages 150 and 160.

[9] Crawford, *Plan of Minneapolis*, 156, 158; *Minneapolis Star and Tribune*, March 2, 1983, p. 18. On the park, see Marjorie Kreidberg's introduction to Lucy Leavenworth Wilder Morris, ed., *Old Rail Fence Corners: Frontier Tales Told by Minnesota Pioneers*, [xvii–xix] (St. Paul, repr. ed. 1976).

[10] Hennepin County Territorial Pioneers' Association, *Hand Book of the Godfrey House and Pioneers' Museum*, 1–3 ([Minneapolis], 1916); *Minneapolis Tribune*, July 1, 1979, Picture Magazine, 12, 13, 15, 16, 18, 20–23; Wirth, *Minneapolis Park System*, 53–54; Lucile M. Kane and Alan Ominsky, *Twin Cities: A Pictorial History of Saint Paul and Minneapolis*, 276 (St. Paul, 1983); Historic American Buildings Survey, National Park Service, *Historic American Buildings Survey*, iv, 190 (Washington, D.C., 1941). Architectural drawings of the buildings are in U.S. Department of the Interior, Historic American Buildings Survey, 1984, [Historic Buildings in Minnesota], photocopies in MHS.

[11] An inventory of structures is in Scott F. Anfinson, *Archaeological Potentials on the West Side of the Central Minneapolis Waterfront*, 173–176 ([St. Paul], 1984). On the Cataract and government mills sites, see pages 105, 114, 115, 155.

[12] Anfinson, *Archaeological Potentials*, 98–100, 154; *Southeast*, May, 1982, p. 6; Association of American Railroads, *Information Letter*, December 18, 1974, unpaged; U.S. Army Corps of Engineers, St. Paul District, *St. Anthony Falls Locks & Dams, Mississippi River: Final Feasibility Report and Environmental Assessment: Hydropower*, February, 1984, p. 24.

[13] U.S. Army Corps of Engineers, St. Paul District, *St. Anthony Falls Locks & Dams*, 23, 28, and *Navigation on the Upper Mississippi River: St. Anthony Falls Lock and Dam*, unpaged brochure (Washington, D.C., 1979).

[14] Minneapolis Housing and Redevelopment Authority, *Three Decades 1947–1977 Renewal in Minneapolis*, unpaged (Minneapolis, n.d.); League of Women Voters of Minneapolis, *Minneapolis Housing and Redevelopment Authority*, 29 (Minneapolis, 1976); "The Changing Face of Downtown Minneapolis," in *Greater Minneapolis*, March, 1961, p. 18, 20, 21; John R. Borchert et al., *Legacy of Minneapolis: Preservation Amid Change*, ix–x (Bloomington, 1983).

[15] On the growing preservation movement, see League of Women Voters, *Minneapolis Housing and Redevelopment Authority*, 3; Roger E. Swardson, "Progress Revisited," in *Twin Citian*, January, 1968, p. 11. For quotations, see *Southeast*, September, 1982, p. 7.

[16] Here and below, see Minnesota Historical Society and Minnesota State Planning Agency, *Historic Preservation for Minnesota Communities*, 12–13, 51 (St. Paul, 1980); June D. Holmquist and Jean A. Brookins, *Minnesota's Major Historic Sites: A Guide*, viii (St. Paul, 1972); U.S. Department of the Interior, National Park Service, *Preservation: Tax Incentives for Historic Buildings*, an unpaged, undated leaflet. Other legislation is summarized in U.S. Department of the Interior, National Park Service, *The National Register of Historic Places, 1976*, vi (Washington, D.C., 1976). On the historic district, see *Minnesota Statutes*, 1971, p. 1703–1707; Nomination Form, National Register of Historic Places Inventory, St. Anthony Falls Historic District, and Russell W. Fridley, Director of MHS and State Historic Preservation Officer, to Jerome Fitzgerald, Minneapolis City Attorney, August 30, 1973 (copy) — both in State Historic Preservation Office, MHS files (hereafter SHPO). On city preservation commissions, see *Minnesota Statutes*, 1971, p. 5057; *Minnesota History Interpreter*, May, 1986, p. 8.

[17] On co-operation see, for example, Charles W. Nelson, Supervisor, Historic Sites Survey and Planning, MHS, to Roy V. Thorshov, Chairman, Minneapolis Heritage Preservation Commission, December 14, 1973, copy in SHPO. On the Heritage Preser

vation Commission, see *Minnesota History Interpreter*, June, 1986, p. 8; *Roots: HPC* [the Commission's Annual Report], 1973, p. 9, 10, 13, 16, 19. For guidelines, see Minneapolis City Planning Department, *Mills District Plan, January*, 1983, p. 26.

[18] For the comparison, see Linda Mack, "Minneapolis Development: Progress, Politics, or Just Plain Chaos?" in *Corporate Report*, April, 1980, p. 69. On the agencies, see Metropolitan Council of the Twin Cities Area, *A Compendium of Agencies and Organizations Concerned with the Major River Corridors in the Twin Cities Metropolitan Area. Appendix B: Major River Corridor Study, September, 1969*. On the MCDA, see MCDA, *A Minneapolis Profile: The Business Guide to the Minneapolis Metropolitan Area*, Structure of Government Section, unpaged (Minneapolis, 1984); "Nicollet Island and East Bank," 6 (June 6, 1985), typewritten report issued by MCDA.

[19] "Public Agencies and Coordination," unpaged and undated, typewritten report issued by MCDA.

[20] Anfinson, *Archaeological Potentials*, 94; Wayne Christensen, "The Americanization of Reiko Weston," in *Corporate Report*, April, 1979, p. 40–42 (quotation cited on p. 41). See also *Minneapolis Star and Tribune*, November 7, 1983, p. 1A.

[21] Minneapolis Riverfront Development Coordination Board, *Saint Anthony Falls Rediscovered*, 44–45 ([Minneapolis], 1980); *Minneapolis Star*, August 5, 1975, p. 1C.

[22] Minneapolis Riverfront Development Coordination Board, *Saint Anthony Falls Rediscovered*, 96–103, 118–119. The quotation is in Riverfront Development Coordination Board, *Central Riverfront Development, Minneapolis, Minnesota*, 10 ([Minneapolis, 1977]).

[23] On Hall's proposals for the falls area, see his "Minnerara Minneapolis Minnesota," in *Twin Citian*, December, 1968, p. 19–24. See also *Pracna on Main (A Minneapolis Landmark): A History of the Saloon*, undated, no pagination; *Minneapolis Tribune*, June 20, 1971, Picture Magazine, p. 10, 12.

[24] *Minneapolis Tribune*, April 26, 1974, p. 1A; *Minneapolis Star*, April 26, 1974, p. 1B; Wayne Christensen, "St. Anthony Main, A New Route for Jefferson Lines," in *Corporate Report*, January, 1978, p. 47; John Kostouros, "St. Anthony Main," in *Architecture Minnesota*, June-July, 1982, p. 27, 60; *Minneapolis Star and Tribune*, November 17, 1985, p. 1D. On public funding, see "Holmes," 2, 3 (June 6, 1985), and an attached, unpaged "Project Activity Summary, Riverfront Development Team" (August 27, 1985) in typewritten reports issued by MCDA. On Hall, see *Roots: HPC*, 1973, p. 6; *Riverfront News*, January, 1980, p. 1; Kostouros, in *Architecture Minnesota*, June-July, 1982, p. 29.

[25] Resources Inventory, in St. Anthony Falls Historic District Files, SHPO; *Southeast*, October, 1977, p. 8, 9; Christensen, in *Corporate Report*, January, 1978, p. 45–48; *Riverfront News*, January, 1980, p. [3]; *Minneapolis Tribune*, Picture Magazine, September 13, 1981, p. 20; *Minneapolis Star and Tribune*, January 24, 1984, p. 5B, December 8, 1985, p. 1G.

[26] Christensen, in *Corporate Report*, January, 1978, p. 46, 47; *Minneapolis Star and Tribune*, October 7, 1985, p. 12M, December 8, 1985, p. 1G. On the park, see *Riverfront News*, October, 1980, p. [2]; Kreidberg in Morris, ed., *Old Rail Fence Corners*, [xix].

[27] *Minneapolis Tribune*, May 26, 1979, p. 11A; *Riverfront News*, August, 1979, p. [2]; *Minneapolis Star and Tribune*, June 16, 1984, p. 1S; *CitiBusiness*, September 14, 1983, p. 37; *Southeast*, September, 1978, p. 1. Boisclair's partners were Kajima Development Corporation and Dai-ichi Seimei America Corporation. On the corporations and project financing, see "Nicollet and East Bank," 7–8 (June 6, 1985), and "Project Activity Summary, Riverfront Development Team" (August 23, 1985) — both typewritten reports issued by MCDA.

[28] *Southeast*, September, 1978, p. 1; *Minneapolis Star*, February 15, 1979, p. 1B, October 26, 1979, p. 1A; *Minneapolis Tribune*, September 11, 1980, p. 8A; *Minneapolis Star and Tribune*, March 5, 1984, p. 1M.

[29] Here and below, see *Southeast*, September, 1978, p. 1, October, 1978, p. 1, June, 1979, p. 1, March, 1980, p. 1, August, 1980, p. 1; *Minneapolis Star*, May 18, 1979, p. 1A, February 15, 1979, p. 1B, October 26, 1979, p. 1, December 26, 1979, p. 5A; *Minneapolis Tribune*, May 24, 1979, p. 4B, February 23, 1980, p. 9A, September 11, 1980, p. 8A; *Minneapolis Star and Tribune*, March 5, 1984, p. 1M. The Historic Riverfront Development Coalition was first called the Ad Hoc Riverfront Development Coalition. See *Southeast*, September, 1978, p. 1. A review of tax increment financing in Minneapolis renewal programs is in William Boudreau, "Developing Discontent," in *Corporate Report*, April, 1982, p. 65–68, 119, 123–130.

[30] The quotation is cited in *Minneapolis Star*, February 15, 1979, p. 1B. See also *Minneapolis Star*, September 21, 1979, p. 1C, June 29, 1979, p. 1C, May 18, 1979, p. 1A, October 1, 1981, p. 1B; *Minneapolis Tribune*, October 23, 1981, p. [16c]; *Minneapolis Star and Tribune*, September 2, 1984, p. 1D; *Southeast*, January, 1982, p. 4, June, 1983, p. 1; *Mississippi Review*, May-June, 1982, p. 1. The De la Barre bust is now in the restored livery stable.

[31] On the development and decline of the island, see Minneapolis Riverfront Development Coordination Board, *Saint Anthony Falls Rediscovered*, 60–64; David L. Rosheim, *The Other Minneapolis, or, The Rise and Fall of the Gateway, the Old Minneapolis Skid Row*, 205–218 (Maquoketa, Iowa, 1978). On the renewal plan, see Miller Dunwiddie Architects, Inc., *Historic Preservation Feasibility Study: Nicollet Island and East Bank Renewal Project*, 123 (Minneapolis, 1974), which was an influential survey commissioned by MHRA. The quotation is in *Southeast*, October, 1978, p. 1.

[32] The islanders' feelings about destruction of buildings and relocation of people are expressed in the Nicollet Island-East Bank Project Area Committee, Inc., *Island in the River*, [8–12], undated, (issued in response to *Mississippi/Minneapolis*, which was published in 1972). On a survey by the Minnesota Historical Society and the Historic Resources Committee of the Minnesota Society of Architects made in 1971, see Miller Dunwiddie Architects, Inc., *Historic Preservation Feasibility Study*, 1. See also Riverfront Development Coordination Board, *Restoration and Preservation Research and Planning Study, Saint Anthony Falls Historic District Located within the Minneapolis Central Riverfront Area* ([Minneapolis], 1979).

[33] *Minneapolis Star*, November 9, 1981, p. 1A.

[34] "Contract for Acquisition and Transfer of Lands for Redevelopment by Public Bodies," between the MCDA and the Park and Recreation Board, May 19, 1983, and Miller Dunwiddie Architects, Inc., to Robert W. Ready, Riverfront Development Coordination Board, August 15, 1978, copies of both in St. Anthony Falls Historic District Files, SHPO; *Minneapolis Star and Tribune*, June 6, 1983, p. 8A, June 13, 1985, p. 1A, August 18, 1986, p. 13A; *Minneapolis Tribune*, September 5, 1978, p. 6A, February 22, 1979, p. 6A, December 6, 1980, p. 10A. The quotation is in *Minneapolis Star and Tribune*, June 21, 1984, p. 28A. More extensive information on the controversy and agreements is in "Nicollet Island and East Bank," 3–4, 13–14 (June 6, 1985), typewritten report issued by MCDA.

[35] Riverfront Development Coordination Board, *Saint Anthony Falls Rediscovered*, 68; *Minneapolis Tribune*, September 17, 1980, p. 1A, December 6, 1980, p. 10A; *Minneapolis Star and Tribune*, August 13, 1985, p. 1A (quotation), September 2, 1985, p. 8A, September 15, 1985, p. 1D, March 18, 1986, p. 5B, August 13, 1986, p. 1B. The building, erected in 1893 by McDonald and Delamater, became the Island Sash and Door Company in 1896.

[36] *Riverfront News*, February, 1980, unpaged; Norman Draper, "A Riverfront Renaissance," in *Twin Cities*, February, 1986, p. 26. On Kerwin, see *Mississippi Review*, July-August, 1982, p. 5; *Minneapolis Star*, March 26, 1971, p. 1B, November 9, 1981, p. 1A; *Minneapolis Tribune*, December 27, 1981, Picture Magazine, p. 4, 5, 8; *Minneapolis Star and Tribune*, June 11, 1982, p. 1C, October 14, 1982, p. 1A, May 12, 1983, p. 1B, August 13, 1984, p. 1B.

[37] "Industry Square," 5–6 (June 6, 1985), typewritten report issued by MCDA; Riverfront Development Coordination Board, *Saint Anthony Falls Rediscovered*, 43–44; *Minneapolis Star and Tribune*, February 20, 1985, p. 15A; *Skyway News* (Minneapolis), February 27, 1986, p. 8. Fraser is quoted in *Mississippi Review*, July-August, 1982, p. 2.

[38] The quotation is cited in *Minneapolis Star and Tribune*, September 10, 1985, p. 12A. See also *Minneapolis Star and Tribune*, September 15, 1985, p. 1D, August 13, 1986, p. 1B; Hayber releases to the media, August 30, 1985, copies in St. Anthony Falls Historic District Files, SHPO; Riverfront Development Coordination Board, *Saint Anthony Falls Rediscovered*, 50–51.

[39] *Southeast*, October, 1983, p. 6; *Minneapolis Star and Tribune*, October 13, 1983, p. 1A, November 7, 1983, p. 1A, November 11, 1983, p. 1B; U.S. Army Corps of Engineers, St. Paul District, *St. Anthony Falls Locks & Dams*, A1–A57, 5, 27, 97; *Minneapolis Star and Tribune*, October 17, 1983, p. 12A. For quotations, see *Minneapolis Star and Tribune*, October 17, 1983, p. 12A; *Minnesota History News*, January, 1984, p. 5.

[40] U.S. Army Corps of Engineers, St. Paul District, *St. Anthony Falls Locks & Dams*, 30, 36, 85, 86, 97–101, 138; *Minneapolis Star and Tribune*, January 6, 1984, p. 1B, February 11, 1984, p. 1B, March 16, 1986, p. 1B, September 4, 1986, p. 3B.

[41] *Southeast*, October 1976, p. 6.

[42] On the walkway, see *Minneapolis Star and Tribune*, September 7, 1986, p. 1B; Nicholas Westbrook, ed., *A Guide to the Industrial Archaeology of the Twin Cities*, 22 (St. Paul, 1983). On the new Hennepin Avenue Bridge, see *Southeast*, March, 1983, p. 1, July, 1983, p. 4; *Minneapolis Star and Tribune*, April 6, 1984, p. 1B, May 11, 1986, p. 14B. On the park, see *Minneapolis Tribune*, October 11, 1981, p. 12A; Draper, in *Twin Cities*, February, 1986, p. 26; *Mississippi Review*, July-August, 1982, p. 1. On the developers, see *Minneapolis Star and Tribune*, August 29, p. 9B, September 29, p. 9M, October 16, p. 1A, 15A — all 1986. On interpretive planning, see Elisabeth Doermann to Nina Archabal and Donn Coddington, July 29, 1986, MHS Files.

43 *Minneapolis Star and Tribune*, May 11, 1986, p. 5D; September 22, 1986, p. 1A; Anfinson, *Archeological Potentials*, 1–3.

[44] Draper, in *Twin Cities*, February, 1986, p. 24, 25, 28; *Minneapolis Star and Tribune*, January 2, 1984, p. 1A; Minneapolis City Planning Department and the Downtown Council, "Metro 2000," draft report, June 2, 1986, unpaged, in Minneapolis History Collection, Minneapolis Public Library and Information Center; John Kostouros, "Riverplace's Japanese Owners Have Some Changes in Mind," in *CityBusiness*, November 19, 1986, p. 6.

Index